MARRYING WELL

AFRICAN STUDIES SERIES 47

Editorial Board
John Dunn, Reader in Politics and Fellow of King's College, Cambridge
J. M. Lonsdale, Lecturer in History and Fellow of Trinity College, Cambridge
A. F. Robertson, Fellow of Darwin College, Cambridge

The African Studies Series is a collection of monographs and general studies that reflect the interdisciplinary interests of the African Studies Centre at Cambridge. Volumes to date have combined historical, anthropological, economic, political and other perspectives. Each contribution has assumed that such broad approaches can contribute much to our understanding of Africa, and that this may in turn be of advantage to specific disciplines.

OTHER BOOKS IN THE SERIES

4 *The Nigerian Military: A Sociological Analysis of Authority and Revolt 1960–1967* Robin Luckham
6 *Labour in the South African Gold Mines, 1911–1969* Francis Wilson
9 *Dependence and Opportunity: Political Change in Ahafo* John Dunn and A. F. Robertson
11 *Islam and Tribal Art in West Africa* René A. Bravmann
14 *Culture, Tradition and Society in the West African Novel* Emmanuel Obiechina
15 *Saints and Politicians: Essays in the Organisation of a Senegalese Peasant Society* Donal B. Cruise O'Brien
17 *Politics in Decolonisation: Kenya Europeans and the Land Issue 1960–1965* Gary Wasserman
18 *Muslim Brotherhoods in Nineteenth-century Africa* B. G. Martin
19 *Warfare in the Sokoto Caliphate: Historical and Sociological Perspectives* Joseph P. Smaldone
20 *Liberia and Sierra Leone: An Essay in Comparative Politics* Christopher Clapham
23 *West African States: Failure and Promise: A Study in Comparative Politics* John Dunn
24 *Afrikaners of the Kalahari: White Minority in a Black Stage* Margo and Martin Russell
25 *A Modern History of Tanganyika* John Iliffe
26 *A History of African Christianity 1950–1975* Adrian Hastings
27 *Slaves, Peasants and Capitalists in Southern Angola 1840–1926* W. G. Clarence-Smith
28 *The Hidden Hippopotamus: Reappraisal in African History: The Early Colonial Experience in Western Zambia* Gwyn Prins
29 *Families Divided: The Impact of Migrant Labour in Lesotho* Colin Murray
30 *Slavery, Colonialism and Economic Growth in Dahomey, 1640–1960* Patrick Manning
31 *Kings, Commoners and Concessionaires: The Evolution and Dissolution of the Nineteenth-century Swazi State* Philip Bonner
32 *Oral Poetry and Somali Nationalism: The Case of Sayyid Mahammad 'Abdille Hasan* Said S. Samatar
33 *The Political Economy of Pondoland 1860–1930: Production, Labour, Migrancy and Chiefs in Rural South Africa* William Beinart
34 *Volkskapitalisme: Class, Capital and Ideology in the Development of Afrikaner Nationalism 1934–1948* Dan O'Meara
35 *The Settler Economies: Studies in the Economic History of Kenya and Rhodesia 1900–1963* Paul Mosley
36 *Transformations in Slavery: A History of Slavery in Africa* Paul E. Lovejoy
37 *Amilcar Cabral: Revolutionary Leadership and People's War* Patrick Chabal
38 *Essays on the Political Economy of Rural Africa* Robert H. Bates
39 *Ijeshas and Nigerians: The Incorporation of a Yoruba Kingdom, 1890s–1970s* J. D. Y. Peel
40 *Black People and the South African War 1899–1902* Peter Warwick
41 *A History of Niger 1850–1960* Finn Fuglestad
42 *Industrialisation and Trade Union Organisation in South Africa 1924–1955* Jon Lewis
43 *The Rising of the Red Shawls: A Revolt in Madagascar 1895–1899* Stephen Ellis
44 *Slavery in Dutch South Africa* Nigel Worden
45 *Law, Custom and Social Order: The Colonial Experience in Malawi and Zambia* Martin Chanock
46 *Salt of the Desert Sun: A History of Salt Production and Trade in the Central Sudan* Paul E. Lovejoy

MARRYING WELL

Marriage, Status and Social Change among the Educated Elite in Colonial Lagos

KRISTIN MANN
Department of History, Emory University

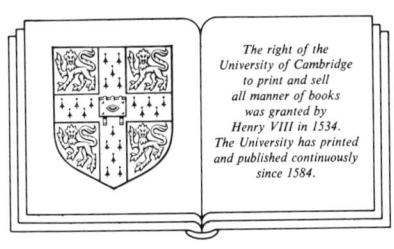

CAMBRIDGE UNIVERSITY PRESS
CAMBRIDGE
LONDON   NEW YORK   NEW ROCHELLE
MELBOURNE   SYDNEY

Published by the Press Syndicate of the University of Cambridge
The Pitt Building, Trumpington Street, Cambridge CB2 1RP
32 East 57th Street, New York, NY 10022, USA
10 Stamford Road, Oakleigh, Melbourne 3166, Australia

© Cambridge University Press 1985

First published 1985

Printed in Great Britain at the University Press, Cambridge

British Library cataloguing in publication data
Mann, Kristin
Marrying well: marriage, status and social
change among the educated elite in colonial Lagos. –
(African studies series, ISSN 0065–406X; 47)
1. Marriage – Nigeria – Lagos – History –
19th century   2. Elite (Social sciences) – Nigeria
– Lagos – History – 19th century
I. Title   II. Series
306.8′1′096691   HQ696.7

Library of Congress cataloging in publication data
Mann, Kristin, 1946–
Marrying well.
(African studies series; 47)
Bibliography; p.
Includes index.
1. Marriage – Nigeria – History.   2. Elite (Social
sciences) – Nigeria – History.   I. Title.   II. Series.
HQ696.7.A25 1986   306.8′5′09669   85–7780

ISBN 0 521 30701 5

To
RICHARD EVANS MANN
THEODOSIA ROSS MANN
THEODOSIA TAYLOR ROSS BAUER

and to the memory of
LECIE EVANS MANN

Contents

List of tables	*page* viii
List of maps	ix
List of figures	ix
Acknowledgements	x
List of abbreviations	xii
Introduction	1
1 The making of the educated African elite	11
2 Yoruba and Christian marriage	35
3 Elite men and the marriage dilemma	54
4 The dangers of dependence: elite women and Christian marriage	77
5 Marriage and the consolidation of status	92
6 Economy, society and marriage	110
Appendix: Educated elite males in Lagos Colony, 1880–1915	128
Notes	133
Select bibliography	177
Index	185

Tables

1.1	Percentage distribution of occupations of elite males at four points in time	25
1.2	Percentage distribution of education of elite males at four points in time	26
1.3	Percentage distribution of the origins of elite males	27
1.4	Percentage distribution of the origins of elite males at four points in time	28
1.5	Percentage distribution of education of elite males by literacy of their fathers	29
1.6	Percentage distribution of occupations of elite males with secondary education or above by literacy of their fathers	30
1.7	Median value in pounds sterling of estates of elite males	33
3.1	Percentage distribution of marriage choices of elite males by origin	63
3.2	Percentage of repatriates and locals practicing Christian and Yoruba marriage	63
3.3	Percentage distribution of marriage choices of repatriates by generation of residence in Yorubaland	64
3.4	Percentage of first- and subsequent-generation repatriates practicing Christian and Yoruba marriage	64
3.5	Percentage distribution of marriage choices of elite males by occupation	65
3.6	Percentage of occupational groups practicing Christian and Yoruba marriage	65
3.7	Percentage distribution of marriage choices of elite males by education	66
3.8	Percentage of educational groups practicing Christian and Yoruba marriage	66
3.9	Percentage distribution of marriage choices of elite males by date of birth	69
3.10	Percentage of cohorts practicing Christian and Yoruba marriage	70
5.1	Percentage distribution of the origins of elite males' Christian wives	93
5.2	Percentage distribution of occupations of fathers of elite males and their Christian wives	93

Maps

1 Africa showing Yoruba and west coast towns 3
2 Town of Lagos about 1880 13

Figures

1.1 Five-year moving averages of palm oil and palm kernel exports by volume 14
1.2 Five-year moving averages of palm oil and palm kernel prices 22
5.1 Abbreviated genealogy of the William Moore family 96
5.2 Abbreviated genealogy of the Josuah Blackall Benjamin family 97

Acknowledgements

Books usually bear the names of individual authors when in fact they represent collective efforts. I wish to acknowledge, and express gratitude for, the abundant help I have received in completing this project. G. Wesley Johnson introduced me to African history and encouraged me to become a professional historian. Kennell Jackson supervised my graduate training and set exacting standards of field and interdisciplinary research. Paul Irwin directed my Ph.D. dissertation, which contained the germ of the present study. Miraculously, he returned each chapter within forty-eight hours and always offered just the right combination of praise and criticism, reassurance and prodding to keep me writing. Ever helpful and enthusiastic, Peter Stansky completed my dissertation committee. Barton Bernstein generously advised and assisted in countless big and small ways. Carl Degler provided moral support and encouraged me to study women and the family. Since we met in 1975, Jean Hay has supported and helped me at every stage in my professional career. A year as a special student in the Anthropology Department at Cambridge University, under the tutelage of Jack Goody, Esther Goody, Polly Hill and Alan Macfarlane, convinced me to focus my study of the Lagos elite on marriage. Participants in the History Department Seminar at Wellesley College, where I taught for two years, helped me see I had a book to write on the subject. Emory University, and particularly its History Department, have given me the home I needed to see the work through. I could not have asked for finer support than my university and department have offered.

At various stages, many colleagues have read part or all of this manuscript. Their comments have made the book much better than it would otherwise have been. I am indebted to Steve Baier, Edna Bay, Sara Berry, John Comaroff, Fred Cooper, John Dunn, Risa Ellovich, Christopher Fyfe, Jane Guyer, Jean Hay, Pat Hilden, Tony Hopkins, Kennell Jackson, Nina Mba, Afolabi Olabimtan, Gabriel Olusanya, Jonathan Prude, Tom Reef and Marcia Wright. During the research I benefited from the help and friendship of three bright, painstaking and resourceful research assistants. In 1973–4 Diipo Gbenro aided me at the Lagos Marriage Registry and Probate Registry. He also helped with interviews and transcribed tapes. In the summer of 1979 Deborah Neff searched Lagos newspapers, and Manju Mehta examined missionary records, each looking for information about marriage. Patricia Stockbridge quickly, accurately and patiently typed more drafts of the manuscript than most mortals could have borne.

I owe my greatest debt to the many people in Nigeria who contributed to the success of this project. I am grateful for the cooperation and patience of the informants listed individually in the bibliography. Their ancestors lived this story; they helped me rediscover it. I also wish to thank the staffs of the Nigerian National Archives, Ibadan; the Africana Collection, the University of Ibadan Library; the African Studies Collection, the University of Lagos Library; the Lagos Marriage Registry; the Lagos Probate Registry; the Lagos High Court Archives; and the Lagos Land Registry. Several persons offered such help and friendship that I wish to mention them by name: Professor J. F. Ade Ajayi, Professor Rebecca Agheyisi, Professor Gabriel Olusanya, Professor Afolabi Olabimtan, Professor David and Mrs Susan Aradeon, Dr Nina Mba, Chief O. A. Ṣobande, the late Mrs J. T. A. Williams, Gladys Agbebiyi, the Hon. Chief Justice Atanda and Mrs Irene Fatayi-Williams and Chief I. A. S. Adewale. These persons made research in the most difficult of cities a rewarding and enjoyable experience. Because of them, I grew to love Lagos.

Over the years my family and friends have made life worth while and sustained me through difficult times. Finally, and most heart-felt, I thank Steven Tipton, friend, companion and fellow scholar. He never doubted I would write this book, and he has given me the first-hand experience with marriage that I have needed to understand what goes on between husbands and wives.

Grants from the Fulbright–Hays Dissertation Research Abroad Fellowship Program; the American Association of University Women; the Committee on Comparative Studies of Africa and the Americas, Stanford University; and the Center for Research in International Studies, Stanford University, supported my dissertation research, from which this study has grown. A Research Training Fellowship from the Social Science Research Council enabled me to study anthropology for a year, which greatly enhanced my understanding of kinship and marriage. Funds from the Center for Research on Women, Wellesley College, permitted me to train and employ Deborah Neff in the summer of 1979. A National Endowment for the Humanities Summer Stipend and an Emory University Summer Research Award sent me back to Nigeria in the summer of 1980 to complete research for the book.

Abbreviations

ASAPS	Anti-Slavery and Aborigines Protection Society Papers
C.M.S.-Y.M.	Church Missionary Society Yoruba Mission Papers
C.O.	Colonial Office Dispatch Books
C.S.O.	Colonial Secretariat Office Records
Carrena	Carrena Papers, Lagos
Coker	Coker Papers, Nigerian National Archives, Ibadan
E & LC	*Eagle and Lagos Critic*
LO	*Lagos Observer*
LS	*Lagos Standard*
LWR	*Lagos Weekly Record*
Macaulay	Macaulay Papers, University of Ibadan Library
N.L.R.	Nigerian Law Reports
Oke	Oke Papers, Nigerian National Archives, Ibadan
Phillips	Phillips Papers, Nigerian National Archives, Ibadan

Introduction

In the nineteenth century Lagos developed into West Africa's leading center of international trade and colonial capital. A small Christian-educated elite emerged there, as in other West African coastal towns, poised at the center of the far-reaching economic, political and social changes then occurring.[1] The men and women who composed such groups knew two kinds of marriage: African, practiced by their ancestors and the majority of the population; and Christian, held up by the Europeans as the only legitimate form of union between man and woman. Very different expectations about polygyny, domestic relationships and roles, and legal rights and duties characterized these two types of marriage. Each stood at the heart of a radically different socio-cultural order. Marriage presented the educated elite with a problem. Questions about how to marry and what marriage should be deeply preoccupied the members of the group, who brooded over them privately, debated them publicly, and struggled to resolve them in their domestic lives.[2] By 1900 hardly a week passed without an article on marriage in the Lagos press, and educated Africans regularly published pamphlets expressing their views on the subject.[3] At the heart of the marriage dilemma lay the role of marriage in elite formation and maintenance and the conflict between men and women over changing marital norms.

This book investigates the history of marriage among the educated African elite that lived in colonial Lagos, the capital of modern-day Nigeria, between 1880 and 1915. The study begins by analyzing the economic, political and social changes that produced the educated elite and shaped its subsequent development, placing the group and marriage in historical context. Chapter 2 contrasts Yoruba and Christian marriage. It sets out their distinctive legal rights and duties, domestic relationships and roles, and attitudes toward polygyny and monogamy. These data define the domestic alternatives open to the elite and explore their social, economic and political implications in a period of rapid change. The book goes on to probe how elite men and women married. It examines the reasons persons formed a customary or a Christian union and the tensions they felt beween the two. I ask why some elite men chose Christian marriage, others Yoruba marriage, and still others Christian and Yoruba marriage, in spite of the contradictions between the two and the fact that combining the two violated church

Marrying well

teaching and colonial law. I then investigate why elite women, unlike elite men, insisted on Christian unions. The discussion of men's and women's marital behavior shows that elite marriage changed in the late nineteenth and early twentieth centuries in response to changing conditions in Lagos. The book ends by reflecting on the interrelation of marriage and economic and social change. It concludes that marriage played a fundamental part in the consolidation of elite status, and that changes in the political economy of Lagos deeply affected marriage and the relationship between the sexes.

This study uses 'educated elite' to refer to men and women at the top of the growing population of educated Africans in early colonial Lagos. Categories employed to discuss inequality in colonial and post-colonial Africa derive from Western social science. They are embedded in bodies of theory and carry specific connotations. For these reasons it is important to make explicit the rationale for treating the group studied here as an elite rather than as a social class.[4]

Marx and Weber defined class stratification as economically determined. Marx saw relationship to the means of production as the key economic variable; Weber, market situation, or the power to dispose of goods and skills for the sake of income. Whereas Weber treated property ownership as a class asset, Marx saw it as the critical aspect of class situation. Weber shrewdly observed that in commercial cities such as Lagos credit often formed the basis of class stratification.[5] Both Marx and Weber distinguished between objective reality, or class position, and subjective understanding, or class consciousness. Marx believed class structure and political power were closely related. He argued that in time the power of the bourgeoisie would extend beyond economic into political life and transform the group into a ruling class.[6]

Weber regarded class as but one form of stratification. In an effort to distinguish other forms as well, he defined status as the positive or negative estimation of honor received by individuals or positions. Honor remained a murky and thus not very helpful concept, but to Weber status clearly rested on perceptions of how much others valued persons or positions. Weber clarified his argument by explaining that status groups are stratified according to principles of their consumption of goods as represented in style of life. Economic factors affect consumption, but other factors, such as religion, education and values, play an equally if not more important part.[7]

Elite theory posits stratification based on skill in performing highly valued roles – political, military, bureaucratic, commercial and so on. All societies need certain important functions to be performed. Persons who excell at a particular activity or set of activities are paid deference and exercise a corresponding measure of influence over the life of the community. In large, complex societies where roles are highly differentiated a number of separate elites may exist. In simpler or smaller-scale societies a single elite may perform a number of different roles, or, as in Lagos, the few persons who perform different roles may form a single elite. Elites are necessarily self-

Introduction

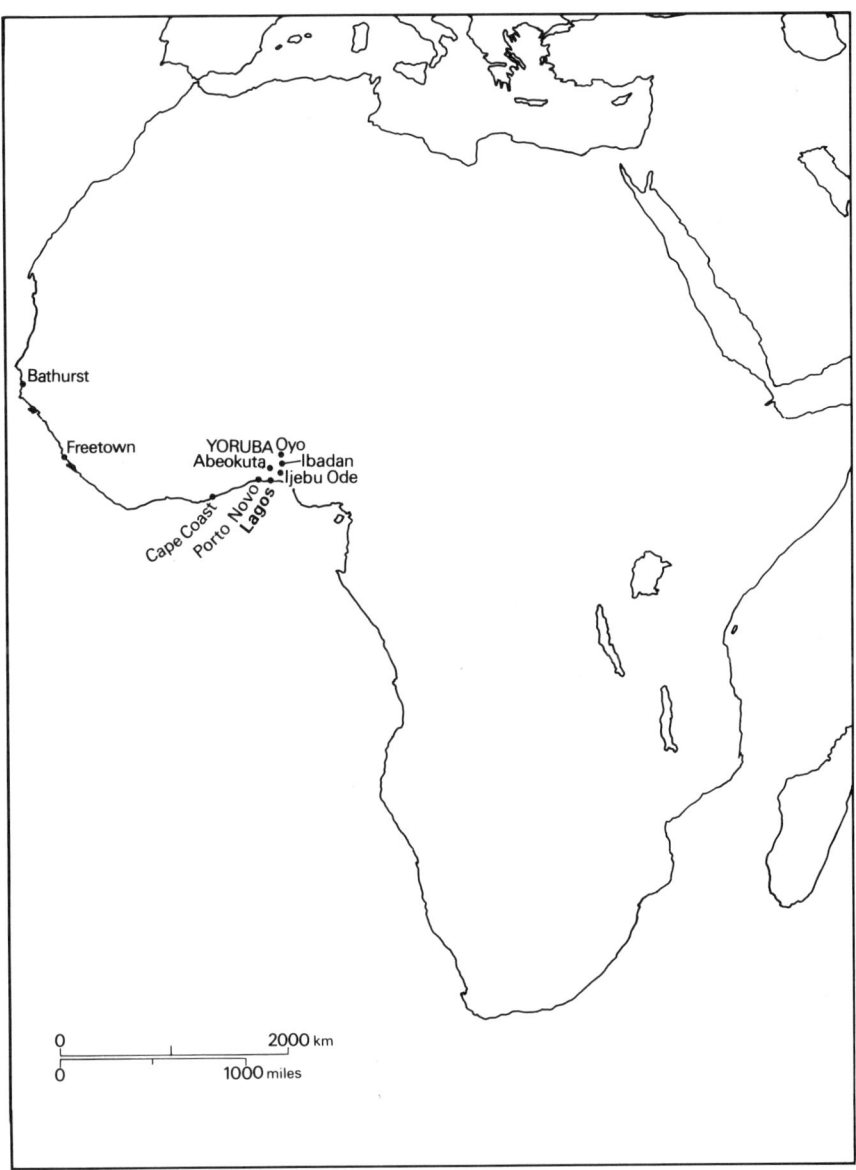

Map 1. Africa showing Yoruba and west coast towns

conscious communities. They share common interests and a common culture. This common culture finds expression in a distinctive style of life learned through similar formal and informal training. Sometimes the culture of elites commands respect, as do the roles that they perform. When this occurs, the deference paid the group and its influence in the community are generalized, and in effect the elite becomes a status group. Elite status brings rewards: influence, power and often wealth. Wealth supports the training and style of life necessary to join the elite, but it is not a sufficient criterion for elite status. Formally, merit in performing important roles determines recruitment into elites. However, if a select group of families monopolizes training and appointment to office, then elite status may become hereditary.[8]

The subjects of this study constituted an elite, not a social class. The group's preeminence derived neither from relationship to the means of production nor from market situation but from Western education and knowledge of British institutions and culture. These attributes enabled the elite to perform vital new roles in the young and rapidly changing colonial society. Until the end of the nineteenth century, Western-educated import–export merchants formed a necessary link in the growing international commerce that bound African and European producers and consumers and led Britain to colonize Nigeria. African colonial servants and professionals performed bureaucratic, legal, medical and other services critical to the development of the new international trade and to the successful operation of the colonial state. How the elite lived was as important for elite status as what it did. The elite created a distinctive style of life built around Christianity, Western education and British manners and customs. In the 1860s, 70s and 80s, this style of life rested on an ideological belief in the moral and cultural superiority of European civilization. The style of life and ideology of the elite united the group and set it off from the rest of the population. They brought this small number of Africans inside the culture of the colonial rulers and legitimized its privileged position in colonial society.

In the nineteenth century the roles and culture of the educated elite gave it influence with Europeans and power over other Africans. In the twentieth century the equation reversed. The elite's special abilities enabled it to lead mass political movements that challenged the colonial government on its own terms and brought the group influence with other Africans and a measure of power within the colonial state. The educated elite derived wealth from trade and employment in the colonial service and professions. Wealth supported the elite's distinctive style of life. It created opportunities in education that gave individuals and their children advantages in the competition for jobs in the colonial service and professions. Thus wealth helped consolidate status and transmit it from generation to generation. But economic position neither defined the elite nor gave it its sense of community. Important economic differences existed within the group. If an African bourgeoisie had begun to develop in the colony, defined either by

Introduction

relationship to the means of production or by market situation, it included elements in the population, most notably wealthy Muslim merchants, that did not share the elite's religion, education, style of life or ideology. Differences in religion and culture affected processes of economic accumulation. They inhibited the development of class consciousness and class-based political action and helped make status a relevant social category in colonial Lagos.[9] In colonial Africa Europeans dominated political decision-making and monopolized force; hence the utter inappropriateness of referring to early educated elites as ruling classes.

Elite theory implies a common set of values, accepted by all, that puts the elite on top. Yet in Lagos no single standard existed. Elite theory also considers processes whereby elites emerge and change. Pareto examined movement into and out of elites – changes in personnel, which he referred to as the 'circulation of elites'.[10] Mannheim explored the emergence of new kinds of elites brought about by fundamental changes in the whole value system of society. He argued that as societies transform they need new talents and develop new ideals. Roles are recast and new elites are created. Mannheim linked this phenomenon to what he called the 'problem of transforming man'.[11] In Lagos the educated elite emerged as part of just such a process of transformation. The growth of international trade and the rise of the colonial state created a demand for new skills and talents and placed a premium on persons who possessed them. This transformation did not occur all at once. Much survived from precolonial Yoruba social and economic life. Indeed, important groups in the population explicitly rejected Christianity, Western education, colonial rule and all that they implied. However, the direction of change was clear. If the educated elite did not embody universally accepted values, it did embody the values of the future. Colonial elites interest scholars in part because they were the social forebears and in some cases actual biological ancestors of groups that dominate independent African nations.

My study raised the difficult methodological problem of how to identify who belonged to the elite and who did not; that is, of how to delineate the boundary of the group. Political scientists who study elites often use a reputational model to identify their subjects. They constitute their groups by determining whom others in the community regard as the elite.[12] No such method could work in a study of colonial Lagos, because no records survive that reveal to the historian who contemporaries believed belonged to the educated elite. As an alternative, I identified occupational roles that clearly brought educated men elite status. Then I determined who filled those positions. This work defines elite males as including all professionals (doctors, lawyers, ministers, headmasters, surveyors and engineers), colonial servants of the rank First Class Clerk or above, and Western-educated import–export merchants who lived or regularly worked in the colony between 1880 and 1915. Also included are a few other occupational groups, such as newspaper publishers and planters, who clearly belonged to the elite

Marrying well

but do not fit neatly into one of the three major occupational categories. This identification scheme had the advantage of emphasizing education and occupation, the major determinants of educated elite status in colonial West Africa. It constituted for investigation a clearly defined group of 200 elite men.[13] The study excludes successful educated traders and high-ranking clerks in mercantile firms because of the impossibility of identifying them, although contemporaries might have counted some such men among the elite. It also excludes Lagos's many teachers, catechists and low-ranking colonial servants. These persons had some Western education, but they did not share the educated elite's values, style of life or privileged position in colonial society.

Elite women proved more difficult to identify. Their special roles lay not in the marketplace or office, but in the home, church and community. Elite women were first wives and mothers, responsible for the all-important task of civilizing home and family life. In their spare time, these women organized Sunday school classes and self-improvement associations and hosted literary clubs and musical evenings to improve the moral and cultural tone of the community. The most prominent elite women show up in written records. But as in most historical settings, elite women wrote less than elite men and their activities attracted less commentary. Hence less information about elite women than men survives in newspapers, private papers and official documents. No records exist that would permit the identification of women or men on the basis of level of education alone. To overcome these limitations, I added the educated sisters, wives and daughters of elite males to the list of women compiled from written records. This approach produced a sizeable if loosely defined group of women, which included all Lagos's leading educated females. Educated men and women of status lower than the elite did not necessarily share that group's marital experiences.

The educated elite was not a fixed social group. The roles that brought elite status did not change in the late nineteenth and early twentieth centuries. Thus the criteria for inclusion in the group remained constant throughout the period. However, the persons who performed these roles changed. New individuals moved into the elite as they completed school and assumed adult responsibilities. I continued to count men and women as members of the elite until death removed them from it, although before that a few men ceased to have elite occupations through retirement or business failure. Chapter 1 analyzes changes in the size and composition of the elite between 1880 and 1915.

Once identified, the fullest possible life history of each member of the elite was compiled, drawing on exhaustive oral and archival research. Written records used in the project included newspapers, colonial dispatches, missionary records and private papers, the standard sources for Nigerian history. They also included wills, baptismal registers, marriage registers and court records, rich but heretofore unexploited documents. Oral data gathered during interviews with more than 150 descendants of the elite fleshed out the archival evidence. Once completed, the life histories of the elite were analyzed for information about marriage, using the method of collective biography. This illuminated both experiences of individuals and regular patterns of behavior within the group, the cumulative result of the separate choices made by its members.[14] By piecing the information from life histories together with what contemporaries wrote about marriage, it was possible to reconstruct the richly textured history of marriage among the elite. The study focuses on the educated elite in Lagos between 1880 and 1915 because by 1880 a distinct, clearly identifiable elite had come into being. Between that year and 1915 the group experienced important changes in its social and economic position and in its marital attitudes and behavior. Because many members of the 1880 to 1915 elite made important domestic decisions before or after those years, the data on marriage presented here illuminate a longer period, stretching roughly from 1860 to 1930.

This study of marriage among the educated elite in colonial Lagos sheds new light on several important topics in African studies – educated elites, marriage and women. Turning first to educated elites, the work depicts how one such group courted, wed and formed families. Significant in itself, this information illuminates a number of larger problems. It shows how the early educated Christians in black Africa's leading city established themselves as an elite. Specifically, the data demonstrate the role of marriage in the creation of a distinctive style of life that united the elite and set it off from the rest of the population. The elite's unique marriage practices created barriers to entry into the group and reinforced exclusivity. They convinced the elite and others of the group's moral and cultural superiority and legitimized its influence and authority in colonial society. Marriage also concentrated education and property within a small number of elite families and cemented a dense web of kinship and affinal relations that promoted the economic and political interests of the group and its individual members. This concentration of resources among elite families facilitated upward social mobility, helped transmit status from parents to children, and fostered the development of an hereditary elite. Through addressing these questions, this work probes the relationship between an important aspect of what Abner Cohen has called the normative culture of an elite and its communal organization and power.[15]

In addition, this study of marriage opens a window on the elite's private life that illuminates its experiences in a period of rapid economic, political and social change. The work uncovers the instrumental and ideological factors that shaped the elite's daily life. It clarifies the responses of the group to African and European culture, a controversial subject in Nigerian historiography.[16] Yoruba and Christian marriage differed fundamentally. They represented different mechanisms for defining social and political identity and for mobilizing and managing a wide range of resources. Europeans made marriage a burning moral issue by pronouncing African marriage barbarous and insisting that African Christians wed in church and embrace Victorian conjugal ideals as outward signs of inward religious and cultural conversion. Members of the Lagos elite confronted questions about marriage repeatedly, each time they or someone close to them made important domestic decisions. Examining the group's responses to this key issue throws new light on its beliefs, needs and interests, and on strategies for social and economic mobility within the political and economic context of colonialism.

Previous studies of West African educated elites focus on the activities of a few prominent persons. Consequently, these works fail to see differences within elites and changes in their dominant characteristics.[17] This study examines the behavior of an entire elite over a critical period in its history.[18] In this way the book analyzes both variation and change in the Lagos elite's religious and cultural outlook and social and economic position. By bringing women into the center of the story and contrasting the sexes' responses to marriage, the study reveals the role of gender in shaping ideology and interest and strategies for mobility.[19]

This study pioneers the history of marriage in Africa, a critical but little-studied topic, owing in part to the difficulty of obtaining reliable data about domestic and kinship relations. The history of marriage itself forms a vital part of the history of the family, a new field in African studies but one well charted in European and American studies.[20] The book describes Yoruba marriage in the late nineteenth century and analyzes how it was changing. It discusses the new form of marriage introduced into Africa by Europeans and documents how this in turn adapted to local conditions. By placing the discussion of marriage in its larger historical context, the work probes the impact on marriage of the growth of international trade, the rise of the colonial state, and the spread of Christianity and Western education. In particular, the study assesses the effects of new ideologies, new processes of social and economic differentiation, and new structures of political and legal authority on domestic relationships and roles, and on beliefs about what was right and valuable in domestic life. In a period of rapid economic, political and social transformation, the book reveals great change as well as great continuity. Finally, the work uncovers the bitter conflict that changes in marriage created between men and women and evaluates the impact of this conflict on the institution of marriage and the relationship between the sexes.

This research on marriage among Lagos's early educated elite illuminates the origins of what some sociologists and anthropologists have called 'modern West African marriage'. Recent studies document that among contemporary educated West Africans corporate lineages have become less important and elementary families more important. As evidence of this change scholars cite the rising incidence of personal choice in mate selection, the growing emphasis on love and companionship as criteria for marriage, and the increasing tendency of couples to reside in their own residences rather than lineage compounds. These works find that although educated couples need to cooperate less than illiterate couples to earn the family living, they want a closer conjugal relationship, involving shared financial decision-making, leisure activities and domestic chores.[21] In Elizabeth Bott's terms, which Christine Oppong borrows in her study of marriage among Ghanaian senior civil servants, the trend has been away from an open kin network and segregated role-relationship and toward a closed kin network and joint role-relationship.[22] Studies of modern marriage also conclude that educated husbands and wives are beginning to accept monogamy as the ideal form of marriage.[23]

Yet these same works show that changes in West African marriage have been gradual and fraught with tension. Few persons want or are able to cut themselves off from relatives. The demands of kin often conflict with the interests of the elementary family, producing antagonisms between spouses that undermine close conjugal relationships. A strong tradition of role segregation survives, and, much as wives want it, many husbands refuse to share financial decision-making and domestic chores. Voluntary associations and social activities remain sex-segregated, moreover, pulling spouses apart during leisure hours and minimizing their shared experiences. Finally, some educated husbands continue to want many children, which makes polygyny attractive. When the tensions in modern marriages become acute, deep-seated mistrust emerges between husbands and wives. Spouses respond by keeping financial and other affairs secret, in hopes of minimizing areas of conflict. In such cases, the very emphasis in modern marriage on a close conjugal relationship creates problems that push couples apart.[24]

Most recent studies describe modern West African marriage rather than explain its origins. At best discussions of causation point to new values and opportunities that have emerged with the rise of education, urbanization and modern occupations; or they analyze the tension that these new values and opportunities create in the context of specific systems of descent.[25] Few works relate changes in marriage to changes in the wider political economy.[26] No work seeks the roots of modern marriage in the past. This study begins to fill the gap. Contemporary educated West Africans have not emerged from an historical vacuum. The changes in marriage that sociologists and anthropologists describe began in fact over a century ago. They have taken place in the context of the incorporation of West Africa into the world economy and of the creation of states, first colonial and then independent. These developments altered the nature of economic opportunities and the character of resources; they transformed processes of economic accumulation and structures of economic and political power. All of these changes affected marriage, just as they were affected by it. Before we can fully understand the nature and origins of modern West African marriage, we need much more information about the history of the institution. This study supplies such information and forges a path for future historical research on a neglected subject.

Marrying well

The book also contributes to knowledge about African women, a subject of rapidly growing interest. Women played an important role in the making of the educated elite; and the history of women and the history of marriage are intimately linked. By contrasting the responses of men and women to marriage, the work reveals how the growth of international trade, the rise of the colonial state and the introduction of Christianity and Western education differently affected the roles and opportunities available to the sexes. These differences in turn shaped relations between men and women and the institution of marriage itself. The study stresses the poignant irony that while Europeans assumed that contact with the West would improve the lot of benighted African women, and while it in fact brought elite women new material comforts, legal rights and prestige, it undermined the autonomy of even these women.[27]

Elite women shaped the world in which they lived.[28] But the structure of opportunities also constrained women's choices. In the early colonial period elite women actively cultivated the foreign conjugal ideals that undermined their autonomy in pursuit of the privileges associated with elite status. Indeed, elite women clung to foreign ideals after elite men began to question them, because these women believed that Christian marriage would best protect their interests. Until the early twentieth century elite women had few other options. After years of disappointment and vulnerability, however, some elite women began to rethink issues related to marriage. These women took steps to improve their economic opportunities and those of other educated women. They rejected the Victorian ideal of idle dependence on a husband in quest of greater economic autonomy, the more usual role of West African women.

This book makes a final contribution, even more important than what it tells us about elites, marriage and women. It depicts a world made by women and men. For twenty-five years we have had studies of African history which have really been studies of men. Recently, as a necessary and valuable corrective to this distortion, we have seen the publication of studies of African women in the past. These works have made too little impact on the mainstream of African history. Most scholars leave the study of women to women's studies and still conceive and write African history as if women did not exist. As yet we have very few works that present the African past as it really was: a world inhabited by men and women and shaped in fundamental ways by the interaction between them. If history is a vision of the past, then this vision will remain imperfect until it comes to include as a matter of course the contributions of women and men to molding their common reality. We will only begin to understand basic problems in African social, economic and political life when we start to examine the relationship between the sexes. Where better to explore this perspective than in a book about marriage? But if the perspective is to fulfill its potential, others must carry it beyond the study of domestic life.

1

The making of the educated African elite

Between the late eighteenth and early twentieth centuries, Lagos developed from a small Yoruba fishing, farming and trading village into a major slave-trading entrepot, and finally into an important port and colonial capital. The growth of international trade, the imposition of colonial rule and the introduction of Christianity and Western education altered the structure of economic and political power in the community. These changes created new opportunities for a small group of Christian, educated Africans in commerce, the colonial service and the professions. This group evolved a distinctive culture, accumulated wealth and other resources, and quickly established itself as a new elite. No sooner had the educated elite emerged than changes in trade and colonial rule undermined its power and authority and threatened its preeminence. The first section of this chapter discusses the local, regional and international changes that first created the educated elite and then assaulted its privileged position in colonial society. The second section summarizes the social and economic characteristics of the elite and analyzes how these changed between 1880 and 1915. Changes in the composition of the elite further illuminate the process and problems of elite formation and maintenance in early colonial Lagos.

LAGOS

Yoruba from the nearby mainland settled the small swampy island that became Lagos some time before the sixteenth century.[1] Numbering only about 5,000 as late as 1800, these early inhabitants lived by fishing, farming and trading. Domestic groups comprising men, their wives and unmarried children, and in some cases slaves or clients, formed the units of economic production.[2] A ruler known as the *Ǫlǫfin* governed the settlement from the neighboring island of Iddo. Patrilineal descent groups founded by sons of the first *Ǫlǫfin* owned the land and fishing rights in and around Lagos. Members of these lineages enjoyed rights of usufruct, while strangers wishing to make their homes there could obtain rights to farm or fish from the heads of the landowning lineages, known as the *Idęjǫ* chiefs. In exchange, these settlers offered fealty and labor or gifts in kind.[3] In time they became incorporated into the landowning lineages; or if they prospered, they established lineages of their own. Material life was simple.

Marrying well

Relatively little inequality existed, although the Ọlọfin and Idẹjọ commanded greater economic and political power than commoners. Farming, fishing or trading ability and wealth-in-people – the number of wives, kin, slaves or clients whose labor and political support one controlled – formed the basis of economic differentiation.[4] As late as the 1860s, Lagos chiefs asserted that 'the wealth and opulence of . . . the Black . . . is of slaves and wives'.[5] Even in this early period, however, rulers may have benefited from certain prerogatives of office, such as fines, gifts or tolls levied on trade.

At the end of the sixteenth century the Kingdom of Benin conquered Lagos. During the seventeenth century Benin appointed its own ruler, founding both the kingship and the lineage that has filled that position to the present day. At about the same time the palace moved from Iddo to Idunganran on the northwest corner of Lagos island, where it still stands at the heart of the old city.[6] Three classes of titled officials began to emerge and joined the Idẹjọ in advising the king. The Ọba, as the king was called, conferred these titles, using them to reward service to the crown and recognize wealth and influence. Often titles became hereditary in the first holder's lineage.[7] The rules of succession to the kingship and the rights and duties of various offices remained fluid, giving rise to political conflict that became chronic in the mid nineteenth century. At stake were both the division of power and authority among offices and the choice of who would fill particular positions. Resources tipping the balance in these contests included political acumen, influence with the Ọba and other officials, and the number and strength of one's wives, kin, clients and slaves.[8]

Lagos became a center of the slave trade in the late eighteenth century and began to change very rapidly. The commerce in slaves created vast new wealth, and concentrated it in the hands of a few big traders. Moreover, this wealth increasingly took the form of slaves, firearms, gunpowder, war canoes and imported luxury goods; the requisites and rewards of the slave trade. A. G. Hopkins's assertion that the Ọba and chiefs maintained monopolistic control over the slave trade wants testing through further research.[9] The famous Madame Tinubu, for example, became a wealthy slave trader before her association with Ọba Akitoye and continued to trade on her own after she returned with him to Lagos.[10] There can be little doubt, however, that participation in the slave trade greatly increased the resources of the Ọba and certain chiefs, who used them to consolidate their political control over Lagos and the surrounding area.[11] At the same time, it may have exacerbated rivalries among wealthy officeholders, who turned their powerful trading organizations to political and military ends. Certainly, resources amassed through the slave trade played a part in the protracted succession dispute between rival claimants to the throne that dominated the political history of mid-nineteenth-century Lagos.[12]

The pace of change quickened in the mid nineteenth century. Great Britain abolished her own slave trade in 1807, and subsequently pressured other nations to do the same. Between 1807 and 1868, the Royal Navy

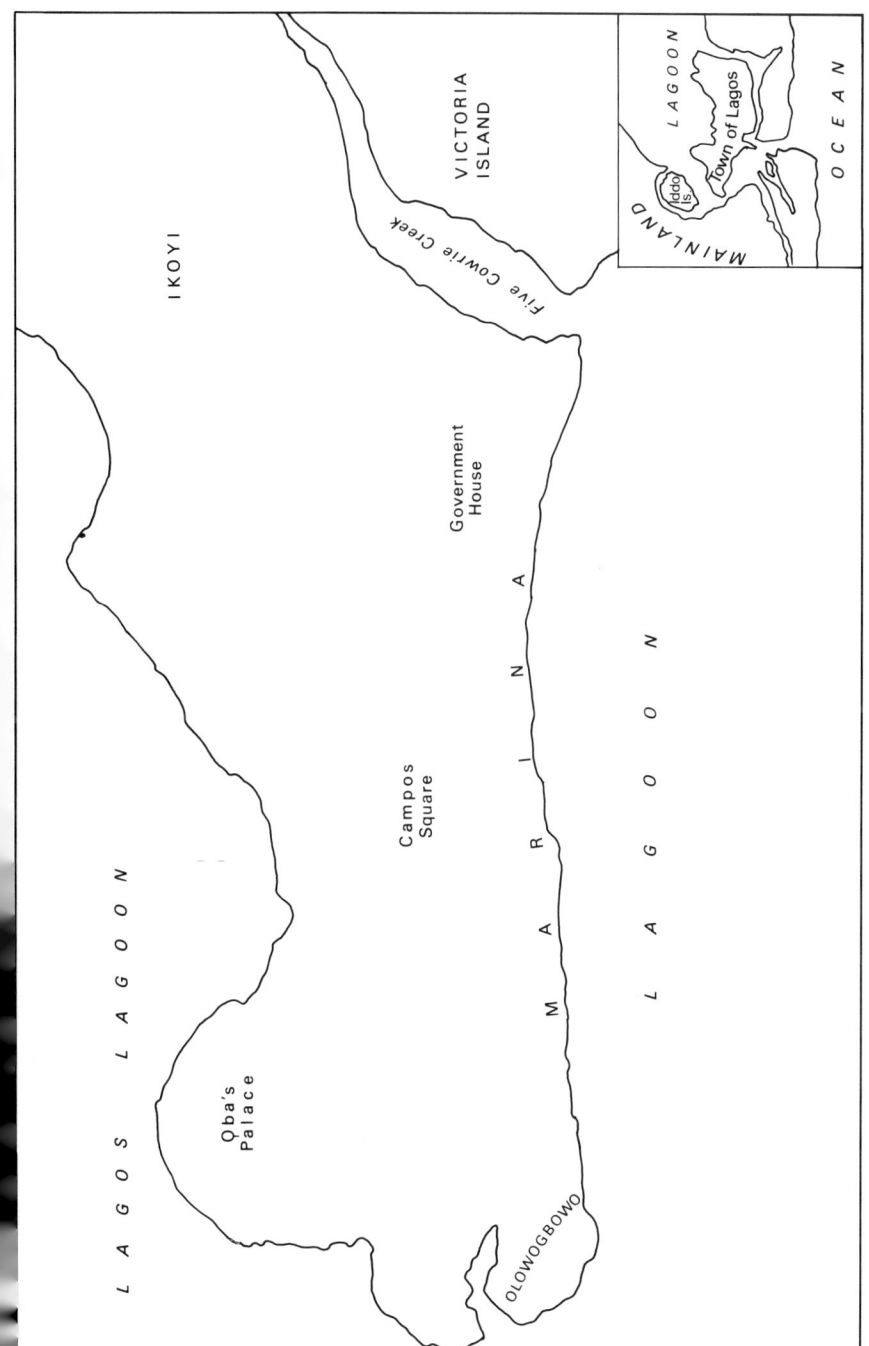

Map 2. Town of Lagos about 1880

patrolled West African waters enforcing anti-slave-trading treaties the Foreign Office concluded with Western and African governments.[13] Also during these years, a market for West African vegetable oils emerged in Europe.[14] In 1849 Queen Victoria appointed a consul to the Bights of Biafra and Benin to help check the slave trade and encourage the growth of legitimate commerce in that area.[15] Soon both the consul and the Navy were drawn into a local political dispute. In 1851 the Royal Navy bombarded Lagos, replacing Kosoko, an Ọba hostile to British interests, with Akitoye, a more compliant claimant.[16] The bombardment dealt a severe blow to the prestige of the Ọba, who now held office at the pleasure of the British. After a decade of continued political instability, Great Britain annexed Lagos island and a small strip of territory on the mainland to suppress the slave trade and further her economic ambitions in the region.[17] Slowly, fitfully, legitimate commerce replaced the trade in slaves. The volume of palm oil, Lagos's first major agricultural export, crept from 4,000 tons per year in the 1850s and 1860s to 12,000 tons per year in the 1890s, while that of palm kernels, a later export, soared from 7,000 tons per year in the 1860s to 48,000 tons per year in the 1890s.

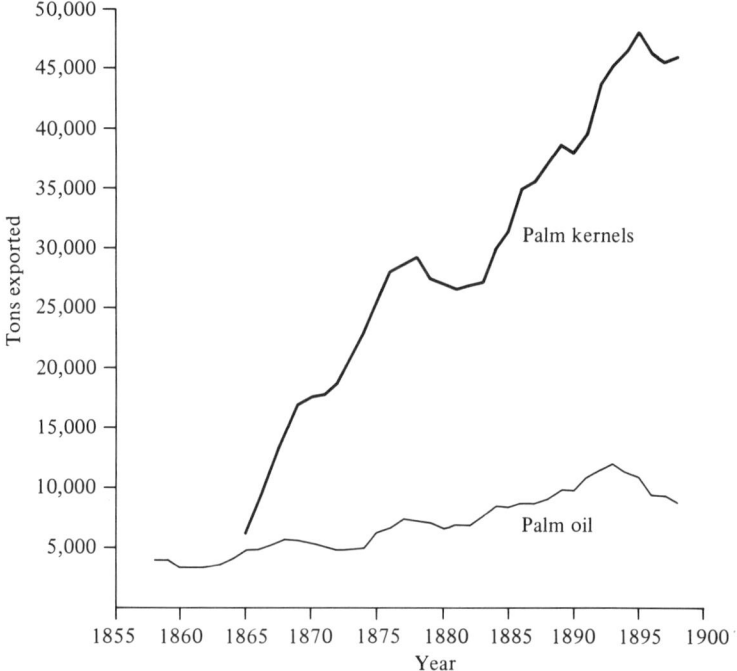

Figure 1.1. Five-year moving averages of palm oil and palm kernel exports by volume. Source: This graph is derived from data in Sara S. Berry, Cocoa, Custom and Socio-Economic Change in Rural Western Nigeria (Oxford, Clarendon Press, 1975), p. 23

The making of the educated African elite

Following the annexation the Colonial Office quickly established direct colonial rule over Lagos. A British governor began building a colonial bureaucracy and legal system that in time usurped responsibility for most aspects of government.[16] By the end of the first decade of colonial rule, Great Britain had created rudimentary executive, treasury, customs, judicial, police, postal, printing, public works and medical departments. Ordinances enacted in the early 1860s introduced a new body of laws – common law, equity and statutes of general application in force in England – and established British courts with jurisdiction over many legal matters.[19] The Supreme Court Ordinance of 1876 stipulated that nothing should deprive Africans of benefit of local law and custom, provided it was not repugnant to 'justice, equity, and good conscience' or incompatible with colonial statute. Yet this ordinance made no provision for the continued functioning of Yoruba courts, and specified that persons who had agreed in any transaction to be bound by English law could not claim benefit of local law.[20] Effectively, the Colonial Office created a new political, administrative and legal order that bypassed the *Ọba* and chiefs and concentrated power and authority in the hands of Europeans, and, to a lesser extent, their African collaborators.

The colonial state grew slowly at first. In 1881 as many Germans as Britons resided in Lagos, and British missionaries and mercantile agents outnumbered colonial servants three to one.[21] In spite of bad years, trade prospered in the 1860s and 1870s with little government interference. A mid-Victorian anti-colonial lobby opposed vigorous development of Britain's West African colonies, arguing that the expansion of trade did not require it and that Her Majesty's government could not afford to assume the white man's burden in the region.[22] In this spirit, a Select Committee of the House of Commons resolved in 1865 that Britain's involvement in West Africa should be kept to a minimum and that attempts should be made 'to encourage in the natives the exercise of those qualities which may render it possible for us more and more to transfer to them the administration of all Governments'.[23] A fiscally conservative Treasury strengthened the anti-colonialists' hand by insisting that colonial expenditure stay within the bounds of colonial revenue, thus limiting the funds available for development.[24] In addition to these constraints, West Africa remained the white man's grave throughout the nineteenth century, because Western medicine had not yet discovered the cause of malaria and other tropical diseases. Between 1881 and 1891 the Lagos death rate for European males in the prime of life stood at five to ten times the rate in England.[25] The cost in human lives of energetic colonial development by Europeans outstripped the potential benefits. The British annexation had cast the die, however, and there would be no turning back. It was only a matter of time before Great Britain assumed a more active role in the development of Lagos Colony.

Historians disagree about the impact on Yorubaland of the shift from the slave to the palm-produce trade. A. G. Hopkins argues that the transition created opportunities for ordinary farmers employing mainly family labor to participate in the overseas exchange economy for the first time, because there were few barriers to entry and economies of scale in palm-oil and palm-kernel production and trade. Competition from below, he asserts, threatened the economic and political power of Yoruba rulers, generating conflict between states, between rulers within states, and between rulers and the ruled.[26] Other historians maintain that economic considerations were subordinate to political ones in nineteenth-century Yoruba warfare and that control of trade was not essential to achieving political power in most Yoruba states.[27] Summarizing the debate, Sara Berry criticizes Hopkins for failing to distinguish between the requirements of export production and export trade. 'While it is probably true', she notes, 'that there were no economies of scale in the production of palm oil . . . it is not clear that this was equally true for the business of transporting and marketing it.' She continues, 'Given the distances and uncertainties of travel, and the highly labor intensive character of inland transport . . . it seems implausible to argue . . . that individual farmers began not only to produce palm oil and kernels for sale but also to compete effectively with large slave-owners who were in a position to transport and market their produce as well.' Berry concludes that without further information on the organization of trade one cannot say whether it began to pass from large- to small-scale middlemen when palm produce replaced slaves as the principal export from Yorubaland.[28]

Lagos was not a typical nineteenth-century Yoruba town. Located on the coast, its inhabitants entered the new international commerce primarily as traders, not producers. Because Lagos lies at the mouth of a vast lagoon and network of creeks that stretch inland to major market towns, Lagosians faced fewer transportation problems than interior traders. Finally, in Lagos the imposition of colonial rule accompanied the shift from the slave to the palm-produce trade, seriously undermining the position of the Ọba and chiefs. While much research remains to be done on both the slave and palm-produce trades in Lagos, the available evidence suggests that the shift to legitimate commerce did erode the economic base of the Yoruba rulers, who found legitimate commerce far less profitable than the old trade in human beings.[29] The fact that Great Britain deprived the Ọba of the right to levy tolls on trade exacerbated his economic problems. With greatly reduced revenue, the local rulers could no longer command the support of large numbers of kin, slaves and clients. As a consequence their political power further declined. At the same time the rise of legitimate commerce created new economic opportunities for commoners and slaves.[30]

During the 1850s, 60s and 70s a type of trade emerged that survived with modifications into the twentieth century. European and African merchants imported textiles, spirits and hardware from England and Germany, often on credit. They broke bulk in Lagos and extended imports or currency, also on credit, to middlemen who sold the imports and bought exports in Lagos

The making of the educated African elite

or inland markets.³¹ In the early colonial period these middlemen were sometimes slaves, but they could also be free traders.³² With the proceeds of their commercial activities, middlemen repaid the Lagos merchants, who exported the palm produce they received and settled their own debts.

Few economic constraints blocked entry into the new legitimate commerce. By the 1880s more than half of the population of Lagos engaged in some kind of commercial activity.³³ Life histories of late-nineteenth-century magnates show that traders could begin buying and selling on a small scale, often on credit, and through hard work, wise investments and luck amass substantial fortunes.³⁴ Business and profits were not distributed equally. A few big European and African importers and exporters handled huge inventories and netted hundreds of pounds annually, while thousands of smaller traders dealt in small quantities of goods and made modest sums.³⁵ Moreover, big traders enjoyed clear advantages. As Berry notes, roads to the interior were hazardous and large caravans found safety in numbers.³⁶ The greater capital commanded by big traders enabled them to withstand economic crises that forced smaller competitors out of business.³⁷ With some important exceptions, however, the leading African merchants in Lagos by the 1880s were neither titleholders nor former slave traders. Most had never owned large numbers of slaves.³⁸ They were a new breed of entrepreneur that had emerged with the rise of legitimate commerce. They owed their success to commercial ability, connections with Europeans and control of capital and land, newly important resources.³⁹

Rapid population growth accompanied Lagos's rise as a center of international trade and a colonial capital. The town grew in size to 25,000 by 1866 and 74,000 by 1911, swelled first by slaves and later by Yoruba and non-Yoruba freemen who flocked to the coast in search of economic opportunities and refuge from the Yoruba wars in the interior.⁴⁰ This rapid population growth surrounded the original inhabitants with strangers. It spawned great competition for economic resources and great fluidity in social relations as newcomers scrambled to make a place for themselves in Lagos.

Between the 1830s and 1880s small but important groups of liberated slaves returned to Yorubaland from Sierra Leone and Brazil. Called Saro and Amaro respectively, these repatriates descended from Yoruba-speaking people. They or their ancestors had been captured in the interior, marched to the coast, and sold into the transatlantic slave trade, often in Lagos itself. The Saro had been freed by Britain's anti-slave trade squadron and set down in Freetown, Sierra Leone, founded as a home for liberated slaves. There some had fallen under the influence of Protestant missionaries, converted to Christianity, and learned reading, writing and Western customs. Others had joined the growing Muslim communities in and around Freetown. In the 1840s and 1850s groups of Saro began returning to Yorubaland, settling first in Badagry and Abeokuta.⁴¹ By 1870 approximately 1,500 made their homes in Lagos.⁴² The Amaro had completed the middle passage and worked as slaves in Brazil, where many had converted to

Catholicism, learned Portuguese, and become familiar with Latin culture. Others had retained their Muslim faith. Through good fortune or hard work, the Amaro had obtained their freedom and then returned to West Africa.[43] Although many had settled in Ouidah and Porto Novo, an estimated 3,000 resided in Lagos by 1886.[44]

The Sierra Leonean and Brazilian repatriates were more heterogeneous than has often been acknowledged. Both groups included Muslims as well as Christians, illiterates as well as literates, and merchants and traders as well as members of other occupations.[45] There is some truth, however, in the stereotype that the Saro built houses in the part of southwest Lagos known as Olowogbowo and earned their living in commerce or as clerks, while the Amaro settled in the center of the island around Campos Square and worked as builders and artisans to shape the face of colonial Lagos.[46] Initially, the local inhabitants reacted hostilely to both the Saro and Amaro, reinforcing their respective identities. But soon some Saro and Amaro forged ties with other groups in the population through intermarriage, patron–client relationships and participation in religious or other voluntary associations. The distinction between these repatriates and the rest of the population began to blur, and religious, educational and economic differences among Saro and Amaro became more important than their shared origins.[47]

Repatriated slaves introduced Christianity and Western education into Yorubaland and drew the first Christian missionaries to the area in the 1840s and 1850s. Saro James White founded the first Church Missionary Society church and primary school in Lagos in 1852. Thomas Babington Macaulay, also a Saro, opened the C.M.S. Grammar School in 1859. The Wesleyan Methodists also established their first church and school in 1852, and the Southern Baptists followed suit in 1854. The Société des Missions Africaines finally sent a missionary to Lagos in 1867, although Brazilian repatriated slaves had introduced Roman Catholicism much earlier and S.M.A. priests had visited Lagos since 1861.[48] At first churches and schools served only repatriates and their offspring, but gradually they began to attract a few of the local inhabitants.[49] By 1886 an estimated 5,000 Christians attended Sunday services at eight C.M.S., five Wesleyan Methodist, one Southern Baptist and two Roman Catholic churches.[50] In 1884 twenty-four primary schools (sixteen C.M.S., five Wesleyan Methodist, one Southern Baptist and two Roman Catholic) and five secondary schools (two C.M.S., two Wesleyan Methodist and one Roman Catholic) in Lagos enrolled 1,861 primary and 156 secondary students. In 1912 some 201 primary and 7 secondary schools throughout southwestern Nigeria taught roughly 14,000 primary and 800 secondary students.[51] As the figures on the number of churches and schools suggest, the Anglicans dominated but did not monopolize missionary activity. By the late nineteenth century an educated Christian subculture existed in Lagos, centering on the churches and schools and including not only Saro and Amaro but also a few local Yoruba. The educated Christians spoke English, knew how to read and write, and observed Christian religious rituals. The best-educated and most well-to-do wore European clothing, understood English institutions, manners and customs, and enjoyed English leisure activities. Many educated Africans held different values than the rest of the population and paid allegiance to the colonial rulers rather than to the Ọba and chiefs. The educated Africans enjoyed influence with Europeans disproportionate to their numbers.

In a recent article, A. G. Hopkins explores the relationship in Lagos between the rise of legitimate commerce, the establishment of colonial rule and the emergence of new property rights. Hopkins argues that European merchants and repatriated slaves settling on the island in the 1850s required land on which to build houses, stores and warehouses. To secure their investments, these settlers treated grants from the Ọba to vacant plots as giving them alienable rights of private ownership, although Yoruba land tenure did not recognize such a thing, and it is very doubtful this is what the Ọba meant to confer. Merchants soon began demanding real estate as security for commercial credit, and a market in land emerged. Hopkins maintains that the further development of these new property rights, which British officials equated with progress and civilization, provided a clear motive for the annexation.[52] In the early years of the colony, individual land rights became widely accepted, land values appreciated, and the colonial state encouraged and protected the establishment of private claims.[53] Wills in the Lagos Probate Registry reveal that by the 1880s land was a major form of investment and repository of wealth in the colony.[54] The pattern of land ownership also changed fundamentally during these years. Many of the most valuable commercial and residential sites on the island passed from the original landowning lineages to recent African and European arrivals.[55] As Hopkins notes, by the 1880s land ownership had become an important basis of inequality in Lagos, and a local *rentier* had emerged.[56]

The far-reaching economic, political and social changes in early colonial Lagos favored educated Christians and fostered the development of an educated elite. Repatriated slaves returned to Lagos well placed to take rapid advantage of new opportunities created by the growth of legitimate commerce, the rise of the colonial state and the emergence of new property rights, in part because they had already witnessed similar developments in their former homes.[57] Some repatriates consolidated their economic position in the colony by acquiring title to choice pieces of real estate before the local inhabitants realized their value.[58] For example, I. H. Willoughby's mother squatted with her children on one of the best business sites in Lagos and successfully defended it against all challengers. Later Willoughby built a lucrative trading establishment on the property.[59] Repatriates used the colonial courts and bureaucracy to protect and extend their interests.

The ability to read and write in English ensured the early educated Christians advantages in a community where the government and private citizens increasingly wrote down, in the language of the colonial rulers, important communications and commercial and legal transactions. Governor Gilbert Carter spoke of the 'divinity' with which illiterate Africans regarded 'a man who [could] write on a piece of paper with a pen'.[60] Illiterate merchants soon found they had to hire literate clerks.[61] Christianity itself provided both men and women an ideology that eased adaptation to new economic and political conditions. Converts could legitimize the accumulation of private property as a mark of civilization, indeed as a sign of God's grace. They could justify collaboration with the colonial rulers as necessary for the spread of the faith. As subsequent chapters will show, Christianity encouraged the development of new forms of marriage, family life and inheritance, crystalized elite identity, and facilitated the concentration and mobilization of valuable resources.

The high European mortality rate and reluctance of Great Britain to commit men and money to colonial development meant good jobs for well-educated blacks in the churches, colonial service and professions. In the 1860s and 1870s, the Anglicans, Wesleyans and Baptists all looked to educated Africans to run their schools in Lagos. By 1881 six of Lagos's seven C.M.S. churches had African pastors. Samuel Crowther, the first African bishop, supervised the work of the C.M.S. throughout much of Yorubaland, although not in Lagos itself.[62] Similarly, the Colonial Office relied on educated Africans to staff the colonial bureaucracy. In 1881 the Civil Establishment employed forty-five Africans and only eleven Europeans. Prior to that date Africans had held such high-ranking posts as Acting Colonial Secretary, Chief Clerk and Treasurer, Assistant Collector and Treasurer, Acting Colonial Surveyor, Postmaster and Superintendent of Police.[63]

Educated Africans played an important part in pioneering the legal, medical and other professions in Nigeria. The colony's first attorneys in private practice read law locally, obtained licenses from the Supreme Court, and represented the legal interests of African and European clients.[64] Christopher A. Ṣapara Williams, Lagos's first British-trained African barrister, was called to the bar in 1879. He moved to Lagos in 1886 after practicing for several years in Cape Coast. By 1915 more than a dozen African barristers worked in the colony.[65] Nathaniel Thomas King, Lagos's first British-trained African doctor, studied at the Universities of Aberdeen and Edinburgh before returning home in 1876. King died in 1884, but in the next three decades thirteen British-trained doctors succeeded him in Lagos.[66] Other professions developed later and more slowly. However, by 1915 Lagos's African population could boast qualified surveyors and pharmacists and even an architect and engineer. The African lawyers, doctors and other professionals possessed technical training and knowledge necessary to perform services vital to blacks and whites in the colony.

African colonial servants and professionals commanded high incomes, which they sometimes multiplied through investment in business, land or more education. Richard Beale Blaize, I. H. Willoughby and P. J. C. Thomas, highly successful merchants, entered trade with money they had

The making of the educated African elite

saved while working for the government.[67] Other colonial servants, including Oguntola Ṣapara, Adeyemo Alakija, Olayimika Alakija and William A. Cole, used their savings to study law or medicine in Great Britain.[68]

Few whites lived in Lagos until after the turn of the century. Those present depended on educated Africans to open Yorubaland to commerce and civilization. These two factors kept racial prejudice in check into the 1890s.[69] The educated elite enjoyed better relations with Europeans during the 1860s, 70s and 80s than at any time until the decade before Nigerian independence. The posts these Africans held and their close association with Europeans gave them influence, authority and access to information that they turned to personal advantage. Educated Africans used their influence with the government to lobby for policies that benefited them individually or as a group. They pressured local governors and the Colonial Office to separate the administration of Lagos from that of the Gold Coast Colony; grant the Oil Rivers to Lagos Colony rather than to the Royal Niger Company; increase expenditure on education and public works; and intervene in interior affairs.[70] African colonial servants sometimes parlayed authority derived from their jobs with the government into private gain. A minor official in the Judicial Department settled a legal dispute outside court and charged a tidy fee for his trouble.[71] An examiner in the Customs Department demanded a bribe before performing a routine service.[72] The Paymaster of the Lagos Constabulary lent money to junior officers and subtracted payments plus 25 percent interest from their wage packets.[73] Herbert Macaulay used his position as Surveyor of Crown Lands to help friends acquire crown grants and persecute enemies by granting their land to others. He and other African colonial servants obtained crown grants under false names and then sold them at a profit.[74] Not all members of the educated elite behaved dishonestly. Because of their close relationship with Europeans and access to the colonial state, most saw opportunities for private gain and did not hesitate to take them.

No sooner had the educated elite emerged than changes occurred which threatened its privileged position in colonial society. An economic depression hit Lagos in the 1880s and persisted into the first decade of the twentieth century. Prices of palm produce fell steadily in Europe after 1870 and reached record lows in the mid-1880s. They remained relatively high in Lagos, however, owing to increased competition for the dwindling supplies coming down to the coast from the interior. By the 1890s, most African merchants had ceased making money on palm produce and either gone out of business or concentrated their activities on imports. Three English firms failed in 1900.[75] Profits on imports diminished at this time, too, because the introduction of currency and banking facilities increased competition in the import sector and undermined barter trade, on which a double profit had been made.[76] To survive, merchants had to operate on a very slim profit margin and ensure a rapid turnover of a large volume of goods. Because merchants still conducted much of their business on credit, success

Marrying well

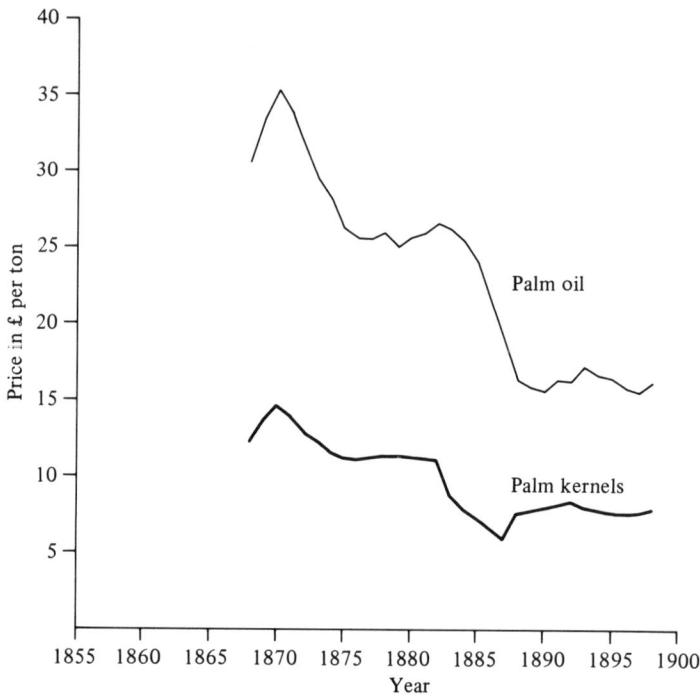

Figure 1.2. Five-year moving averages of palm oil and palm kernel prices. *Source:* This graph is derived from data in Sara S. Berry, *Cocoa, Custom and Socio-Economic Change in Rural Western Nigeria* (Oxford, Clarendon Press, 1975), p. 23

depended in part on establishing stable business relations with a large number of reliable traders who took imports regularly, sold them quickly, and repaid their debts promptly.[77] Economic conditions during these years clearly favored large European firms with capital to finance stock and credit over long periods of time, and to survive sudden downturns in trade.

Contemporaries in Lagos and Britain blamed the economic depression not on falling palm-produce prices in Europe and rampant competition in Lagos but on warfare among Yoruba people in the interior, which they believed had interrupted the supply of palm oil and palm kernels to the coast.[78] Business interests in Manchester, Liverpool and Lagos pressed the Colonial Office and the local government to restore peace in the interior so that trade could flow freely again.[79] John Payne Jackson, editor of the *Lagos Weekly Record*, expressed the sentiments of many Lagosians when he wrote, 'the strong arm of Her Majesty's Government is alone capable of reducing the interior country to that condition of peace and quiet essential to its future well-being' and, he might have added, to the future well-being of the colony.[80]

In 1892 Governor Carter responded to public opinion, with which he personally agreed, by sending a military expedition fifty miles inland to pacify the bellicose Ijebu. A year later, with the Ijebu defeat still fresh in the minds of the interior people, Carter swept through Egba, Oyo and Ibadan country signing treaties with the local rulers.[81] Although Carter's aggression brought virtually all of Yorubaland under the British Protectorate, it did not have the desired effect on the economy of Lagos. As the Yoruba wars subsided, the volume and value of imports and exports rose, but prices of palm oil and palm kernels remained depressed, competition on the coast intensified, and Lagos merchants continued to lose money. In 1898 a businessman told a commission investigating trade that while his turnover had greatly increased since the mid-1880s, his profits had fallen from 15 to 30 percent to 1 to 2 percent annually.[82]

In other respects, Carter's expedition had a profound effect on Lagos, forming what A. G. Hopkins has called 'the thin edge of the imperial wedge'.[83] The colony became the administrative headquarters of a vast hinterland, necessitating a larger, more effective bureaucracy in Lagos. This administrative expansion fatefully coincided with the arrival at the Colonial Office of Joseph Chamberlain, bent on more rapidly exploiting Africa's vast underdeveloped estates.[84] It shortly preceded advances in tropical medicine that made Lagos a healthier place for Europeans. Between 1911 and 1920 the death rate for whites in the colony fell to 13 per 1,000, not much higher than in England.[85] As a consequence of these changes, the number of Europeans and the size of the Civil Establishment in Lagos increased more than fourfold between 1891 and 1911. By 1911 the European population totalled 608; by 1905, the last date for which figures on Lagos alone are available, the Civil Establishment numbered 592 (187 Europeans and 405 Africans). The scope of government activity also expanded dramatically.[86] Expenditure on communications, public works and sanitation soared, financed both by growing revenues and the first colonial loans. In the 1890s alone, work either began or was completed on electric lighting, improved sewage disposal, a bridge between Lagos and the mainland, and a railway line linking the colony with the Niger.[87] By 1911 the colonial government had added agriculture, audit, education, forestry, railroad and telegraph departments and was well on its way toward building an effective regional civil service. British attitudes toward the colonial government's role in Lagos changed markedly during the 1890s and the first decade of the twentieth century. Policy-makers in London and Lagos now assumed that Great Britain would remain in the colony indefinitely and that in future whites would play a larger and educated Africans a smaller part in colonial development.[88]

Educated Africans had agitated for more vigorous colonial expansion during the 1880s and 1890s, expecting to be Britain's partners in progress.[89] They had not anticipated the heightened racism that accompanied the change in policy. As more Europeans, including women and working-class males, arrived in Lagos, educated Africans began to be systematically excluded from new jobs created and old positions they had held.[90] The changing attitude of the Church Missionary Society became apparent as early as 1891, when Bishop Samuel Crowther was succeeded by a white. It was painfully obvious in 1915 when the society summarily dismissed J. S. Fanimokun, principal of the C.M.S. Grammar School for eighteen years, and replaced him with a European.[91] The percentage of Africans in the Civil Establishment remained roughly the same and the number of blacks who were First Class Clerks or above actually increased, because the colonial government grew rapidly in the 1890s and first decade of the twentieth century. At this time, however, the government closed to Africans certain top-ranking clerical positions and segregated the West African Medical Staff.[92] In 1897 and again in 1903 the Lagos Chamber of Commerce split along racial lines. These divisions reflected growing conflict of interest between European and African merchants and deepening racial antipathy between whites and blacks. After 1903 the Lagos Chamber of Commerce excluded Africans altogether.[93] In the early twentieth century, racial discrimination in social life became quite common, epitomized by the establishment in 1909 of a colonial church open to whites only.[94] William MacGregor, governor between 1899 and 1904, slowed some of the worst of these changes, arguing that 'Segregation would . . . be disastrous here.'[95] Walter Egerton, MacGregor's racist successor, encouraged them by providing separate facilities for Europeans and stipulating that blacks should never hold positions superior to whites.[96]

Educated Africans continued to enjoy many opportunities after the 1890s, but conditions were not as propitious as they had been before. Trade improved between 1906 and 1919. The organization of trade, however, still favored large European firms.[97] Toward the end of this period, moreover, European oligarchies began pursuing non-competitive business practices in an effort to force African merchants out of business.[98] The elite meanwhile faced increasing competition in the colonial service and the professions from Europeans and the growing number of educated Africans in Lagos. Overt discrimination blocked advancement in many fields, while hardening racial attitudes deprived the group of easy access to Europeans and influence with them. Africans in government employment were more closely supervised than ever before. It is true that lawyers Kitoyi Ajasa and Adeyemo Alakija, colonial servant Henry Carr, merchant Samuel H. Pearse and a few others retained the confidence of whites. But most Europeans now regarded most educated Africans with deep disdain. Typical of this attitude, Acting Governor G. C. Denton asserted in 1895 that he had never met an African in a position of trust who did not abuse it.[99] These changing historical circumstances undermined the educated elite's position in colonial society and affected its religious, cultural and political views. Each of these developments had implications for marriage.

Table 1.1. *Percentage distribution of occupations of elite males at four points in time*[a]

Occupation	Date			
	1880	1891	1902	1915
Merchants	57	48	38	18
Colonial servants	22	15	21	32
Professionals	11	26	32	38
Others	9	11	9	11
N	(54)	(80)	(85)	(117)

[a] Unless otherwise specified, data in this and subsequent tables are derived from interviews with descendants of the elite, newspapers, *Blue Books, Government Gazettes* and other private and public documents cited in the bibliography.

Because of rounding, percentages in tables may not total 100.

'Professionals' includes clergy, lawyers, doctors, surveyors, headmasters and engineers. 'Others' includes newspaper publishers, pharmacists, planters and locally trained lawyers.

THE EDUCATED ELITE

The educated elite grew steadily between 1880 and 1915. Elite males numbered 54 in 1880, 80 in 1891, 85 in 1902 and 117 in 1915, and totalled 200 persons during the entire thirty-five-year period. Occupational criteria were used to identify elite men; by definition they worked as import–export merchants, colonial servants or professionals or in other modern occupations. While 57 merchants, 60 colonial servants, 61 professionals and 22 members of other occupations belonged to the elite during the entire period, the percentage in the three major categories changed markedly from decade to decade, as Table 1.1 indicates. These figures show a shift from an elite dominated by merchants in 1880 to one dominated by professionals and colonial servants in 1915.[100] Among the reasons for this change were the growing demand for educated blacks in the colonial service and the professions; the increasing availability in West Africa of secondary education needed to pursue professional training abroad; and, perhaps most important, the changing economic climate in Lagos, which enhanced the attractiveness of law, medicine and the colonial service. When business became unprofitable, educated young men sought other outlets for their talents, and parents saw secondary and advanced education as a sound investment.[101]

Quantitative data on elite women are unavailable, owing to the greater difficulty of identifying and obtaining information about them. Always fewer than elite men, elite women also increased in number during the years studied. The ideal was for elite women to be 'housewives', rather than to work outside the home. By the 1880s many such women achieved this ideal.

Table 1.2. *Percentage distribution of education of elite males at four points in time*

Education	Date			
	1880	1891	1902	1915
Primary	41	32	21	8
Secondary	39	44	47	52
Advanced	20	24	32	39
N	(54)	(80)	(85)	(117)

Those who did work taught school or took in sewing. Teaching offered an exception to the ideal that educated women should not work outside the home. The elite admired ladies who entered the classroom to share their training with young girls. Until the twentieth century, even teachers usually stopped work after marriage. Sewing probably attracted educated young women because it enabled them to earn a little cash without leaving home. A few elite women traded, the most common economic activity of Yoruba women, but usually on a small scale.[102] Fanny Barber and Rebecca Phillips Johnson, substantial women traders, stand out as exceptions.[103] A number of Lagos's educated women traders complained that the Royal Niger Company drove them out of business when it was granted a charter to administer the Niger River in 1886.[104]

The elite was very highly educated compared with the population as a whole, only a fraction of which could read and write.[105] All elite males had gone to primary school, at least 80 percent had attended secondary school, and roughly 30 percent had received advanced education at Fourah Bay College in Sierra Leone or at a medical training hospital, the Inns of Court or a university in Britain.[106] As the changing occupations of elite men suggest, the proportion with secondary or advanced education increased as the period progressed.

Elite women were not as highly educated as elite men. None received professional or university training between 1880 and 1915. Even so, all elite women had attended primary school, many had gone to secondary school in Freetown, Abeokuta or Lagos, and some had completed their education with a few years at an English girls' school. The proportion of elite women with secondary education increased during the period, as was true of elite men. For both men and women, education became an ever more important criterion for entry into the elite.

Until the colonial governments established schools for Muslims in Freetown in 1890 and Lagos in 1896, religious organizations controlled all the Western educational institutions in these two towns.[107] The curriculum in most schools included religious instruction, and school attendance clearly

Table 1.3. *Percentage distribution of the origins of elite males*[a]

Saro	68 ⎫	
Brazilian	8 ⎬	82 repatriates
Other	6 ⎭	
Local Yoruba	12 ⎫	18 locals
Other Nigerians	6 ⎭	
N	(165)	

[a] The origins of 35 elite males could not be determined.
'Other' includes Ghanaians, Gambians, Afro-Americans and a Liberian. 'Other Nigerians' includes Gun, Nupe and Igbo.

fostered conversion to Christianity.[108] The long exposure of the elite to Western education helps explain why all of its members were Christian, although less than a quarter of Lagos's population embraced the white man's religion.[109] Of the 157 elite males whose religious denomination could be determined, 43 percent were Anglican, 29 percent were Wesleyan, 2 percent were Baptist and 8 percent were Catholic. After 1888 a number of African churches split from the European denominations for political and constitutional reasons.[110] Only 18 percent of the elite males joined one of these African churches. Elite women came more overwhelmingly from the Anglican faith than did elite men. Very few elite women joined the African churches.

Anglicans dominated the elite because of their numerical superiority in the colony and because the C.M.S. operated more and better schools than the other religious organizations. The C.M.S. far surpassed the Wesleyans, Baptists and Catholics in educational opportunities for women. But in addition the C.M.S. enjoyed a preferred status with the colonial rulers, and this made it attractive to educated Africans. Anglicanism became associated with elite status. A disproportionate number of the group attended St Paul's Breadfruit Church and Christ Church in central Lagos. However, religious denomination did not determine status. Wesleyans, Baptists and Catholics all occupied influential positions in the colony, and some of them commanded as much power and respect as any Anglican. Upwardly mobile members of these minority denominations rarely felt the need to convert to Anglicanism to ease movement into the elite. This said, it is worth noting how few of the elite ever joined the African churches. The loyalty of the group to the European denominations reflects a deep-seated preference for foreign religious institutions and a strong belief that African Christianity did not suit the elite.

The educated elite came primarily from the Christian Saro, not surprising given this group's early and intimate contact with Western education and culture. Saro made up 68 percent of the elite males, while Sierra Leonean, Brazilian and other repatriated slaves together made up 82 percent of their

Marrying well

Table 1.4. *Percentage distribution of the origins of elite males at four points in time*

	1880		1891		1902		1915	
Saro	73		73		71		61	
Brazilian	12	92	13	91	11	89	5	72
Other	6		6		7		6	
Yoruba	4	8	6	9	8	11	18	28
Other Nigerians	4		3		3		10	
N	(48)		(69)		(73)		(97)	

number. The dominance of the repatriates diminished during the period, however. Saro fell from 73 percent in 1880 to 61 percent in 1915, and repatriates as a whole declined from 92 percent in 1880 to 72 percent in 1915. An increase in the number of local Yoruba and of other Nigerians made up the difference.[111] Elite women were even more predominantly Christian Saro than elite men, and among elite women the proportion of Saro hardly diminished during the period.

Important sub-ethnic divisions existed among the Yoruba. Many repatriates or their ancestors had come originally from Yorubaland. On returning to Lagos, some Saro and Amaro traced their roots in the interior. Unfortunately, information on sub-ethnic identity proved impossible to obtain for more than a few elite men and women. Thus it is impossible to say what percentage of the elite would have identified as Egba, Ibadan, Ijesha or Ijebu. Each of these groups could claim sons among the elite, the Egba more than the rest and the Ijebu fewer.

Data on place of origin demonstrate that it is misleading to use 'educated elite' and 'Saro' interchangeably, as some authors have done.[112] Most Saro did not belong to an educated elite, even loosely defined, and many were neither literate nor Christian. Moreover, elite males included a significant number of non-Saro. Education and Christianity rather than place of origin provided the key mechanisms of elite formation, and therefore emerged as the distinctive characteristics of the group. Whatever their origin, members of the educated elite had more in common with one another socially, economically and culturally than they did with illiterate or Muslim Saro.

Children born in Lagos or the interior of Saro and Amaro parents are usually counted as Saro and Amaro in scholarly works, and they have been treated that way here.[113] However, 46 percent of the elite males who were Saro and Amaro had been born in Yorubaland. Much smaller in the 1880s and 1890s, this proportion increased to almost 60 percent by 1915, signaling a change from a primarily foreign-born to a largely locally born elite. The proportion of elite males born in Lagos itself grew from 9 percent in 1880 to 44 percent in 1915. Very few of these men came from old, established Lagos

The making of the educated African elite

Table 1.5. *Percentage distribution of education of elite males by literacy of their fathers*

Education of elite males	Literacy of their fathers	
	Illiterate	Literate
Primary	23	12
Secondary	53	45
Advanced	23	43
N	(30)	(83)

lineages, but more could claim connections with lineages in the interior. Moreover, once persons settled in Lagos, they began building kin groups of their own, some of which became large and powerful.[114]

In colonial Lagos extended kin often played an important part in raising, educating and opening opportunities to children.[115] Evaluation of the family backgrounds of the educated elite, therefore, depends on information about grandparents, aunts, uncles and siblings as well as about parents. While the family histories necessary to provide these data are only partially complete, they indicate that many elite men and women came from families in which a parent or other relative already had had close contact with Europeans and accepted the value of education and other aspects of Western culture.[116] This helps explain the willingness of these families to encourage and support lengthy schooling. Information could be obtained about the fathers of 113 elite males. Almost three-quarters of this number were literate. Twenty-one percent worked as clerks, catechists or clergy, while 50 percent worked as merchants or traders. Only 29 percent made their living as farmers, craftsmen, chiefs, warriors or cult priests, traditional occupations. The percentage of elite men's fathers who worked as clerks, catechists and clergy was higher than the average in 1880 but lower than the average in 1915, while the reverse was true of the percentage that worked in traditional occupations. Taken with data on origin and place of birth, this suggests that the social base of elite males had begun to broaden by the end of the period.

The relationship between elite men's education and the occupation and education of their fathers further illustrates the relevance of family background to status. Table 1.5 shows that elite men with literate fathers were more likely than elite men with illiterate fathers to receive advanced education. Table 1.6 demonstrates that among elite males with secondary education or above, sons of illiterates were more likely than sons of literates to become merchants or colonial servants; while sons of literates were more likely than sons of illiterates to become professionals. The professions, and to a lessser extent the higher ranks of the colonial service, remained the preserve of children of educated Saro throughout the period. No close

Table 1.6. *Percentage distribution of occupations of elite males with secondary education or above by literacy of their fathers*

	Literacy of their fathers	
Occupations of elite males	Illiterate	Literate
Merchant	30	19
Civil servant	50	33
Professional	20	48
N	(20)	(67)

relationship existed between the occupations of elite males and those of their fathers. Sons of merchants and traders did not enter commerce and sons of clerks did not join the colonial service in disproportionate numbers.

Quantitative data on the fathers of elite women are unavailable, but qualitative data suggest that these women came from even better families than elite men. Fewer elite women than men had illiterate fathers and more had fathers who worked as clerks, clergy or import–export merchants. It is not surprising that elite women should have come from better backgrounds than their male counterparts. Most families invested greater resources in the education of sons than of daughters. Only families that attached great importance to Western education, wanted to protect the status of their daughters, or found the cost of schooling no obstacle gave girls sufficient education to assure them a place among the educated elite.[117]

Detailed data on the economic status of different social groups in Lagos must await further research on the social and economic history of the town. Nevertheless, it is important to go as far as possible toward locating the elite economically. Overall, these men and women came from prosperous families, although the economic status of their kin varied widely. Dr Ayodeji Oyejola's parents died while he was a young child, and he was raised by aunts who worked as petty traders.[118] Mojola Agbebi, a local minister, helped him attend Colwyn Bay Institution in Wales and then study medicine in Edinburgh.[119] In contrast, persons such as Dr S. A. Leigh-Sodipe, Eric Olawolu Moore, Olaşeni Moore, Candido da Rocha, Annette Oyinkan (Bucknor) Edun, Arabella Ibiremi (Vaughan) Moore, Victoria (Davies) Randle and Stella (Davies) Coker were children of wealthy merchants.[120] The high economic status of the elite's families gave them access to education and other opportunities. Some elite men and women inherited wealth, which they then turned to economic advantage. Candido da Rocha's share of his father's £1,500 estate helped him launch a successful business career; while Josiah Henryson Doherty's sizeable inheritance consolidated wealth he had accumulated personally.[121] Charlotte O. (Blaize) Obasa inherited a fortune from her father; while Hannah Matilda

(Williams) Benjamin inherited valuable land and houses from each of her parents.[122] The families of most elite men and women had made their money relatively recently from legitimate commerce, salaried employment, rents or farming, not from the slave trade, tolls or other customary prerogatives. Daniel Akitoye, Samuel Sogunro Davies and M. A. Akinṣemoyin, descendants of Ọbas, and William K. Fafunwa, Henry Glover and A. A. Oshodi, sons of important chiefs, were exceptions rather than the rule.[123]

Government records indicate that the annual wage of regularly employed unskilled laborers in Lagos averaged about £12 in the 1890s and first decade of the twentieth century.[124] A. G. Hopkins has estimated that the average earnings of skilled craftsmen varied between £36 and £60 during the same period.[125] The average profits of traders cannot be determined, but the difficulty the government faced in attracting laborers suggests that even petty traders must have netted more than unskilled workers.[126] Many traders undoubtedly made far more. At the upper end of the scale, the Ọba of Lagos received a stipend of no more than £400 during most of the years between 1880 and 1915.[127]

Compared with these figures, data on elite males indicate their high annual incomes. Rectors and headmasters earned £75 to £150 per year, varying from decade to decade and denomination to denomination. Both of these occupational groups received perquisites that supplemented their salaries – free housing and reduced school fees for their children. Substantially greater, the annual income of colonial servants averaged £212 between 1880 and 1915. Salaries fluctuated from decade to decade, but they remained relatively constant from department to department, with the exception that doctors always earned much more than clerks. Elite males in the clerical service took home an average of £213 in 1880, £174 in 1891 and £252 in 1913, while those in the Colonial Medical Service averaged £250 in 1891 and £393 in 1913.[128] Both clerks and doctors occasionally received horse, house or personal allowances that supplemented their salaries. Some doctors in the colonial service enjoyed additional income from private practice.[129]

The incomes of private doctors and of lawyers are much harder to document. Little can be said but that they sometimes charged hefty fees, had ample work, and lived very comfortably. The government paid lawyer Ṣapara Williams, to cite an example, 600 guineas for a case that took only a fraction of his time for a few months. In another matter, Williams received £335 without ever appearing in court.[130] When transferred to the interior, doctors in the Colonial Medical Service complained of a substantial fall in income due to loss of private practice.[131]

Turning to merchants, I. H. Willoughby grossed an average of £393 per month in the summer of 1887, before his trade began falling off.[132] Zachariah Archibald Williams reputedly grossed £60,000 in 1884, before retiring from business in 1889.[133] A. G. Hopkins calculated that I. B. Williams netted £550 a year in the 1880s and that Josiah Henryson Doherty, one of Lagos's wealthiest men, made £2,374 in a single year at the height of his career.[134] David Augustus Taylor earned upwards of £600 per annum before he began losing money and abandoned trade at the end of the century.[135] Profits made in random years by other merchants could be cited, but they would tell us all too little. Until further research has been done it is safest merely to conclude that merchants had the highest potential incomes of any occupational group among the elite, but that they also faced the greatest risks.

Elite women did not often earn substantial incomes from their own economic activities. Teaching paid very poorly. In the 1880s schoolmistresses' salaries varied from £7 to £36, with most in the £7 to £15 range.[136] Some teachers received small supplemental allowances, but salaries rose little during the next two decades.[137] Seamstresses cannot have earned much more, given the abundance of men and women with their skills. A few women traders made substantially greater sums, but these women could rarely compete with leading male merchants.

Many elite men and some elite women invested in real estate, and supplemented other earnings with rental income varying from several pounds to several hundred pounds per year.[138] Wills indicate that while most of the elite owned only two or three houses or farm plots, a few of the richest men and women owned dozens of pieces of real estate, including large farms and valuable commercial property.[139] I. B. Williams retired from trade in 1890 and supported himself and his wife quite luxuriously off rents. When he died in 1925, Williams received more than £400 per year for five large houses in central Lagos, which he rented to African and European firms.[140] In 1895 Z. A. Williams rented one building to the colonial government and another to a European firm. At that time he allegedly owned more than 3,000 acres outside the colony.[141] Lawyer Adeyemo Alakija owned more than sixteen parcels of choice real estate when he died in 1952.[142]

Land made an attractive investment not only because it generated income, but also because it could be used as collateral, turning a hard asset into liquid capital. Merchant Seidu Olowu mortgaged the same property to three different parties in 1909, in return for £1,500 cash and £500 credit.[143] A. G. Hopkins documents that in the largest single land deal in nineteenth-century Lagos, J. P. L. Davies mortgaged all his real estate for annual credit of £60,000.[144] In 1919 P. J. C. Thomas took out a £100,000 mortgage on his property.[145] The fact that land appreciated dramatically in value during the colonial period added to its attractiveness. Abigail Macaulay obtained a property for £3 6s. 6d. in 1870. The government requisitioned the land in 1893, and in 1936 paid her family £21,105 compensation.[146] By the 1880s land had become an important basis of the educated elite's wealth.[147]

Probate records kept by the Lagos Supreme Court measure wealth imperfectly. The valuation of an estate reflects only what the deceased owned at the time of death, giving no indication of wealth already transferred to kin.[148] Wills sometimes list real estate and personal effects owned

Table 1.7. *Median value in pounds sterling of estates of elite males*

Merchants	1,499	(37)
Professionals	300	(30)
Colonial servants	34	(20)

when the document was written, but lost later in life.[149] Probate records do, however, provide a rough indication of the worth of the educated elite relative to that of all persons who appear in probate records. They also further illuminate the comparative economic status of elite men and women and of the major occupational groups among elite men. Lagos probate records begin in 1886. The median value of the approximately 2,550 estates brought before the court between that year and 1945 was £25.[150] The median value of the estates of the 98 elite males who appear in probate records was £300, more than ten times as great.[151] Only thirteen elite women turned up in probate records, reflecting the fact that fewer elite women than men owned substantial property and that succession to elite women's property raised fewer problems than succession to elite men's. The median value of the thirteen women's estates was £150, half that of elite men's.[152]

Table 1.7 breaks down the median value of elite men's estates by occupation, and demonstrates that merchants accumulated far more wealth than professionals or colonial servants. The court valued lawyers' and doctors' estates at £1,425 and £800 respectively, however, indicating they died almost as wealthy as merchants and far wealthier than other professionals. Only one elite woman left an estate valued at greater than £1,500.

Economic data demonstrate that the elite's wealth varied considerably. Men accumulated greater wealth than women. Among elite men, certain occupational groups accumulated greater wealth than others. As a group elite men were wealthy relative to the population as a whole. This wealth gave the elite and their children advantages in the quest for education and elite occupations. It supported a distinctive style of life expressed through the consumption of ideal and material goods such as European clothing and furniture, and in leisure activities such as dances and concerts and public ceremonies such as weddings. The elite's distinctive style of life defined the group, set it apart from the rest of the population, and gave content and meaning to elite status.

The growth of legitimate commerce, the rise of the colonial state and the introduction of Christianity and Western education altered the structure of economic and political power in Lagos. A small group of Western-educated Christians took advantage of these changes to accumulate wealth and other resources and establish itself as a new elite. No sooner was the educated elite established than economic depression, heightened imperialism and racial discrimination threatened the group's position in colonial society. Elite males adjusted to changing conditions in trade by seeking careers in the colonial service or professions. In time, heightened imperialism and racial discrimination provoked the emergence among the elite of cultural nationalism and political opposition.

2

Yoruba and Christian marriage

Yoruba and Christian marriage differed fundamentally. They rested on different assumptions about polygyny, domestic relationships and roles, and legal rights and duties. Each type of marriage had emerged in a particular cultural context and been shaped by specific processes of historical change. Each stood at the heart of a distinct socio-cultural order and had distinct economic, social and political implications. This chapter describes Yoruba marriage as practiced in the nineteenth century and by some Yoruba-speaking people still today. It then analyzes the new form of marriage introduced into Yorubaland by repatriated slaves and Christian missionaries. The discussions of Yoruba and Christian marriage define the domestic options open to the elite. They show the alternatives that underlay domestic decision-making and shaped the daily lives of elite men and women.

As used here Yoruba and Christian marriage represent ideological constructs – terms employed to make a point. Neither was a unitary social form, as the data clearly show, and the adjectives that describe them do not actually explain what they were. Neither Yoruba nor Christian marriage remained static and unchanging. Changes in the wider economy and society affected these two types of marriage, just as they were affected by them. That Yoruba and Christian marriage are ideological constructs makes them no less useful tools of analysis. Indeed, emphasizing this aspect of terminology underscores the fundamental differences between Yoruba and Christian marriage and strengthens the overall argument about marriage among the elite.

YORUBA MARRIAGE

In the nineteenth century, Lagos Yoruba shared an ideology of patrilineal descent. In the precolonial period, bounded, exogamous groups of patrilaterally related kin played a major part in the social and political organization of the town. These remained important after the annexation, in spite of the change in government and rapid influx of immigrants. Headed in principle by the eldest male, patrilineages regulated their internal affairs and mediated between lineage members and the wider society. Yoruba inhabited the world as members of corporate descent groups, not as individuals.[1]

Residence was patrilocal. Male and unmarried female kin lived together in large compounds along with slaves and clients, often recent immigrants. Women moved to their husbands' homes when they married. If a lineage outgrew its compound, it segmented and established a new residence. This second household remained part of the lineage and recognized the authority of its head, but became a separate administrative unit. Wealthy men often built homes of their own, while continuing to belong to the lineage.[2] By the turn of the century, wealthy polygynists sometimes provided each wife a separate dwelling, believing this would minimize conflict among the women.[3]

Descent exhibited strong bilateral tendencies, which grew more pronounced in the last half of the century. Married women retained membership in their own lineages, and female kin who lived nearby sometimes played an active role in lineage affairs. A woman's relatives felt a strong social obligation to her and her children, who could exercise rights through their mother's line. Cognates formed the circle of relatives active in most life-cycle ceremonies, including marriage.[4]

In the precolonial period, lineages held corporate rights to land and titles, although persons could acquire individual rights to other kinds of property. Lineage members enjoyed rights to use as much land as they needed, but could not alienate it.[5] While private ownership of land became common in colonial Lagos, family title also survived.[6] Strictly speaking, rights to family land were not heritable. Parents' claims died with them, and children acquired rights of their own at birth. The property a man used during his lifetime devolved to his junior siblings or children, depending on the nature of the property, the structure of the family and the wishes of kin. Interests in privately owned land, on the other hand, passed to children, sometimes becoming family property. If a man was a polygynist, his estate was divided *per stirpes*; that is, into portions determined by the number of his wives. All of the children of one wife then shared a single portion. Children of concubines or fleeting liaisons inherited as long as the deceased had acknowledged paternity of these offspring. The legitimacy of a child depended on recognition by its father, not on the status of its mother. Daughters inherited as well as sons, sometimes equally, sometimes not. Privately owned property could be partitioned, giving children absolute title to their portions. Spouses had limited rights to one another's property during life, and did not inherit from one another. Wives devolved to men's younger brothers and sons, although women past childbearing age sometimes returned to their own families.[7] After the annexation, the emergence of new property rights and the establishment of colonial courts created opportunities for Lagosians to press claims at odds with these customary norms.[8]

The Yoruba regarded marriage not as an isolated event but as a protracted process through which lineages alienated productive and reproductive rights in female members in exchange for bridewealth, goods and services transferred from the man's kin to the woman's kin prior to marriage. On other occasions this same process enabled lineages to give bridewealth and acquire rights in wives essential to the perpetuation of the group. The Yoruba saw bridewealth as compensating the woman's kin for the loss of her productive and reproductive capacities. Asked to interpret Yoruba customs, a committee of educated Africans observed that bridewealth 'is a sort . . . of gift on the part of the husband to the wife's family as a compensation for the loss of her services'.[9] This exchange of women for prestations created a web of obligations between recipients that extended far beyond marriage and gave each lineage a stake in the union. The Yoruba looked to their affines for assistance during life-cycle ceremonies, at times of economic hardship and when pursuing political goals. A contemporary writer asserted that 'the binding force' of marriage rested in the 'joint obligations' it created.[10]

Consistent with this emphasis on exchange, the Yoruba viewed marriage as a union of lineages, not individuals. Locals repeatedly spoke of marriage as a 'family contract'.[11] Kin often arranged first marriages, in some cases when the parties themselves were children. Even in subsequent marriages relatives exercised considerable control over the selection of spouses and regarded the consent of both families as a necessary preliminary to marriage. A contributor to a local newspaper wrote, '[C]onsent of parents or of persons *in loco parentis* plus the bestowal of necessary dowry constitutes validity of marriage according to native law.'[12] Jacob Kehinde Coker, a member of the educated elite, mirrored this sentiment when he wrote, 'Marriage means the choice of husband and wife with the approval and consent of the parents and families of [both] part[ies].'[13] Elsewhere Coker wrote, 'To the African a woman not given to the husband by those responsible for her is not regarded lawfully married.'[14] In this and subsequent phases of the marriage process immigrants without relatives near Lagos often relied on patrons or friends to perform the duties of kin.[15]

Relatives weighed many factors when evaluating marriage partners. First they observed rules of exogamy. Next they wanted to ensure that prospective mates would fulfill conjugal responsibilities – bear children, work diligently, and meet obligations to affines. To this end, kin investigated spouses and their lineages looking for biological or social disabilities such as barrenness, laziness, insanity or indebtedness, all of which the Yoruba regarded as hereditary.[16] Because marriage established alliances between lineages, relatives also weighed political or social factors. One observer commented, 'families . . . [wanted] to see that the union fulfilled its intended purpose of enhancing the family prestige on both sides and strengthening the family connection by widening its ties in directions deemed desirable'.[17]

N. A. Fadipe, a Yoruba sociologist, studied marriage in southwestern Nigeria in the early 1930s and wrote very perceptively about his own people. Fadipe claimed that kin attached little significance to the sentiments existing between the couple prior to marriage. He stated, 'The romantic element in

Marrying well

Yoruba marriage was almost non-existent.'[18] It is true that the Yoruba did not regard love as a prerequisite to marriage, although they did believe that love might grow out of marriage. The Yoruba also thought that persons' most intimate companions should be friends of the same sex, not spouses.[19] Whether for emotional or other reasons, however, young men and women in late-nineteenth-century Lagos sometimes expressed strong feelings about whom they wanted to wed. Occasionally they forced kin to heed their wishes. Barikisu Laniwan, for example, resolved to marry a young trader named Sani Giwa. When a relative objected, she obstinately refused to marry anyone else and finally got her way.[20] Even when families arranged marriages, they usually permitted the couple a veto.[21]

Lineages took a final precaution before consenting to marriage. They consulted *Ifa,* the Yoruba oracle, and sanctioned the union only if it communicated a favorable response. When kin disapproved of a marriage, they could block it, saying *Ifa* had sent a negative reply.[22] The educated elite who practiced Yoruba marriage often preferred to dispense with *Ifa* consultation, but non-Christian relatives sometimes performed the ritual for them.[23]

Once a man's relatives had agreed to a union, a series of rituals ensued which symbolized the unification of the two lineages and exchange of rights between them.[24] These rituals began when the head of the man's lineage, usually the eldest male, visited the woman's kin and asked for her in marriage. A contemporary asserted, '[I]t is the duty of every head of a family to ask for a bride for the males under his direct control.'[25] The woman's relatives did not give an immediate reply but took time to discuss the marriage and consult *Ifa*. If the woman's lineage ultimately consented to the union, representatives of both families met to negotiate bridewealth. Men's paternal and maternal relatives contributed prestations for first marriages, giving them a measure of control over the timing of the union and selection of the spouse. Men themselves usually paid bridewealth for subsequent marriages.

The first exchange occurred at *iṣihun,* a ceremony marking the couple's formal betrothal. On this occasion representatives of the man's lineage gathered at the compound of the woman's lineage and offered kola, bitter kola, refreshments and possibly a small amount of currency, which the woman's cognates shared to show that they accepted the betrothal. When Christians entered customary unions the man presented his fiancée with a Bible and gold wedding band, signs of the couple's new religious faith.[26] During this and subsequent Yoruba marriage rituals, Christians might also say prayers or read passages from the Bible.[27]

Iṣihun publicly symbolized the transfer of rights in the woman. Afterwards each lineage had widely recognized obligations to the other. The man enjoyed exclusive sexual access to the woman, whom he now called wife (*iyawo*), and he could claim any children she bore. Each year until the woman finally moved to her husband's home, he presented her father agricultural produce and small amounts of currency, which she might share. The man was also expected to help if his affines needed labor to clear land or build houses or had bridewealth, funeral expenses or large debts to pay. The cumulative value of these prestations could be great. At the end of the century, a colonial official accused women's kin of protracting these payments to maximize gains from marriage.[28]

The man's kin paid *idaanǫn*, the final installment of bridewealth, shortly before the woman moved to her husband's household. *Idaanǫn* means the creation of affines, and this exchange marked the final union of the two lineages. Without it Yoruba marriage was incomplete. A contemporary explained, 'Until the *ano* has been given and received, nothing is considered binding.'[29] In the precolonial period *idaanǫn* included kola, bitter kola, alligator pepper, honey and cloth, each with symbolic significance.[30] During the colonial period, the Yoruba began exchanging cash and spirits as well, signs of the emergence of a money economy and of increasing economic differentiation. Many men complained that the cash payments, varying from a few shillings to several pounds, imposed economic hardship. In 1889, Lagos traders begged the colonial government to legislate an upper limit of fifteen shillings sixpence.[31] The woman received the cloth and possibly a share of the currency, while her cognates divided the rest.

The bride moved to her husband's residence during a ritual known as *igbeeyawo*, which in first marriages occurred when the woman was two or three years past puberty and the man was in his late twenties. On this occasion the woman's female relatives groomed and dressed her. She then promenaded through the compound, receiving blessings and domestic utensils from her parents and kin. As the bride departed, the head of her lineage told her to obey her husband, affines and co-wives. Her companions then escorted her to her new home, bearing the gifts she had been given. On arrival, older wives in the husband's lineage greeted the party, lifted the bride onto their shoulders, and carried her inside. This act, *igbeeyawo*, marked the woman's entrance into her husband's household.[32]

Domestic groups formed the basic unit of economic production in Yorubaland.[33] These were headed in theory by husbands and comprised also wives, unmarried children and perhaps slaves, clients or pawns. Marriage marked the moment when sons stopped working for their fathers and established domestic groups of their own, although children of both sexes had lifelong economic obligations to their parents. A sexual division of labor characterized most domestic groups. However, the precise economic activities of men, women and slaves depended on how the group made its living. In farm families, males cleared the forest, burned the bush, and tilled the soil. They also hunted and gathered palm nuts. Females helped with the harvest, processed food crops, traded agricultural surplus, and performed domestic labor. Slaves worked in the field, market or home.[34] The scale of men's economic activities depended in part on the amount of labor they controlled. Wives formed an important economic asset because they both worked themselves and reproduced labor by bearing and rearing children. The services associated with bridewealth enabled women's fathers to tap the labor of younger men.[35]

The Yoruba regarded polygyny as the ideal form of marriage. It is impossible to calculate a polygyny rate for the nineteenth century, but few men had more than two wives simultaneously. Only the richest elders and chiefs had upwards of ten wives at a time.[36] Even so, polygyny contributed to social and economic differentiation. Wives and children created wealth and enhanced power. The greater the number of a man's wives and children, the greater the size of his labor pool and the wider his network of political alliances. Because only rich and powerful men could make multiple marriages, the number of a man's wives and children also marked his prestige.

In ordinary families, meeting domestic needs required a degree of cooperation between husbands and wives. Spouses had clearcut economic obligations to one another. The Yoruba expected husbands to provide their families with a place to live, give their wives capital to begin trading, meet their obligations to affines, and contribute to their children's upkeep. The Yoruba expected wives, on the other hand, to help support themselves and their children and to fulfill responsibilities to their husbands' kin. After meeting these responsibilities, spouses enjoyed considerable autonomy. Each could pursue independent economic activities and accumulate wealth. Neither had a right to use the other's property, nor interfere in its management.[37] A newspaper article on the status of African women remarked, 'In the ownership of property women have equal rights with men . . . A woman may hold property as distinct from her husband and may hold it inalienably.'[38] The 'Report on the Yoruba' by the committee of educated Africans asserted, 'The husband has rights to his wife's person but none to her property.'[39] Certain social structural features encouraged wives to protect their autonomy. In polygynous households, each wife and her children (ọmọiya) formed a separate unit. Wives not surprisingly wanted to conserve resources for use by themselves and their children, and to minimize obligations to their husbands. In addition to this, wives remained members of their own lineages after marriage. They did not join their husbands' lineages. If women wanted to play an active role in public affairs, they used their own lineages as a base of support. In these circumstances women preferred to invest resources in their own relatives, rather than in their husbands or affines.[40]

This discussion has emphasized Yoruba norms – the way the sources say marriage ought to have been. Many Yoruba marriages in Lagos conformed to these ideals. However, Yoruba marriage was changing in the second half of the nineteenth century. Individual behavior often deviated widely from socially accepted norms. Indeed, a discussion of norms obscures the fluidity of Yoruba marriage in colonial Lagos and masks the latitude in everyday life of individual domestic choice. Recent anthropological research emphasizes that marriage can be analyzed on two levels, as a set of rules or 'related

Yoruba and Christian marriage

principles which give form to the socio-cultural universe' and as a lived reality.[41] Rules constrain options and explain why some practices are subject to greater deviation than others. Social behavior, the cumulative result of individual actions, shapes rules.[42] Two areas of conflict between rules and actual behavior emerge from a study of Yoruba marriage in turn-of-the-century Lagos: the control of kin over marriage and the division of responsibility between husbands and wives.

In 1911 a Lagos chief called to give evidence on marriage testified, 'In olden times no man [could] act independently of his family . . . Some are acting independently now, others not.'[43] In that same trial another chief complained, '[G]irls go to live with husbands of their own choice. We are not finding a remedy the time is past.'[44] Still another chief worried that kin were losing their control over marriage: 'As to now-a-days, whatever the people like, that is what they do.'[45] These statements show that by the late nineteenth century some Lagos men and women asserted independence of kin in domestic affairs. Relatives could not always control the selection of spouses, the terms and timing of marriages, or the character of conjugal relationships and roles. Some men and women treated the web of rituals and obligations surrounding marriage as a matter of choice to be invoked when deemed desirable and avoided when not. In many instances couples formed unions without the consent of kin. Bridewealth changed hands after the fact, if at all, to give the unions greater legitimacy. Analyzing one such union, a writer commented, 'It is intriguing to note how . . . ancestral wisdom is preserved . . . clothing the *de facto* marriage with the . . . status of *de jure* . . . [A]fter the expiration of one month . . . [the] bridegroom . . . shall dispatch "peacemakers" or "Pardon Seekers", . . . who shall convey the requisite dowry [and] endeavor to appease the wrath . . . of the parents of the bride.'[46] Couples such as this took marriage into their own hands and acted independently of kin. In the case cited, the husband and wife attempted to placate the bride's family by conforming belatedly to Yoruba norms. When it suited the man and woman they would undoubtedly assert their autonomy again.

Conjugal relationships and roles sometimes also deviated from Yoruba norms. Spouses often fought and bargained over domestic responsibilities, manipulating and redefining obligations to one another in an effort to maximize benefits and minimize costs. The precise relationship and roles of husbands and wives depended on their personal ambitions, feelings for one another and ability to enforce social norms. Some men and women lived up to cultural ideals, voluntarily or under pressure from kin, patrons or friends. Others fulfilled only minimal obligations.[47] Wives and children were occasionally so autonomous that they formed independent units of economic production.[48] Men and women moved in and out of marriage with comparative ease, which underscores the fluidity of the marriage bond. Many persons passed through several unions in a lifetime.[49]

It is important to view behavior that deviated from Yoruba ideals in the context of certain other characteristics of Yoruba marriage. John Comaroff's work on marriage payments notes that much research has treated marriage as a single, undifferentiated category of relationships. Persons are either married or unmarried, and unions are either formal and legitimate or informal and illegitimate. All marriages are regarded as having the same social structural significance. In fact, Comaroff demonstrates, many societies recognize taxonomies according to which unions may be classified.[50] Early colonial Yoruba distinguished among Yoruba, Muslim, and Christian marriage and concubinage. Moreover, they appreciated variations within each type of marriage depending on the origins of the union, the status of the parties involved and the character of subsequent relationships between spouses and their kin. In 1911 the Reverend James George Campbell wrote to a local newspaper, 'Society in Lagos is on the whole composed of three grades: (1) Those who marry according to European custom whether sincerely or simply to keep up with the times (2) Those who marry according to Native custom (3) Those who live any how.' He continued, 'There are three kinds of wives in native polygamous life. The Dowry Wife. The Gift Wife. And the Slave Wife [sic].'[51] Chiefs who testified in the trial cited above distinguished between wives called *iyawo* and *aya* and concubines called *ale*.[52] Fadipe defined four types of Yoruba marriage.[53] Each kind of union entailed different conjugal, kin and affinal relationships and roles and imparted different values. The nature of conjugal, kin and affinal responsibilities in turn helped define the status of a union. Unions themselves represented contrasting ways of locating couples and their offspring in the social universe. Concubines did not have the same standing in the eyes of the community as customary wives, and 'dowry' wives did not have the same standing as 'gift' wives.

The status of unions was sometimes ambiguous, because Yoruba marriage was a process and marital behavior often deviated from social norms. Persons did not always know whether couples were married, or if married, precisely how they were married. Occasionally observers disagreed about the status of unions. Asked about the marital standing of a particular woman, a witness in the trial *In re Ṣapara* testified that some persons would call her *iyawo*, but he would not.[54] To complicate matters further, the status of unions could change as couples observed or neglected conjugal and affinal responsibilities. A chief noted, 'A man may take a woman, and they live together and get children, and [he] may make her *iyawo* by giving the *ano* afterwards.'[55] Another chief asserted that if a couple lived together without consent or bridewealth payment, the man became the woman's 'husband' if her kin accepted gifts from him when one of their relatives died.[56] Similarly, marriages could end without the return of the bridewealth, the key transaction in Yoruba divorce. Men and women could shed their status as husbands and wives slowly by ceasing to fulfill conjugal duties. Thus the boundary between 'Those who marry according to Native custom' and 'Those who live any how' was fluid and not always clear. In this situation, persons enjoyed great latitude to redefine the status of unions to suit their own ends by manipulating outward behavior. Dr Oguntola Ṣapara paid a modified form of bridewealth for Adel Coker and lived with her for seven years as if she were his Yoruba wife. In order to wed another woman in church, Ṣapara then claimed that what he had paid was not in fact bridewealth, and that Adel was only his mistress.[57] Deviation from Yoruba marital norms sometimes reflected a self-conscious effort to redefine the status of a union or to leave its status deliberately ambiguous.

Many late-nineteenth and early-twentieth-century Lagosians did not like what they saw happening in domestic life. They blamed changes in marriage on the coming of Europeans. A 1907 article in the *Lagos Weekly Record* asserted, 'It is not generally conceived the extent to which the native marriage custom has been violated and perverted under the new order of things.'[58] A 1911 article lamented, 'In the confusion which has overtaken the social order of native life, marriage which is at the foundation of society . . . has . . . lost all sanctity and meaning.'[59] Twenty years later Fadipe wrote, '[M]arriage is one of the social institutions of the Yoruba which has been most in a state of flux as a result of the diffusion of foreign ideas and the quick process of economic growth.'[60] Contemporaries were right. The final chapter of this book considers the impact on Yoruba marriage of colonial economic, political and social changes.

CHRISTIAN MARRIAGE

In the mid nineteenth century, Christian repatriated slaves and European missionaries introduced a new form of marriage into Yorubaland. This type of marriage had emerged in England as part of a long process of historical change.[61] It brought attitudes toward polygyny and expectations about domestic relationships and roles and legal rights and duties that were antithetical to Yoruba marriage. Many Christian marriage practices were Victorian rather than explicitly Christian, as some of the educated elite came to realize. But with characteristic ethnocentrism, most Victorians equated their own form of marriage with Christianity and civilization. Missionaries demanded that educated Africans conform to English marriage practices as an outward sign of inward religious and cultural conversion.[62] Henry Carr, a member of the educated elite who accepted the missionaries' teaching, referred to Christian marriage as a 'positive law of Christianity'.[63] An article in a Lagos newspaper commented, 'The educated native, under the influence of missionary teaching has become imbued with the idea that acceptance of the English marriage system was indispensable to conversion to Christianity and admission to heaven.'[64]

Christian marriage did not have wide appeal in Lagos, even among Christian converts. Between 1880 and 1907, an average of only fifty Christian unions occurred each year out of a Christian population that grew from about 5,000 to about 10,000.[65] Not all members of the educated elite

Marrying well

practiced Christian marriage; and some men and women who did not belong to the elite entered Christian unions. However, the educated elite embraced Christian marriage more enthusiastically than any other segment of the population. Christian marriage played a major role in identifying and defining the elite. It contributed in important ways to elite formation and maintenance.

No African customs except human sacrifice and slavery offended Victorians more than polygyny. Missionaries in Lagos, no matter what their denomination, viewed monogamy as the most fundamental characteristic of Christian marriage. They made it a condition of baptism and treated polygyny among converts as grounds for excommunication. Charles Phillips, a Yoruba bishop, wrote, 'I fail to see the difference in the scriptural treatment of polygamy and slavery. Both are . . . evils that afflict society. Both originate from the corruption of the human heart.'[66] The colonial government reinforced the missionaries' stand on polygyny by passing marriage ordinances that regulated Christian marriage. Two 1863 ordinances provided for licensing and registering Christian unions.[67] The Marriage Ordinance of 1884 went further by specifying that persons already married according to Yoruba custom could not marry someone else in church, and that those married in church could not wed again according to Yoruba custom. Thus, the 1884 ordinance prohibited polygyny among men who practiced Christian marriage. It gave Christian wives a legal right to monogamy.[68]

In addition, Europeans in Lagos spread Western values about the proper conjugal and kinship relationships. They taught that Christian marriage united two individuals, not two lineages, and that it should be based on love and companionship. Europeans also held that personal happiness rather than family welfare should form the primary motive for marriage. Abigail C. Oluwole, wife of a Yoruba bishop, wrote a pamphlet entitled *Christian Marriage* for the Mother's Union, an Anglican organization founded to 'uphold the sanctity of marriage' and 'lead . . . families in purity and holiness of life'. Mrs Oluwole instructed her readers, 'God instituted marriage *between only two persons, a* man and *a* woman.' She continued, 'Marriage should be based on *love* . . . No calamity is greater than for two persons to be united who do not love one another.'[69] A letter from a mother to her daughter's guardian also illustrates the significance attached to love as a criterion for marriage. The woman wrote that she could not consent to her daughter's marriage until she returned to Lagos and determined that the couple loved one another.[70] Asked to write an essay on Christian marriage, a Church Missionary Society catechist argued, 'Wife is a helpmate for the husband, as she is as well a partner, an equal (in certain respects) . . . she is a co-sharer of troubles with her husband; she is the tightest friend that [he] could get in life . . . she . . . freely exposes to him . . . that which she could not make any other in the world acquainted with.'[71] Another writer commented that Christian marriage must be based on 'genuine . . . affection' and 'should be a source of real happiness'.[72].

Beyond introducing new ideas about the proper conjugal and kinship relationships, Europeans transmitted to educated Christians middle-class Victorian values about the ideal roles of husbands and wives. They portrayed husbands as economic providers and wives as mothers and homemakers. In the section of *Christian Marriage* devoted to the 'pecuniary duties' of wives, Mrs Oluwole told her readers that the good Christian wife was 'very industrious in cleaning her house, having well-cooked and punctual meals, mending and making the clothes of the household, [and] if possible having the washing done at home'.[73] She suggested that before marriage girls might find useful employment as governesses, cooks, housekeepers and nurses, perfecting skills they would need as wives. In marked contrast to Yoruba norms, however, Mrs Oluwole implied that after marriage women ought not work outside the home. Mrs Oluwole advised her readers, 'What man is there who on his return from business finds a warm welcome awaiting him from a wife who is also ready to minister to his comforts and to sympathize with him in the joys or troubles he may have had in his day's work, who would not look forward to his wife's society?' She added, 'Never let anyone do for your husband what you can do yourself.'[74]

The curricula at boys' and girls' schools illuminate what Europeans expected of educated men and women. Local secondary schools taught boys English, arithmetic, geography, history, algebra, geometry, natural science, philosophy, political economy and bookkeeping to prepare them for careers as clerks, businessmen or professionals. The Church Missionary Society Female Institution, until 1907 Lagos's only secondary school for girls, taught its pupils domestic economy, needlework, religious instruction, drawing and singing, in addition to English, arithmetic, geography and history.[75] A letter in a local newspaper expressed the philosophy behind women's education. '[I]n establishing a High School or any other school for girls . . . the kind of education required is such practical training as will . . . make them competent to take care of their homes, and be good wives and mothers.'[76] An elderly widow explained, 'Our parents and teachers did not want us to work. We went to school to learn cake baking, needlework, French and drawing so we could be "housewives". All we were expected to do was marry and take care of our husbands' homes.'[77]

In addition to their responsibilities as mothers and homemakers, missionaries depicted Christian wives as moral exemplars – custodians of society's moral values. The advice a man sent a woman about to open a school for girls reveals the degree to which the educated elite had internalized this European outlook. The man wrote,

> I always think that girls . . . need much to be looked after sooner than boys for in them . . . are to be instilled the virtues of true womanhood, patience and self-control and purity of life . . . We of course do not want our ladies to

become lawyers and doctresses and educationists and philosophers and statesmen, but we do want them to attain to that which is noble and true and holy.'[78]

In a similar vein, a Lagos woman cautioned her Sunday school class, '[A]lthough women are the weaker vessels, on them depends in extenso, the Purity of our land.'[79] A contributor to a Lagos newspaper explained, 'It is woman's sphere to mould and fashion society . . . Behind the throne she is powerful, and even more powerful than the monarch himself . . . men may make institutions and laws, but women make men.'[80]

Another Western value influenced the educated elite. Europeans assumed that marriage formed a conjugal estate and created an identity of interests between spouses. Husbands and wives toiled dutifully in their separate spheres for the welfare of the elementary family, neither for themselves alone nor for their kin groups. It is true that Victorians vested husbands with autocratic authority within the family. But Victorians also believed that in good marriages husbands would respect their wives and take their wishes into account when making decisions. Many elite men and women embarked on Christian marriage with the idea that husbands and wives ought to share common interests. As subsequent chapters will show, the new domestic ideals that Christian marriage embodied proved difficult for the educated elite to achieve.

In Christian courtship practices and marriage rituals, the educated elite adopted much that was foreign but retained much that was Yoruba as well. Consistent with the emphasis in Western marriage on love and companionship, the educated elite enjoyed new independence when choosing Christian mates. Young men and women met at church, clubs and social events. Parents and friends then hosted dances and picnics where couples could get better acquainted, develop emotional attachments, and decide if they wanted to wed.[81] Asked how the educated elite selected Christian spouses, an informant replied, 'We chose for ourselves because of our love.'[82] Christian marriages were arranged only when persons had difficulty finding suitable mates, and then by respectable Christians rather than by kin. A man pressed Stella (Davies) Coker, 'When are you finishing the arrangements for me to get married – any polished girl will do?'[83] Rebecca Phillips Johnson and Charlotte O. (Blaize) Obasa, two elite women, enjoyed great reputations as matchmakers.[84]

Few of the educated elite came from large local patrilineages. Most elite men and women traced descent through the male and female lines, and many helped build and maintain close-knit cognatic kin groups. While the elite's relatives accepted love and companionship as the basis of Christian marriage, they continued to regard marriage as a union of two families.[85] Among the elite, kin retained a measure of control over the selection of spouses by ensuring that young persons socialized only with friends of the right social status. Families of the elite still viewed consent as a vital preliminary to matrimony and vetoed unsuitable mates. Merchant J. P. L.

Yoruba and Christian marriage

Davies prevented his willful daughter Victoria from marrying a Mr Lewis from Sierra Leone. Years later Victoria blamed her father for forbidding her to wed the man she loved and forcing her into an unhappy match.[86] A few fathers attempted to control children's marriages from the grave, by including clauses in their wills disinheriting them if they wed particular suitors.

Prior to Christian marriage, kin investigated prospective spouses to determine their suitability, much as before Yoruba marriage. Indeed, Mrs Oluwole urged this Yoruba practice on her readers, lamenting that 'one cannot always know a person's character from appearance'. She wrote,

> In the days of our grandparents no one would give a girl in marriage, or allow a son to marry, without first making full and strict enquiries as to character, religion, health, etc. . . . But it is a most difficult thing to get this done now . . . The result we have today is, unhappy marriages, separation, divorce, and hatred of the marriage tie.[87]

Conducting a pre-nuptial investigation, J. P. L. Davies asked his wife, 'Let me know all about Miss Anna Lynch and whether it is likely she can make a wife for James Johnson our clergyman.'[88] The Reverend Charles Phillips objected to a proposed marriage on the following grounds:

> I feel strongly that the object of your love is not worthy of your love and of admittance into the family. She is decidedly the most objectionable person. I assure you that whatever suspicions or ill feeling you may have against me, I am speaking to you out of love and concern and solicitude for your future happiness . . . I hereby most lovingly and correctly protest in the name of the family against your marriage. Yea in the name of your mother, brother, and sister and in the name of our Heavenly Father. I beg you to try to put off the marriage before it is too late.[89]

When considering Christian marriage partners, kin may have looked for signs of barrenness, sterility, insanity, indebtedness and intemperance, as before Yoruba marriage. Prior to Christian marriage, however, families also weighed new factors – education, social status and Christian reputation. Relatives wanted to ensure that persons came from the right social background to make good Christian mates. This meant fulfilling Christian marital ideals and, in the case of husbands, comfortably supporting their families. Desirable marriage partners usually came from wealthy, well-connected families. But because Lagos offered abundant opportunities for upward and downward mobility, kin generally placed greater emphasis on the characteristics of spouses than on the position of their families. Well-educated Christians of sound reputation would marry well no matter what their family background.[90]

Christian marriage rites began in a manner similar to customary rites. A representative of the man, known as his *alarena,* approached the woman's parents or guardian and asked for her in marriage. Usually the head of the man's family performed this duty, but if that person was away from Lagos or not a practicing Christian then a patron or respected friend might assume the

Marrying well

responsibility.[91] In the 1870s, discussions preceding Christian marriage occurred orally. Early in that decade five different men asked Charles Phillips about his sister Zenobia.[92] By the turn of the century, educated Africans usually broached the subject of marriage in a letter. Albert E. Carrena sent P. Nogueira a typical request.

> I am now approaching you on a subject which relates to the future welfare of my son Amatus. My son has unfolded his wishes with regard to the relations existing between him and your daughter Miss Florentina Nogueira to me, and I beg to assure you that his intention towards your daughter is a sincere one. He has assured me that he would spare nothing undone to make the future of your daughter a happy one.
>
> I therefore feel it a very great pleasure to approach you and to ask you for the hand of your daughter Miss Florentina Nogueira in marriage to my son Amatus.
>
> I pray and sincerely hope that the unification of the two families will be a happy and fruitful one and receive abundant blessings from the Almighty.[93]

In two weeks Carrena received the following reply:

> I am directed by the members of my family to acknowledge with pleasure the receipt of your letter . . . asking for the hand of our daughter Florentina in marriage to your son Amatus.
>
> I am to express that having known your family as we do, we do not hesitate to give our consent as we have the feeling of full assurance that by the will of God both families will not have cause to regret this betrothal and that the two parties especially concerned will find pleasure and happiness in each other's company.[94]

Many such letters survive, and they share a number of characteristics.[95] First, they imply that a close relationship existed between the couple before the man's kin raised the subject of marriage. Next, they suggest that the couple's happiness hinged on the marriage. Finally, such letters indicate that relatives still saw marriage as unifying families, not just individuals – note the use of 'my family' and 'our daughter' in the second letter. Nogueira's reply hints that his family agreed to the union because it knew Amatus and his kin and found them socially acceptable. Families took this exchange of letters very seriously. On one occasion a suitor wrote to his beloved's father, explaining that he had made 'private contracts' with the girl. The father rebuked the young man, saying he had no objections to the match, but the request would have to be made 'in the usual way' or it could not be considered.[96] Had the man's kin refused to write a letter of proposal, the marriage negotiations could not have proceeded. A. K. Ajisafe, a noted student of Yoruba culture, wrote, 'It is not decorous . . . for the man himself to go direct to the girl's parents to ask for her.'[97]

If the woman's family agreed to the marriage, members of the man's family called on them for the formal betrothal. The man's paternal and maternal relatives presented the woman's cognatic kin with kola, bitter kola, alligator pepper and honey, included in *iṣihun* and *idaanọn*. They also offered refreshments and sometimes cash. The man gave his future bride a

Bible and gold wedding ring. Wealthy men often provided these prestations themselves, enhancing their marital autonomy.[98] The couple played a more active role in this ceremony than in Yoruba betrothal. The age of marriage had risen among the elite owing to education and other factors, women being in their early twenties and men in their late twenties or early thirties.[99] Moreover, the pair had chosen one another and were already well acquainted. After the engagement the woman's parents permitted the man to come to their home courting, a privilege not enjoyed before customary marriage.[100]

The interlude between the betrothal and Christian wedding varied from weeks to years. Colonial servant P. J. C. Thomas wrote a friend, 'Since leaving Lagos ... events unexpected and unanticipated ... have transpired. One was that within three weeks I was engaged and married.'[101] Dr Ayodeji Oyejola, on the other hand, waited several years for his fiancée to finish school before he wed.[102] During this period, the man sometimes made gifts to the woman's relatives or offered financial help or other services. As important, he gave the bride-to-be gifts of currency, jewelry, cloth or clothing.[103] Some men financed their fiancées' education in England.[104] Others transferred land to their future wives. Sarah Forbes Bonetta Davies, Margaret C. Hoare and Felicia Ayodele Wright all received real estate when they married.[105] The pre-nuptial exchange culminated shortly before the wedding when the groom presented the bride with a trousseau or money to buy one. In the early 1870s, Charles Phillips ordered Marianne Bailey the following items from England: a white lace dress trimmed with satin ribbon and frills 'in the latest fashion', a bridal wreath, a white bonnet, a black cloth jacket, a purple dress with white lace, a bonnet to match, a pair of stays, four yards of embroidery, two pairs of kid boots, ladies' drawers, two pairs of stockings, a white fan, a purple fan, a sun shade 'in the French style' and a black lace cloak. For all of this Phillips paid £13.[106] A 1914 article in the *Lagos Standard* asserted that trousseaux varied in cost from £5 to £42, averaging about £15.[107]

Important differences existed in the property transactions before Yoruba and Christian marriage. In both cases the kola, bitter kola, alligator pepper and honey marked the betrothal, symbolized the unification of the families, and created a shared interest in the marriage. The educated elite did not view Christian marriage as an exchange of women for bridewealth or see bridewealth as compensation for the loss of women's productive and reproductive capacities. Yet some families may have regarded the gifts preceding Christian marriage as just reward for all that they had invested in educating, clothing and otherwise preparing their daughters for Christian marriage.[108] The exchange prior to Christian marriage also took on important new meanings. It asserted the participants' Yoruba identity and affirmed their commitment to basic Yoruba values, at the very moment that they gave their sons and daughters in a new kind of marriage. In the absence of corporate descent groups, moreover, this exchange played an important role in defining kinship relations. Kin became those who contributed marriage prestations, and affines those who received them.[109]

In contrast to Yoruba bridewealth, the most valuable items exchanged before Christian marriage passed from the man or his relatives direct to the woman, forming a conjugal fund for her benefit and that of her children. These goods constituted neither bridewealth nor dowry, since dowry involves property that devolves to a woman from her own kin. Jack Goody calls exchanges such as that before Christian marriage indirect dowry.[110] In a community where there was competition for well-educated Christian women, these prestations assured wealthy educated men wives of the right social status. By demanding a substantial outlay prior to marriage, the transactions helped women's relatives determine the economic position of suitors and thus protect the women's status after marriage. When husbands transferred land to their wives, it gave the women a measure of financial security. Saro probably brought the practice of giving a trousseau from Sierra Leone. This exchange may have derived from the Yoruba custom whereby men gave their fiancées cloth prior to marriage. Or it may simply have inverted the source of the trousseau that Victorian parents typically provided their daughters. Whatever its origins, the trousseau ensured the bride a symbolic currency, Western clothing, essential to her role as a Christian wife. A newspaper article referred to men who believed that 'unless his opposite sex . . . [wears] a guinea gown, embroidered gown, lace gown, velvet gown, a splendid silk shawl, and other up to date garments that fall to the lot of well-to-do Westerners, she is not worth call[ing] civilized not withstanding her high education'.[111] The trousseau also symbolized the husband's willingness to assume financial responsibility for his wife and children.

The Marriage Ordinance of 1884 provided for civil ceremonies, but the educated elite's ordinance weddings always took place in church. These ceremonies closely followed the Western marriage rites, as illustrated by the following description entitled 'Marriage in High Life'.

> The contiguity of the bride's parents' residence to the Chapel happily rendered her entrance into the sacred edifice a mere walk over: leaning on her father's arm and attended by thirteen bride's maids . . . the bride's train [was] borne by . . . [her] brothers . . .
> The groom latterly arrived and met his best man . . . Mr Herbert Macaulay of the Public Works Department, and the ceremony immediately commenced, performed by the Rev. A. T. R. Bartrop assisted by the Revs. J. B. Thomas and Brian Roe; Mr Hoare [gave] his daughter away.
> Mr O. E. Macaulay most effectively rendered Mendelssohn's 'Wedding March' and Master Edmund Johnson played a variety of lively airs.
> . . . the company repaired to the residence of the bride's parents where a reception was held and light refreshments partaken of.[112]

Once couples had married in church, locals knew them as *alarede*. *Alaredeerẹ* designated a man's Christian wife.

Yoruba and Christian marriage

Christian wives typically moved to their husbands' homes after the church wedding.[113] Ideally couples established households of their own and did not live with the husband's kin. Henry Carr explained, 'the educated Native young man ... postpones his Christian marriage until ... he has a competence and can comfortably support a home'.[114] Wealth enabled many of the elite to achieve this goal. Couples who could not set up housekeeping on their own resided with whoever offered the most suitable accommodations, often one of the wives' relatives. Such couples usually moved to dwellings of their own as soon as they could afford it. Soon after his transfer to Lagos, customs official George Smith asked the government for a house allowance. He argued, 'I do not intend to depend on my mother-in-law to house me.'[115] Even when elite couples lived in separate households, they maintained close contact with relatives through regular visits. Most elite couples brought aunts, siblings, cousins, nieces or nephews to live with them at some point in their lives. Moreover, most Yoruba kinship obligations transcended residential boundaries.[116]

Europeans and many educated Africans believed that Christian marriage gave men, women and their children a new status. Justice Brandford Griffith expressed this point of view in 1898 when he argued, 'Christian marriage imposes on the husband duties and obligations not recognized by native law. The wife throws in her lot with the husband, she enters his family, her property becomes his ... Christian marriage clothes the parties to such a marriage and their offspring with a status unknown to native law.'[117] To protect this status the colonial state backed certain European marriage customs with the force of colonial law, fundamentally altering the legal rights of Christian husbands and wives and of their children. The Marriage Ordinance of 1884 made Christian marriage and polygyny mutually exclusive and gave Christian wives a legal right to monogamy. This ordinance contained a second equally important provision that changed the inheritance rights of spouses and children. This provision specified that when persons 'subject to Yoruba law and custom' married under the ordinance and died intestate, their self-acquired property should be divided according to English law governing succession to the personal property of intestates.[118] At that time English law of intestacy held that a wife's personal property passed to her heirs, subject to her husband's right to use it for life. One-third of a husband's personal property devolved to his wife for life, while the remaining two-thirds went to his heirs. For the purpose of intestate succession, heirs included legitimate children or next of kin.[119] Unless persons wrote wills specifying otherwise, Christian marriage radically altered Yoruba inheritance practices by giving spouses rights to each other's estates and by making Christian wives and their children sole heirs to men's self-acquired property. Marriage under the ordinance disinherited siblings and offspring by customary wives or concubines.

To regulate Christian marriage, the Marriage Ordinance of 1884 created Marriage Registries and licensed churches for the celebration of marriage.

Marrying well

The ordinance required couples who wanted to wed in church to give the Marriage Registrar notice, which he then posted for twenty-one days prior to issuing a marriage license. During this interval anyone who knew 'just cause' why the wedding should not take place could block the issue of the license, pending judicial hearing. Before the Registrar could grant a license, the applicants had to satisfy him by affidavit 'that neither . . . [was] married by Native law or custom to any person other than the person with whom such marriage is proposed'. As a further check, the ordinance specified that Christian marriages could take place only in Marriage Registries or licensed places of worship. The law forbade ministers to celebrate weddings if they knew any impediment that made the couple ineligible for Christian marriage. Finally, the ordinance empowered the Supreme Court to punish violators by fining them £100 or imprisoning them for two to five years.[120]

The educated elite certainly understood these provisions of the Marriage Ordinance. In the late nineteenth and early twentieth centuries, numerous pamphlets and newspaper articles complained that Christian marriage prohibited polygyny and interfered with Yoruba inheritance. George Alfred Williams, editor of the *Lagos Standard,* printed the following rhymed warning to bachelors: 'He who courts and goes away may live to court another day, but he who weds and courts girls still, may get in court against his will.'[121] Announcing the Christian marriage of Christiana Robbin and Samuel A. Wright, Williams had earlier alluded to the ordinance in a clever *double entendre,* 'Young bachelors – A charming CHRISTIAN(a) is ROBBIN(g) us of our (w)right.'[122] Most commentators adopted a more serious tone. A 1909 article in the *Lagos Weekly Record* cautioned, 'It is obvious that where the law sanctions and gives recognition only to "the voluntary union for life of one man and one woman to the exclusion of all others", such law is not only unadapted to people living under polygamous conditions but is in conflict with the bottom principles upon which the social life of such people is founded, and must mean . . . the disruption and overthrow of the social fabric . . . The object of the law is manifestly defeated where instead of promoting social order it works to produce social chaos.'[123]

Successive Supreme Court ordinances extended English law to matrimonial disputes between couples who wed under the Marriage Ordinance, changing the legal rights of Christian husbands and wives in other important ways.[124] Even highly educated Africans, however, were unfamiliar with the complexities of English family law, so that the full legal consequences of Christian marriage emerged only slowly as judges decided local cases in the courts. Whatever the law, the educated elite believed that Christian marriage gave wives new rights to maintenance and their husbands' property. They thought this perhaps because of the portion of the Anglican marriage ceremony where the groom said to the bride, 'with this ring I thee wed, with my body I thee worship, and with all my worldly goods I thee endow'.[125] One man asserted, 'the foreign form of . . . [marriage] I cannot understand . . . I cannot endow [my wife] with all my earthly goods.'[126] Another maintained that he preferred Yoruba marriage because 'there is no endowment by the bridegroom of all his earthly goods'.[127] A stanza in a doggerel satirizing the Christian wife's 'Ten Commandments' to her husband demanded, 'Thou shalt in a manner mild and meek, Give me thy wages every week.'[128] The educated elite undoubtedly realized that Christian marriage gave husbands new rights to their wives' property. This change received little comment, however, perhaps because elite women were not as outspoken as elite men or perhaps because elite women owned little property.

The educated elite also believed that ordinance marriage made divorce more difficult to obtain. They knew that Christian couples could end their marriages legally only by going to colonial court. Moreover, they understood that Christian husbands could sue for divorce only on grounds of adultery, while Christian wives could sue only in cases of adultery aggravated by incest, bigamy, desertion or cruelty.[129] Some contemporary observers maintained that in the past Yoruba divorce had been virtually impossible to obtain.[130] By the late nineteenth century, however, the educated elite saw Yoruba marriages ended commonly and easily. The 'Report on the Yoruba' commented, 'There is a great facility for divorce.'[131] N. A. Fadipe remarked on the 'popularization of divorce' in the colonial period.[132]

Yoruba and Christian marriage carried different expectations about polygyny, domestic relationships and roles, and legal rights and duties. They had very different economic, social and political implications. The Christian marriage rites and domestic relationships and roles became an important part of the distinctive style of life that defined the educated elite and set it off from the rest of the population. Until the elite's religious and cultural attitudes and values began to change at the end of the nineteenth century, and to a certain extent later, belief in the moral and cultural superiority of Christian marriage formed a central tenet in the ideology of the group. As subsequent chapters will show, Christian marriage concentrated valuable resources within the elite and created a dense network of kinship and affinal relationships that promoted the economic and political interests of the group.

3

Elite men and the marriage dilemma

Marriage confronted the educated elite with a dilemma. Christian marriage played a vital role in elite formation and maintenance. Europeans and many educated Africans insisted on the moral and cultural incompatibility of Christianity and Yoruba marital norms. Yet many elite men saw compelling advantages to Yoruba marriage and felt deep-seated tension between Yoruba and Christian conjugal ideals. Moreover, elite men and women responded differently to Christian marriage, because colonial economic, social and political changes differently affected their roles and opportunities. This compounded the marriage problem. Disagreement over marriage produced conflict between elite husbands and wives that had a lasting impact on the relationship between the sexes and the institution of marriage itself. In time, a few of the boldest elite men and women challenged the moral superiority of Christian marriage and the identification of Christianity with Western conjugal ideals. These new attitudes emerged slowly, however, after years of struggle over marriage – struggle that raged within individuals and between the sexes. Even then Christian marriage remained an important element in elite formation and maintenance.

This chapter explores the responses of elite men to the problem of how to marry, while the next probes the responses of elite women. The analysis takes an actor-oriented approach, which focuses attention on domestic behavior and the motives underlying it. Such an approach uncovers the appeal of Christian and Yoruba marriage to elite men and women. Ideology and interest shaped domestic decision-making. Gender played an important part in determining ideology and interest. Elite men's and women's marital attitudes and behavior changed in the early colonial period, but at different times, in different ways and for different reasons. Changes in marriage occurred in response to changing economic, political and social conditions in Lagos. An examination of the domestic life of the elite illuminates the link between marriage and the wider economy and society. It highlights the different impact of colonial economic, political and social changes on elite men and women.

Research on the life histories of elite males produced extensive data about the marriages of 113 members of the group. Marriage registers, newspapers and wills revealed that an additional 36 elite males made Christian marriages. Further information about the domestic lives of these men proved impossible to obtain, however, and in many cases disappeared forever with the deaths of their children. There are no biases in the kinds of men about whom information is missing. Available life histories and abundant written records provide ample evidence for the historian to recreate the rich and subtle tapestry of elite men's domestic lives.

Of the 113 elite males about whose marriages extensive data are available, 45 (40 percent) made Christian marriages only, 14 (12 percent) made Yoruba marriages only, and 54 (48 percent) married in church and also formed 'outside' unions, as contemporaries called them. Looked at slightly differently, 99 (88 percent) made Christian marriages at some time in their lives, and 68 (60 percent) at some point entered customary or outside unions. Outside unions often began with Yoruba marriage rites and had the status of customary unions. Sometimes they began informally and later acquired the status of Yoruba marriages. Occasionally outside unions remained extra-marital liaisons. The status of outside unions, like Yoruba marriages, could change or remain deliberately ambiguous.[1]

Many elite men believed fervently in the moral superiority of Christian marriage. These persons had listened to the religious arguments of their preachers and teachers and accepted that Christian marriage was the only legitimate form of union between a man and woman. Henry Carr wrote, '[I]f any man will seriously reflect . . . he will perceive that . . . Christian . . . marriage is . . . one of those great conquests over nature, one of those eternal moral landmarks which man should on no account let go again.'[2] George Alfred Williams, editor of the *Lagos Standard,* referred to educated Africans who practiced Christian marriage 'to make the home a sacred altar fit [for] God to dwell in'.[3] When making decisions about marriage, men such as these acted out of a profound commitment to what Christian missionaries had taught them was morally right.

A more generalized belief in the superiority of Western culture often accompanied a strong religious preference for Christian marriage. In the last half of the nineteenth century many educated Africans accepted Victorian ideas about evolution and progress. These persons regarded Africa as more backward than Europe and believed that the continent could progress only if its people embraced Western values and institutions.[4] This conviction spurred some elite males to adopt Christian marriage. A writer in a local newspaper pleaded, 'It has been admitted by the highly cultured of Africans that our native customs . . . such as polygamy . . . [are] inconsistent with . . . civilization.'[5] John Payne Jackson, editor of the *Lagos Weekly Record,* told his readers in 1894 that they must accept monogamy without compromise. The 'universal law of the survival of the fittest', he claimed, applied to morals. '[T]he Negro, if he desires to survive, must fashion his ideals after the highest standards and endeavor to work up to them.'[6] The alternative, another writer warned, 'was to sink into the mire of barbarism'.[7]

Some elite males lacked strong religious and ideological convictions and practiced Christian marriage for purely instrumental reasons, while others found that instrumental concerns reinforced their religious and ideological preferences. Contemporaries spoke of persons who 'married according to European custom . . . simply to keep up with the times' or 'for the sake of doing what everybody else does'.[8] They might also have mentioned men who made Christian marriages as a mark of elite status and a path to it.

In late-nineteenth and early-twentieth-century Lagos marriage formed an act of social definition. As such, it not only shaped domestic relationships and roles and legal rights and duties, but also located persons in the social universe. Christian marriage was neither a necessary nor a sufficient criterion for elite status. It served as much to consolidate elite status as to foster movement into the group. But Christian marriage, with its distinctive rituals and family life, became closely associated with the elite. The community expected elite men and women to court, wed and conduct domestic affairs in a certain way. Conforming to these expectations helped identify persons as members of the group. As Abner Cohen has pointed out in his study of the Creoles of contemporary Sierra Leone, Christian marriage and other distinctive cultural practices defined the elite as a group, gave it social cohesion, and distinguished it from the rest of the population.[9] In addition, Christian marriage brought educated Africans in Lagos economic and social benefits that facilitated upward mobility.

The Christian wedding itself provided the educated elite with an occasion to display religion and style of life, wealth and social standing. The elite's Christian weddings always took place in church and followed elaborate foreign ceremonies. The costly wedding attire and church decorations indicated just how much the groom's and bride's families could afford to spend on the affair. The number and identity of the guests demonstrated the size and influence of the couple's social network. Influential Europeans and educated Africans attended the most important weddings, while the Ọba, chiefs and Muslim associations paraded to the church *en masse* when they wished to honor families.[10] After hosting a Christian wedding, merchant J. P. L. Davies noted in his diary that he was heartily pleased by the crowd that turned out, because it reflected 'his position in the social world'.[11]

Lagos newspapers chronicled society weddings in minute detail, so that their social impact reached well beyond their immediate audience. When the Reverend James Johnson wed Sabina Leigh, daughter of merchant Jacob Samuel Leigh, the *Lagos Weekly Record* waxed eloquent.

> The preparations in honor of the event were of the most elaborate character . . . At an early hour Thursday morning . . . the street from the residence of the bride's father all along to St Paul's Church was thronged with gaily dressed groups in European and native attire . . . Long before . . . 2 o'clock, the large Church of St Paul's was crowded beyond its capacity, the gallery and every inch of room from the nave to . . . the chancel being occupied. The Church was tastefully decorated with palms and flowers . . . while a line of many coloured flags and pennants hung high along the middle . . . of the Church. Scrolls bearing appropriate mottoes adorned the walls on all sides, that on the front of the gallery being enclosed in a tapestry of flowers and palms.

> Punctually . . . the bridegroom . . . arrived . . . [and] was received with a murmur of applause. A quarter of an hour after, the bride made her appearance attired in a dress of rich white satin, the underskirt of which was organ pleated at the back, the overskirt in front consisting of three Honiton lace flounces and the train of which was of white velvet lined with satin . . . She wore suede 8 button gloves and shoes . . . and [a] long tulle veil, and carried a fan of ostrich feathers with mother of pearl sticks. Her train was borne by two pages dressed in . . . Fountbery ruby coloured suits and caps to match: and [she] was followed by 10 bridesmaids arrayed in pink sura silk Princess shaped dresses with cream silk lace over bishop's sleeves: cream lace hats trimmed with pink roses and ruby velvet ribbon . . . parasols of blonde lace lined with pink and finished off with bows of ruby velvet and ribbon, bronze shoes, and pink gauze fans each carrying a gilded wicker basket of flowers . . . Just as the ceremony was about to commence, Prince Oyekan entered . . . accompanied by the White Cap Chiefs and retainers.[12]

Later the article noted that the couple received 'numerous and costly' gifts.[13] Surely this was a wedding fit for a king. A local critic of Christian marriage claimed that it remained popular even after marital attitudes and behavior began to change in the 1890s, because the 'pomp and show' of Christian weddings 'constitute an irresistible attraction to our young people'.[14]

Until the racial and political climate began to change in the 1890s, and to a certain extent later, many educated Africans believed that making a Christian marriage would create an image in the eyes of Europeans that would improve their opportunities in colonial society. The educated elite's privileged position in colonial Lagos depended on European favor. Yet educated blacks knew that most whites regarded Africans and their culture as inferior. Some educated African men hoped to demonstrate that they were worthy of confidence and sought greater influence and authority by showing their colonial masters that they had assimilated European culture.[15] Christian marriage stood as the perfect symbol of assimilation. Contemporary observers acknowledged that this strategy sometimes bred hypocrisy, pointing to men who practiced Yoruba marriage secretly but condemned it publicly to create a good impression with whites.[16]

Christian marriage also brought men more tangible rewards. Most elite women in Lagos insisted on Christian marriage, and kin supported them in this position.[17] Men who wanted elite wives had little choice but to enter Christian unions. A firm believer in Yoruba marriage, Dr Oguntola Ṣapara may have agreed to wed Ore Green in church because she refused to marry him any other way.[18] From the perspective of elite males, elite wives had many compelling advantages. These women shared their husbands' values, experiences and interests, and hence understood them better than other women. Educated Christian wives alone could satisfy the Western companionate ideal. Elite wives also could establish homes where rising merchants, colonial servants or professionals would feel comfortable entertaining Europeans and other educated Africans. On these occasions men and women could establish and strengthen useful social connections. Then too, elite women could accompany their husbands to church, parties and Government House, where an educated, fashionably turned-out wife by a man's side served as a persistent reminder of his status.[19] Wives' activities reflected on their husbands' reputations. The Church Missionary Society censured Thomas Babington Macaulay, principal of the C.M.S. Grammar School, because his wife traded, arguing that commerce was not a suitable occupation for a woman of Mrs Macaulay's social standing.[20] On the other hand, Governor William MacGregor cited the charitable activities of lawyer Christopher A. Ṣapara Williams's wife as a reason for nominating him to the Legislative Council.[21] In addition to these advantages, elite wives could teach men's children the language, customs and values of the colonial rulers, enhancing their chances of educational and occupational success and helping to transmit status from one generation to the next. Finally, entering a Christian union with an elite woman provided a means of creating useful affinal connections with influential educated Africans, connections which could themselves facilitate upward social mobility.

Among educated Christians monogamy itself had clear advantages. Yoruba custom took shape in an agrarian context, where polygyny mobilized labor and other important resources. Wives and children created wealth and enhanced power and prestige. Education, occupation and style of life determined status in colonial Lagos, a commercial and administrative city. Among the educated elite wealth took the form of privately owned land, houses and luxury goods. It derived from trade, rents and, increasingly as the period wore on, employment in the professions and colonial service. Educated Christians who were concerned about upward social mobility strove to maximize educational and hence occupational opportunities for themselves and their children. Wives occasionally played a part in merchants' commercial success. They contributed to the success of colonial servants and professionals only indirectly, as described above. Educated wives and children rarely contributed to the family income, but rather constituted a drain on it. In this new social and economic setting, educated men had good reason to want to limit the number of their wives, children and affines, in hopes of doing as much as possible for themselves and their dependents.

Occasionally educated wives inherited substantial wealth. Under colonial law, men who made Christian marriages should have enjoyed rights to their wives' property. In Lagos, parents frequently entailed bequests to daughters so that this did not occur.[22] Even so, men fortunate enough to marry wealthy educated women usually benefitted from their wives' resources. Wives of independent means met many of their own expenses and helped support their children.

During the protracted marriage debate, elite men who advocated Yoruba marriage defended in detail their reasons for preferring it. What these men wrote, coupled with how they lived, vividly illuminates the attractions of

Yoruba marriage for elite males. Polygyny proved the most irreconcilable difference between Yoruba and Christian marriage. Not surprisingly it emerges as a major concern in marital decision-making. Elite men saw many advantages to plural marriage. First it ensured men offspring. The Yoruba regarded dying childless as a terrible calamity.[23] Yet barrenness condemned many monogamists to this fate. While visiting Lagos, the influential Liberian scholar and statesman Edward W. Blyden recognized this fact and argued that monogamy would last in the colony 'only as long as the forces which gave it birth . . . continued to exercise their . . . influence'. 'If you will carefully watch events in the lives of our [monogamous] predecessors and contemporaries', he reasoned, 'you will see that there is no reproduction. One Bishop Crowther, then a full-stop; one Bishop Johnson, another full-stop; one Henry Carr, again a full-stop. No system that does not help the swarm is good for the bees.'[24]

Elite men who defended polygyny also maintained that it protected women, although few elite women expressed this point of view. Such men asserted that by enabling all girls to marry, polygyny eliminated the plight of spinsters, deprived of woman's natural calling and dependent for life on the charity of relatives. These men worried that monogamy had created a surplus of women driven to prostitution to survive. An 1897 article in the *Lagos Weekly Record* proclaimed that in 'purely African cities' one could not find that plague of Europe, 'the professional outcasts, whose . . . living it is, to seduce and destroy innocent and unwary youth'.[25] Elite men also argued that polygyny safeguarded widows. In polygynous societies, widows could devolve as wives to their husbands' brothers or sons, who would ensure that the women were cared for. These societies need not worry about the problem of neglected old women.[26] But most passionately elite men argued that polygyny provided a form of birth control, which benefited women and children. The Yoruba held that women should not have sexual intercourse during the two to three years that they nursed their offspring, and regarded this period of sexual abstinence as a means of spacing children vital to the health of mothers and babies.[27] During this interval polygyny gave husbands a legitimate sexual outlet – other wives. Monogamy, critics charged, drove men to fornicate or violate the taboo against sex during lactation, equally unattractive alternatives. In *Polygyny Defended* Jacob Kehinde Coker commented, 'adultery and fornication must be used in the majority of monogamous marriages to bolster it up'.[28] Newspaper articles and pamphlets warned that too frequent childbearing, the fault of monogamy, was killing elite women and children. A 1901 letter to the press cautioned, 'The climatic conditions [in Africa] are such as to make child bearing a very serious affair, and under the unregulated methods of the Europeanized native, the child born is in the majority of cases but a weakling and soon dies off.'[29] A 1913 article entitled 'The Strenuous Life of Modern Civilization' spoke of 'the large and increasing number of deaths of young women who succumb to the ordeal of childbirth'.[30] Many elite men viewed with horror and pity the experience of a woman such as Zenobia (Phillips) Johnson, who bore eleven children in twenty-two years and saw seven die in childhood.[31] Women and children, men protested, ought not be abused in this way.

In nineteenth-century Yorubaland wives and children formed a valuable economic and political asset. The importance of wealth-in-people, including wives and children, declined in colonial Lagos as legitimate commerce became the mainstay of the economy and privately owned land and capital emerged as important economic resources.[32] The careers of Richard Beale Blaize, Jacob Samuel Leigh, I. B. Williams and other monogamous entrepreneurs demonstrate that by the late nineteenth century neither economic success nor political influence depended on polygyny.[33] All the same, some elite males continued to see social and economic advantages to having many wives and children and favored polygyny for this reason. Wives and children could still contribute valuable labor and services.[34] Moreover, plural marriage made possible a wide and diverse network of potentially useful alliances. Defending Yoruba marriage, Jacob Kehinde Coker wrote, 'In polygyny . . . large relations [are] kept up.'[35] Furthermore, some men believed that the greater the number of their children, the greater the likelihood that one would achieve success to the benefit of the family.[36] Polygyny and monogamy presented quite different alternatives with respect to the number of men's children and the number and social origins of their wives and affines. Assuming men felt no overriding religious or ideological commitment, the choice between these alternatives rested on how men perceived and evaluated their needs and interests and on how they hoped to meet them.

Quite apart from the issue of polygyny, elite males sometimes chose Yoruba marriage because they preferred the customary conjugal relationship and roles. These men dismissed the European ideal of companionate marriage as unrealistic, and wanted wives who would contribute to the household economy and retain a measure of financial independence. A letter to a local paper asked why 'aborigines' and Muslims amassed greater wealth than Christians and found the answer in 'the disadvantages of Christian marriage'. The author reasoned, 'the native heathen . . . has no family to be responsible for *to any extent*, beyond that having so many wives he looks up to each of them to provide his meals for him'. The Christian, on the other hand, 'is under a burden to make all ends meet, feed his children, wife, and family and sometimes provide for the family of his wife . . . secure the highest education possible . . . for the children, provide for them a profession . . . find them proper . . . raiment . . . and with all provide comfortable dwelling and sleeping places for them'.[37] Newspaper articles and pamphlets routinely criticized elite women for shunning domestic labor, demanding a retinue of servants, and thinking only of finery and frivolity. One man complained, 'It is wrong in [women] to leave all the drudgery and domestic works . . . to servants whilst, as is commonly the case at present,

Elite men and the marriage dilemma

they . . . sit down . . . reading a novel, or playing the piano, or sewing a pair of canvas slippers or enjoying the chat of a friend.'[38] Another moaned, 'The passion for dress . . . amounts almost to a mania with them.'[39] Men such as these blamed Christian marriage for creating impossible expectations in wives and leading to disappointment and bitterness when husbands failed to meet them. To avoid such demands some members of the elite entered only customary unions.[40] Mojola Agbebi defended Yoruba marriage, saying, 'The idea that a woman was to be a burden to her husband had no existence in the mind of the African . . . until he came in contact with [European] civilization. Let him who has money make his wife a queen.'[41]

Elite males also chose Yoruba marriage because they objected to the impact of Christian marriage on their legal rights and duties. One man refused to wed in church because of the irrevocable character of the Christian marriage contract.[42] Others complained that Christian marriage turned the 'native law of succession' topsy-turvy.[43] Still others feared that Christian marriage gave wives rights to their husbands' property. Most elite men knew that they could circumvent the problem of inheritance by writing wills, and many used testaments to recognize children born outside Christian marriage or disinherit Christian wives.[44] However, some men preferred to avoid troublesome legal problems altogether by forming only customary unions. Anglican officials acknowledged that the section of the Marriage Ordinance which dealt with succession constituted a barrier to Christian marriage, and in 1906 they petitioned the government to revoke this part of the law.[45]

Yoruba marriage had a final attraction for elite males. The status of customary unions was sometimes ambiguous and customary conjugal relationships and roles and legal rights and duties could be manipulated and redefined. Men could go so far as to assert that they were married on one occasion and that they were not on another.[46] This meant that elite men enjoyed considerable freedom to shape customary unions to their own ends. Customary marriage gave men greater latitude in their domestic lives than did Christian marriage.

Elite males saw a host of advantages to Yoruba marriage. A few believed so strongly that Yoruba marriage best suited local social and economic realities that they wanted to practice it openly, regardless of the religious or social cost. For just this reason, Dr Oguntola Ṣapara, Josiah Henryson Doherty, David Augustus Taylor and James George, pillars of the Christian community, refused to wed in church and made no secret of their Yoruba marriages.[47]

If these are the reasons why elite males made Christian or Yoruba marriages, why did almost half the group wed in church and also form outside unions, in spite of the fact that this violated church teaching and often colonial law? Most simply, these men felt the appeal of Christian and Yoruba marriage. They could enjoy the benefits of both by marrying in church and taking outside wives. An examination of the circumstances in

Marrying well

which men entered Christian and outside unions further illuminates this phenomenon.

Some elite males began adult life committed to Christian or Yoruba marriage. In the course of these men's lives, however, their needs and interests or attitudes and values changed, and they felt moved to enter the other kind of union. Domestic crises often pushed elite men to dual marriage. Christian unions sometimes broke down from unhappiness. When this happened men rarely obtained legal divorces and made second Christian marriages but instead entered outside unions, sometimes maintaining a connection with their Christian wives, sometimes not. Few men wanted second Christian marriages because most blamed the troubles with their first wives on foreign conjugal expectations.[48] Elite men also made outside marriages if their Christian wives failed to produce offspring. The Yoruba desired children so strongly that elite women often forgave husbands who took outside wives for this reason. Outside marriage, after all, provided a way for barren women to bring children into the home. A telling family portrait survives showing an elite man and his Christian wife surrounded by a group of children. One would never know from the picture that the Christian wife bore no offspring and the man had fathered the children by other women.[49] Professional advancement or a move from one occupation to another could also make a different form of marriage attractive. Clerks and school teachers who left customary wives behind when they went abroad to study law or medicine usually wanted Christian marriages to elite women when they returned home transformed into lawyers or doctors.[50] Colonial servants who preferred customary unions while junior clerks in the bush sometimes felt they needed educated Christian wives when promoted and transferred to Lagos.[51] Finally, elite men occasionally made one kind of marriage first because they preferred it, and later were persuaded by a woman to form a second different kind of union.[52]

Other elite males set out quite self-consciously in early adulthood to enter both Christian and outside unions, as a means of maximizing resources and opportunities. These men saw dual marriage as just one more strategy for adapting domestic circumstances to personal needs.[53] This strategy proved especially common among men who hoped to make good Christian marriages at some time in their lives, but could not afford Christian marriage or find suitable Christian wives when they were ready to wed. Rather than postpone marriage or wed unsuitable women in church, these men entered customary unions or extra-marital liaisons. Later they wed educated Christian women in church.[54] In such cases, dual marriage enabled men to meet their immediate needs without sacrificing their long-term interests. So long as men left the status of outside unions vague, they could pursue this strategy without violating the letter of the Marriage Ordinance.

Quantitative data from the life histories of the 113 elite males on whom full data about marriage are available show that some kinds of men proved

Table 3.1. *Percentage distribution of marriage choices of elite males by origin*[a]

	Origin	
Marriage choice	Repatriates	Locals
Christian only	42	26
Yoruba only	8	30
Christian and outside	49	44
Total	99	100
N	(87)	(23)

[a] 'Repatriates' includes Saro, Brazilians, Gambians, Liberians, Afro-Americans and Ghanaians. 'Locals' includes local Yoruba, Gun, Nupe and Igbo.

more likely to choose one domestic option than another. Origin, occupation, education, father's religion and education, Christian wife's religion and education, and age at Christian marriage all affected marital behavior. Table 3.1 demonstrates that a greater percentage of repatriated slaves (42 percent) than locals (26 percent) practiced Christian marriage only, while a smaller percentage formed Yoruba marriages only. Roughly equal percentages entered Christian and outside unions. Moreover, Table 3.2 indicates that a greater proportion of repatriates (91 percent) than locals (70 percent) made Christian marriages at some time in their lives, while a smaller proportion ever formed Yoruba or outside unions. Thus the data show a correlation between repatriates and Christian marriage and locals and Yoruba or outside marriage. Little information survives about sub-ethnic identity. Therefore it is impossible to say definitively whether sub-ethnic divisions had any bearing on marriage practices. None of the available evidence suggests that this variable played an important part in shaping marital behavior.

Table 3.2. *Percentage of repatriates and locals practicing Christian and Yoruba marriage*[a]

	Origin	
Marriage	Repatriates	Locals
Christian	91	70
Yoruba or outside	57	74

[a] The figures in this table were derived by adding the percentages in Table 3.1 for 'Christian only' and 'Christian and outside' and for 'Yoruba only' and 'Christian and outside'.

Table 3.3. *Percentage distribution of marriage choices of repatriates by generation of residence in Yorubaland*

Marriage choice	Generation of residence	
	First	Second and third
Christian only	53	38
Yoruba only	—	14
Christian and outside	47	48
Total	100	100
N	(32)	(50)

Table 3.4. *Percentage of first- and subsequent-generation repatriates practicing Christian and Yoruba marriage*[a]

Marriage	Generation of residence	
	First	Second and third
Christian	100	86
Yoruba or outside	47	62

[a] The percentages in this table were derived by adding the figures in Table 3.3 for 'Christian only' and 'Christian and outside' and for 'Yoruba only' and 'Christian and outside'.

Among repatriates length of residence in Yorubaland influenced marital behavior. Table 3.3 shows that 53 percent of the first-generation repatriates entered Christian marriages only, while just 38 percent of the second- or third-generation repatriates made that choice. None of the first-generation repatriates practiced Yoruba marriage only, while 14 percent of the second- and third-generation repatriates formed customary unions only. Again equal percentages of these groups entered Christian and outside unions. Table 3.4 illustrates that all of the first-generation repatriates made Christian marriages at some time in their lives, while fewer than half ever formed Yoruba or outside unions. In contrast just four-fifths of the second- or third-generation repatriates ever entered Christian unions, while three-fifths ever made Yoruba or outside unions. With longer residence in Yorubaland, a measure of social integration occurred and repatriates became more likely to practice Yoruba marriage exclusively or in combination with Christian marriage.[55]

The marital behavior of the three major occupational groups among elite males differed markedly. Table 3.5 demonstrates that professionals, colonial servants and merchants, in that order, were most likely to make

Table 3.5. *Percentage distribution of marriage choices of elite males by occupation*

	Occupation			
Marriage choice	Professional	Colonial servant	Merchant	Other
Christian only	53	43	29	22
Yoruba only	5	14	16	22
Christian and outside	42	43	55	56
Total	100	100	100	100
N	(38)	(28)	(38)	(9)

Table 3.6. *Percentage of occupational groups practicing Christian and Yoruba marriage*[a]

	Occupation			
Marriage	Professional	Colonial servant	Merchant	Other
Christian	95	86	84	78
Yoruba or outside	47	57	71	78

[a] The figures in this table were derived by adding the percentages in Table 3.5 for 'Christian only' and 'Christian and outside' and for 'Yoruba only' and 'Christian and outside'.

Christian marriages only. Professionals proved less likely than colonial servants or merchants to make Yoruba marriages only, while merchants proved more likely than colonial servants or professionals to enter Christian and outside unions. Table 3.6 indicates that professionals were more likely than colonial servants or merchants ever to enter Christian unions, while merchants, colonial servants and professionals, in that order, were most likely ever to form Yoruba or outside unions. Figures on the marital behavior of these different occupational groups do not change significantly when origin and generation of residence are held constant.

Education also affected marital behavior. Tables 3.7 and 3.8 illustrate that a greater percentage of elite males with advanced education than with primary or secondary education practiced Christian marriage exclusively or in combination with outside unions. A smaller percentage practiced Yoruba marriage exclusively or in combination with Christian marriage. Table 3.7 also demonstrates that a smaller proportion of elite males with advanced education entered both Christian and outside unions. Thus the data show a relationship between Christian marriage and post-secondary education in Sierra Leone or Great Britain.

Marrying well

Table 3.7. *Percentage distribution of marriage choices of elite males by education*

	Education	
Marriage choice	Primary or secondary	Advanced
Christian only	33	50
Yoruba only	16	7
Christian and outside	51	43
Total	100	100
N	(69)	(44)

Table 3.8. *Percentage of educational groups practicing Christian and Yoruba marriage*[a]

	Education	
Marriage	Primary or secondary	Advanced
Christian	84	93
Yoruba or outside	67	50

[a] The figures in this table were derived by adding the percentages in Table 3.7 for 'Christian only' and 'Christian and outside' and for 'Yoruba only' and 'Christian and outside'.

With a single important qualification, religious denomination does not emerge as a major determinant of marital behavior. Members of the African churches were more likely than others to make Yoruba marriages exclusively or in combination with Christian unions. Catholics formed a very small percentage of the elite. They did not behave differently from Protestants in domestic life. Among Anglicans and Wesleyans, the two major Protestant denominations, a greater percentage of Anglicans (51 percent) than Wesleyans (29 percent) made Christian marriages only, but a greater percentage (9 percent versus 3 percent) also made Yoruba marriages only. Two-thirds of the Wesleyans as opposed to two-fifths of the Anglicans entered Christian and outside unions. Paradoxically, Wesleyans were more likely than Anglicans at some time to make Christian marriages and more likely also at some time to enter Yoruba or outside unions.

Other factors bore on marital behavior. Second- and third-generation educated Christians made Christian marriages and Christian marriages only more often than did other elite males.[56] Men whose Christian wives were well educated and came from Christian homes formed outside unions more rarely than did men whose Christian wives were semi-literate and came from non-Christian homes.[57] In addition, elite males who postponed Christian marriage until after thirty were twice as likely to enter outside unions as those who made Christian marriages before thirty. This was true in spite of the fact that the after-thirty group included a disproportionate number of professionals, the occupational group least prone to outside unions. Economic considerations clearly affected elite men's responses to marriage, as the evidence has already shown. Neither qualitative nor quantitative data, however, indicate a direct correlation between wealth and marital behavior.

What accounts for these differences in the marital behavior of elite males? What do answers to this question reveal about variations in the experiences of the group? What do they show about how the pressures for and against Christian and Yoruba marriage operated in the lives of different kinds of men? Repatriates, men with advanced education and second- and third-generation educated Christians may have felt greater religious and ideological commitment to Christian marriage than did other elite males. First-generation repatriates and men educated abroad had had unusually long and intense exposure to European culture. Moreover, this exposure had occurred outside Yorubaland, in situations where persons felt pressure to embrace Christianity and European culture, and where they were relatively free of countervailing pressures from within their own culture.[58] Gratitude to Great Britain for their freedom reinforced some Saros' belief in the religious and ideological superiority of European culture.[59] Second- and third-generation educated Christians often had grown up with Christian marriage. From childhood, parents or guardians had socialized them to accept European conjugal ideals. These men may have felt the attractions of Yoruba marriage less keenly than did first-generation educated Christians. Moreover, second- and third-generation educated Christians sometimes encountered staunch opposition from kin when they tried to form Yoruba or outside unions.[60]

Pragmatic considerations reinforced repatriates', professionals' and colonial servants' commitment to Christian marriage. Especially in the first generation, repatriates lacked ties of kinship, clientage and friendship with the local population. Vulnerability led some such persons to look for support to Europeans and other educated Africans. Christian marriage provided these men with a mechanism for asserting their identity with whites and for creating alliances with educated blacks.[61] By the same token, repatriates may have made unattractive Yoruba marriage partners for local women, because they were outsiders who lacked ties to the local population. Professionals and colonial servants depended for occupational advancement on the approval of Europeans and influential educated Africans. Whites could damage the careers of ministers, doctors, lawyers and colonial servants merely by hinting at character defects.[62] Relative to commerce, these occupations demanded propriety and respectability. Europeans and many educated Africans expected professionals and colonial servants to embody the highest in 'civilized' values.⁶³ For this reason, professionals and colonial servants attached particular importance to the image that Christian marriage created, and they found the cost of customary or outside unions especially high.

Two other factors influenced elite men's marital behavior – their Christian wives' educational and religious background and their own age at Christian marriage. Elite women made Christian marriages in part because they favored monogamy. When men with well-educated Christian wives tried to establish outside unions, they often encountered determined opposition from their wives and their wives' relatives. The Christian wives did not always emerge victorious from these confrontations, but they did have some power to shape their husbands' domestic behavior.⁶⁴ Turning to the question of age, men who made Christian marriages in their twenties felt less need than men who postponed Christian marriage until their thirties to enter outside unions to avoid delay in establishing homes and starting families.

Analysis of why certain kinds of men proved more likely than others to form Yoruba or outside unions suggests a number of conclusions. Locals, first-generation educated Christians and men with only primary and secondary education often had stronger and deeper ties to Yoruba culture than did other elite males. These men had had less intense exposure to European culture, and their exposure usually had occurred within the confines of their own culture. Such men may have seen the attractions of Yoruba marriage more clearly than did others. Moreover, locals and first-generation educated Christians experienced great pressure from kin, patrons and friends to conform to Yoruba marital norms.⁶⁵ Stronger ties to the local population may have made locals and first-generation educated Christians more attractive Yoruba marriage partners and given them greater freedom to deviate from foreign conjugal ideals.⁶⁶ The fact that more second- and third-generation repatriates than first-generation repatriates made Yoruba marriages suggests that social integration occurred with longer residence in Lagos. Once better integrated into the local community, repatriates felt the appeal of Yoruba marriage more keenly, made more attractive Yoruba marriage partners, and felt greater freedom to deviate from Christian marriage. Merchants and colonial servants proved more susceptible than did professionals to the economic advantages of Yoruba marriage – merchants because wives and affines could contribute to commercial success, and both merchants and colonial servants because Yoruba marriage imposed fewer financial burdens than Christian marriage.⁶⁷ Colonial servants earned the smallest incomes of the three major occupational groups and may have attached special importance to having wives who would contribute to the family economically. A disproportionate number of the elite males who joined the African churches made Yoruba or outside marriages, because these denominations attracted educated Christians at odds with the European churches over marriage. The African churches accepted polygyny and Yoruba and outside unions, as subsequent discussion will show. Finally,

Table 3.9. *Percentage distribution of marriage choices of elite males by date of birth*

	Date of birth	
Marriage choice	1810–50	1851–90
Christian only	54	35
Yoruba only	8	12
Christian and outside	38	53
Total	100	100
N	(24)	(74)

elite males with non-elite Christian wives felt less domestic pressure to conform to foreign conjugal ideals than did elite males with elite Christian wives. Moreover, non-elite women probably found it harder than elite women to enforce their new status as Christian wives.

The quantitative data demonstrated that greater percentages of merchants, first-generation educated Christians and men with only primary and secondary education than of other elite males entered both Christian and outside unions. This suggests that such men felt the tensions between Christian and Yoruba marriage more acutely than did others, and that they may have seen greater advantages to forming both kinds of unions. These men may also have felt fewer pressures that constrained them from making outside marriages. The data also showed that a greater percentage of Wesleyans than Anglicans made both Christian and outside unions. The two denominations adopted similar official policies toward marriage. Possibly the Wesleyan church tolerated outside unions unofficially, in a way that the Anglican church did not. No direct evidence supports this argument, and the fact that more Anglicans than Wesleyans made Yoruba marriages only tends to contradict it. A greater percentage of Wesleyans than Anglicans made their living in commerce, and a smaller percentage had advanced education. Most likely, occupational and educational differences between these groups explain the differences in their marital behavior.

How and why did the marital behavior of elite males change? What do answers to these questions reveal about changes in the group's needs and interests and attitudes and values? What do they tell us about how elite males responded to changing conditions in Lagos?

Dates of customary marriages and extra-marital liaisons could rarely be obtained. Consequently, the only way to measure change in marital behavior is to compare trends between different cohorts. Tables 3.9 and 3.10 contain information about the marriages of elite males born between 1810 and 1850 and between 1851 and 1890. The data in these tables illustrate that

Table 3.10. *Percentage of cohorts practicing Christian and Yoruba marriage*[a]

Marriage	Date of birth	
	1810–50	1851–90
Christian	92	88
Yoruba or outside	46	65

[a] The figures in this table were derived by adding the percentages in Table 3.9 for 'Christian only' and 'Christian and outside' and for 'Yoruba only' and 'Christian and outside'.

the percentage of each cohort who practiced Yoruba marriage only, or whoever practiced Christian marriage, remained relatively constant, rising from 8 percent to 12 percent in the first case and falling from 92 percent to 88 percent in the second. Table 3.9 shows, however, that the percentage practicing Christian marriage only fell from 54 percent among the 1810 to 1850 cohort to 35 percent among the 1851 to 1890 cohort. This table also indicates that the percentage forming both Christian and outside unions rose from 38 percent among the first cohort to 53 percent among the second cohort, contributing to a 20 percent increase in the proportion that ever entered Yoruba or outside unions.

This trend toward more Yoruba and outside unions, whether or not men also married in church, runs counter to the predictions of theories of marital and family change that stress evolution, acculturation and modernization.[68] These findings remind us that change is not linear. The complex economic, political and cultural factors that shape it can themselves change or recombine so that older social norms come to look more compelling rather than less. As conditions in Lagos altered, the moral force and economic and social appeal of Yoruba marriage increased for the educated elite, the group that had been most deeply influenced by contact with Europe. No single factor explains the trend toward more Yoruba and outside unions among the 1851 to 1890 cohort. Indeed, it is impossible to say which of several phenomena may have been most important. In the late nineteenth and early twentieth centuries, economic, cultural, religious and political developments all helped make Yoruba marriage more attractive to elite males who reached marriageable age during or after these years.[69]

A severe trade depression struck Lagos in the 1880s and lasted until the first decade of the twentieth century. As opportunities in trade declined, a growing number of elite males sought careers in the colonial service and professions. In the 1890s, the trade depression led Great Britain to colonize the Yoruba interior, and resulted in a larger and more aggressive imperial presence in Lagos. Soon the educated elite encountered blatant racial discrimination in jobs and social life. By the time commerce picked up in the twentieth century, the structure of trade had changed so that African merchants experienced great difficulty competing with European firms.[70] All these changes threatened the educated elite's position in colonial society; all affected marriage.

Adverse economic conditions influenced the marital behavior of elite males in a number of ways. Low profits and uncertain career prospects led some men to postpone expensive Christian marriage and instead enter customary unions or extra-marital liaisons.[71] They also heightened men's awareness of the financial burdens of Christian marriage and benefits of Yoruba marriage. In the late 1890s, complaints about Christian wives' economic expectations increased in number and vehemence.[72] After the turn of the century, several merchants entered customary unions to cement favorable business relationships. Because profit margins were slim and business was conducted on credit, a merchant's commercial success depended in part on his ability to build and maintain a large clientele of traders who bought goods regularly, sold them quickly, and repaid their debts promptly. Forming marriage alliances with reliable and successful traders contributed to this end. When wives and affines obtained trade goods from a merchant, they remained economically independent. Yet they were less likely than other traders to transfer their business to a competitor without good economic reasons, because ties of marriage as well as profit bound them to their supplier. Marriage alliances also minimized the risks associated with credit. Wives and affines could not easily abscond, leaving unpaid debts.[73] In a time of economic uncertainty, moreover, elite males may have attached new importance to the web of diverse affinal relationships that polygyny made possible. These relationships both created economic opportunities and gave men a kind of security.

The heightened imperialism and new racism after the mid-1890s also affected the marital behavior of elite males. E. A. Ayandele and Fred Omu have shown that these developments helped provoke a cultural nationalist movement among the educated elite. In the mid-1890s, educated Africans began to study Yoruba language, history and social institutions. Study fostered new pride in Yoruba culture. Several authors have documented that during these years influential members of the elite renounced English names in favor of Yoruba names and shed European dress in favor of African apparel.[74] No cultural question aroused greater passion than marriage. A careful study of the press, pamphlet literature and private papers from the late nineteenth and early twentieth centuries reveals a virtual obsession with marriage, the institution which in the words of one man lay 'at the foundation of society'.[75]

The emergence of cultural nationalism in Lagos had two larger consequences. First, it stimulated educated Africans to rethink the meaning of civilization and eventually led them to a position of cultural relativism. Beginning in the 1890s and gaining momentum after the turn of the century, influential educated Africans began to argue that customs were culturally determined; that one custom was not better or worse than another, only more or less well suited to a given cultural environment. European names, dress and marriage might be right for Europeans, but they were neither inherently superior nor right for West Africans.[76] In defense of Yoruba dress, John Payne Jackson wrote, 'In the world around and above us, every beast has its skin and every fowl its feathers. The beneficent creator covered the back of the sheep with wool in the wintry clime and deprived it of wool in the tropics . . . Every creature for its habitat and every costume for its clime.'[77] On the subject of Yoruba marriage, George Alfred Williams argued that 'only the ignorant and conceited' would 'contend that a man to be morally good must be a monogamist'. He continued, 'By morality we mean . . . respect for the rules on which existence of a society is based . . . As these rules vary with time and place, morality appears . . . to be a very variable matter.'[78] Dr Moyses da Rocha summarized the relativist position: 'civilization is a relative term . . . The Chinaman, the Jap, the Yoruba, the Zulu – each in his own way is as civilized as the Briton, the Frenchman, the German or the Spaniard.'[79]

Second, the emergence of cultural nationalism provoked educated Africans to reevaluate the impact of European culture on West Africa. The results, these persons concluded, had not all been good. Critics blamed the introduction of European culture for spreading hypocrisy and immorality.[80] They associated moral degeneracy with physical degeneracy, disease and death, and they worried that contact with Europe had endangered the very race.[81]

Discussions of the negative effects of European culture on West Africa often focused on marriage. Commentators asserted that the emphasis in Christian unions on love and individual happiness had undermined the control of kin and dealt a blow to 'age, experience and authority'.[82] They accused Christian husbands and wives of turning domestic liberty into license, and of destroying the sanctity of marriage and the family.[83] Critics of Christian marriage also complained that monogamy had bred prostitution and adultery, far greater evils than polygyny.[84] The Lagos press expressed the concern that many educated Africans felt about marriage. One article asserted, 'where this [European] marriage system has been introduced . . . it has . . . produc[ed] a state of social and moral corruption quite terrorizing in its blighting destructiveness'.[85] Another lamented that Christian marriage had 'impelled [Africans] on the road to perdition'.[86] Still another article proclaimed that thanks to Christian marriage West African coastal towns were 'rotten before they [were] ripe'.[87] Drawing the connection between immorality and physical degeneracy, a final article commented, 'Western marriage has produc[ed] morally *hypocrisy* and *deceit,* and [physically] *disease* and *death.*'[88] The cultural nationalist movement, then, not only led educated Africans to a deeper appreciation of Yoruba marriage, but also convinced them that Yoruba marriage was in no way inferior to Christian marriage and that Christian marriage itself had done great harm in

West Africa. Each of these new attitudes contributed to an increase in Yoruba marriage among the 1851 to 1890 cohort.

Between 1888 and 1901 a number of African churches in Lagos broke away from the European denominations. The establishment of the African churches occurred independently of the cultural nationalist movement, but the two reinforced each other and shared many concerns. The African churches split with the European denominations for political and constitutional reasons, rather than over the issue of polygyny. However, the founders of these churches included men such as Mojola Agbebi, Hezekiah Africanus Caulcrick, George Alfred Williams, James George Campbell, Samuel A. Coker and Jacob Kehinde Coker, who had long felt troubled by the stand of the European denominations on polygyny.[89] These men studied the scriptures at length, looking for passages that proved polygyny antithetical to Christianity. Finding none, they concluded that polygyny did not violate the law of God.[90]

The founders of the African churches carried their defense of Yoruba marriage a step further. In sermons, pamphlets and newspaper articles, they asserted that the European denominations represented European marriage customs as Christian doctrine, but that the two were not synonymous. These religious leaders argued that marriage and other social customs were rooted in culture, not Christianity; and that the European denominations were wrong to deny polygynists the sacraments. Edward W. Blyden, who deeply influenced Lagos's African church movement, asserted that no law of God existed on the subject of marriage.[91] In 1897 John Payne Jackson reversed the stand he had taken on monogamy three years earlier. In an influential editorial he asked, 'Are [West Africans] to be held in their marriage arrangements to the terms of a contract composed hundreds of years ago in a distant country and for an entirely different race, especially when there is no warrant whatever in the Bible for such terms?'[92] The following year the *Lagos Weekly Record* reprinted an article from the *Gold Coast Aborigines* which questioned the right of the Wesleyan church to say, 'We will not admit you . . . unless you marry as the English do.'[93] Almost a decade later the paper echoed these themes, '[T]he missionary has invariably . . . given his convert to understand that Christian marriage was ordained by God and [is] indispensable to Christian . . . virtue . . . A little thought must suffice to suggest both the unreasonableness and presumptuousness of identifying God with a social contract between a man and a woman.'[94]

The African churches did not advocate Yoruba marriage. They merely accepted polygynous members and defended the right of African Christians to marry as they chose. All the same, the establishment of the African churches in Lagos contributed to a rise in Yoruba marriage among elite males born between 1851 and 1890. The religious defense of Yoruba marriage articulated by the founders of the African churches enabled even those elite males who remained within the European denominations to reconcile Yoruba marriage with their Christian faith. It gave men moral courage to defy what the Europeans had taught them was right and to practice Yoruba marriage when Yoruba marriage best suited their domestic or other needs. Finally, the establishment of the African churches offered elite males an alternative. For the first time, they could practice Yoruba marriage openly and remain members in good standing of a Christian church.

The laity in the African churches responded to changing cultural and religious beliefs about marriage by proclaiming a new kind of marriage, 'Native Christian' or 'parlour marriage'. Members of the African churches regarded such unions as Christian, but accepted that they might be polygynous and expected that the conjugal relationship and roles would conform more nearly to Yoruba than European norms.[95] Native Christian weddings usually occurred in the parlor of the bride's home and combined Yoruba rituals and Christian prayers. Clergymen in the African churches often blessed the marriages, which were neither recorded in the Marriage Registry nor bound by the Marriage Ordinance. After Emily Taiwo Vidal and E. Adolphus Fowler celebrated the first Native Christian marriage in 1896, a few elite males entered Native Christian unions.[96] Native Christian marriage did not replace Christian marriage among the educated elite. It merely gave religious recognition to the kind of customary unions that educated Africans had long been making.

The late nineteenth and early twentieth centuries witnessed the emergence of political opposition among the educated elite. This, too, affected the marital behavior of elite males, although perhaps less directly than the economic, cultural and religious changes already discussed. Between 1895 and 1915, members of the educated elite fought the colonial government over a host of issues – taxation, segregation, land policy and freedom of the press.[97] Agitation subsided during World War I but revived around new issues after 1917.[98] In this climate of growing political opposition, making a Yoruba marriage became for some elite men an act of cultural resistance.[99]

Practicing Yoruba marriage had additional political significance. When members of the educated elite began to challenge the colonial government, they sought to strengthen their power base in the local community by leading a number of popular political causes.[100] Yoruba marriage provided these men with a means of identifying with their new followers, the Yoruba masses. Making a Yoruba marriage said symbolically, 'We may be educated Christians, but we are Yoruba like you.' The educated elite also used Yoruba marriage to create alliances with important local families. Both strategies effectively countered the frequent British criticism that the educated elite was unqualified for political leadership because it lacked roots in the local culture and ties to the local population.[101]

Political considerations probably influenced the marital behavior of Herbert Macaulay, one of Lagos's earliest opposition leaders. According to popular legend, Macaulay mourned his Christian wife's death during her first childbirth by vowing never to marry again. Macaulay never did marry again in church, but subsequently he took numerous customary wives and concubines.[102] Macaulay's public vow marked him as a deeply bereaved Christian widower. At the same time, it conveniently freed him from the possibility of a second Christian marriage and opened the way for politically expedient customary and extra-marital unions.

With such compelling reasons for the increase in Yoruba marriage among the 1851 to 1890 cohort, perhaps the more puzzling historical problem is why no decrease occurred in the percentage of elite males that ever made Christian marriages. Several factors help explain this phenomenon. Elite women insisted on Christian marriage throughout the period. Elite males who wanted wives of the same social background as themselves had little choice but to make Christian marriages. While economic depression and heightened racial discrimination may have made the financial burdens of Christian marriage seem more onerous, these changes also may have made the benefits of Christian marriage appear that much more important. But perhaps most significant, Christian marriage remained a mark of elite status and an expression of the distinctive culture of the group. Christian marriage continued to help identify individuals as members of the elite and to distinguish the group from the rest of the population. Right conduct in family life, based as it was on Christian teaching and European institutions and values, convinced the elite and others of the group's moral and cultural superiority and hence of its right to power and authority in colonial society. All but a tiny minority of the elite males hesitated to abandon Christian marriage because it expressed and legitimized their status.

Christian and Yoruba marriage had different economic, social and political implications. They represented different mechanisms for defining social and political identity and mobilizing and managing a wide range of resources. As elite males strove to establish themselves in early colonial Lagos, they saw advantages to each form of union. Men chose one or the other or tried to combine them by entering Christian and outside unions. Beliefs, needs and interests, and strategies for social and economic mobility all shaped domestic behavior. While some elite males moved easily between Yoruba and Christian marriage, others felt deep-seated tensions between them. These tensions arose out of conflicting needs and interests and conflicting beliefs about what was right. Such tensions pushed some men to modify their marital behavior and others to rethink their beliefs. They confronted elite males as a group with a very real cultural dilemma. As men's beliefs, needs and interests, and social and economic strategies changed, so too did their marriage choices.

The role of marriage in identifying, defining and legitimizing the elite helps explain why the whole problem of marriage aroused such passion among the group. Weber pointed out that stratification by style of life makes submission to fashion critically important. Positively privileged status groups demand deportment of their members, because deportment symbolizes 'the beauty and excellence' of these groups.[103] Members of the elite could neither deviate from Christian marriage nor challenge its superiority without at the same time questioning the superiority of the status group. Questioning the superiority of the educated elite proved particularly threatening at a time when it had already come under attack from the British power structure. In the late nineteenth and early twentieth centuries, a growing number of elite males responded to changing economic, political and social conditions by entering customary or outside unions and rethinking Christian marriage. They could not do so without provoking a serious crisis within the elite.

Conflicting views of the response of the educated elite to African and European culture run through the historical literature on Nigeria. One interpretation sees this group as 'Black Englishmen', cut off from Africa and deriving its religious and cultural beliefs from Europe. E. A. Ayandele, a leading proponent of this view, argues that the members of the educated elite were 'black in their skins', but 'white in their cultural and social ambitions'.[104] He maintains that the educated elite regarded illiterate Africans as benighted heathens and Europeans as saviors bringing light to the heart of darkness in the form of Christianity, Western education and colonial rule. Ayandele asserts that the educated elite willingly collaborated in colonial rule and hoped to share power with the British only in the very distant future.[105]

A second view depicts the educated elite as hybrids, products of its African origins and European contact. M. J. C. Echeruo writes that the elite stood at the 'cross-roads of civilization'; that it felt 'a sincere sense of attachment' to Yoruba culture and a 'deep-felt appreciation of European life'.[106] Authors of this persuasion maintain that the educated elite saw colonialism as a blessing, but that it bitterly resented inefficiency and misguided policies and wanted full rights of British citizenship.[107]

Each of these views is too monolithic. Jean Herskovits's study of the Sierra Leoneans in Yorubaland recognizes that not all educated Africans responded in the same way to African and European culture. Herskovits posits a scale of reactions determined by degree of acceptance of foreign values and government policies. However, she fails to see that reactions of individuals changed from situation to situation and during the course of their lives, and that the dominant mood of the elite changed at the end of the nineteenth century.[108] Fred Omu's study of the Lagos press offers the best explanation of how and why the elite's cultural outlook changed. But perhaps because Omu investigated only the press, he glosses over differences within the elite.[109] The responses of elite males to marriage, a key cultural issue, show the complexity of individual cultural reactions and the diversity of experience within the group. The responses to marriage also point to significant change in the dominant mood of the elite during a formative period in its history.

4

The dangers of dependence: elite women and Christian marriage

Elite women responded to Christian marriage more unambiguously than did elite men. Of sufficiently high social status to pick and choose marriage partners, elite women insisted on Christian unions.[1] A witness in the famous court case *Savage* v. *Macfoy* testified that he warned the defendant not to try to make a 'native marriage' because 'our girls prefer English form'.[2] An article in the Lagos press commented that educated women regarded Christian marriage as *'ultima thule'*, the ultimate accomplishment.[3] After the first Native Christian marriage, a man told the bride's father that he was lucky to have a daughter who did not insist on ordinance marriage.[4] Elite women's preference for Christian marriage continued throughout the period, although around the turn of the century a few such women began to rethink aspects of Christian unions.

Elite women's attitude toward marriage was reinforced by that of their parents. Jacob Kehinde Coker spoke of the 'desire on the part of many West African Christians, especially mothers, that their daughters should marry in foreign marriages and their sons in native custom'.[5] Parents' efforts to ensure that daughters made good Christian matches further illustrate the importance attached to this kind of union. A thorough European education, including if possible a few years at an English boarding school, provided the best protection money could buy, because foreign-educated women were in great demand as Christian wives for elite men. A few parents worried so much about girls' marriage options that if forced to choose they sent daughters abroad for schooling instead of sons. One father maintained that his boys could succeed in trade or the colonial service with a local education, but his girls required a foreign education so they could make good Christian marriages.[6] An informant explained that parents strove to educate daughters in England to give them 'a little something extra for protection'.[7] Elite women formed customary or outside unions only if they had some blot on their reputations that made them unattractive Christian wives, or if they were widowed or separated and had no other means of support. Lower-status women used customary unions to form alliances with elite men, but elite women did not view this type of marriage as a viable domestic option.[8]

Elite men and women made Christian marriages for some of the same reasons. Missionaries, teachers and in some cases parents had socialized them to believe in the religious and cultural superiority of foreign marital norms, especially monogamy. When asked if she, her sisters or her friends would have made Yoruba marriages, Mrs C. O. Blaize replied, 'How could we? That would not have been marriage. We were Christian and believed only in Christian marriage.'[9] Similar pragmatic concerns also moved many women and men. Christian marriage clearly displayed the religion and style of life of elite women and the wealth and social standing of their parents. It helped identify women as members of the elite and enhanced their prestige.[10] In addition, elite women used Christian marriages to form advantageous alliances with socially and economically prominent families in Lagos and other British West African colonies, just as did elite men. These factors do not explain why elite women responded to Christian marriage more positively than did elite men. Nor do they tell us why parents thought it more important for daughters than sons to wed under the ordinance. Answers to these questions lie in a consideration of issues of special concern to women.

Colonial rule and the growth of international trade adversely affected the status of West African women. Men dominated the production and trade of lucrative new export crops, even in areas where women played an important part in agriculture.[11] The expansion of trade created new opportunities for women in commerce, but in most places men took the lead in the import–export business and women engaged in petty retailing or local commerce.[12] Colonial governments ignored or failed to see women's political roles and undermined their political power and influence.[13] Colonial administrations introduced new laws and established new courts that sometimes gave women new legal rights or created new opportunities for them to contest male authority. But often women could not enforce their new rights or obtain access to the colonial courts.[14] When colonial governments began to codify customary law, male elders sometimes seized the opportunity to redefine local laws to their advantage.[15] Christianity and Western education spread ideologies that undermined women's personal autonomy and economic independence. Education for women lagged behind education for men, restricting access to modern occupations.[16] Elite women's response to Christian marriage makes sense only in the context of the impact of colonial rule on their status. Analyzing women's response to marriage in turn uncovers the effects of Christianity, Western education and certain colonial economic and legal changes on women's roles, ideology and opportunities.

Europeans and educated repatriates brought to Lagos Victorian ideas about the separate spheres of men and women. Profoundly influential among the elite although not among the lower orders, these beliefs held that a woman's place was in the home caring for her husband and children. The perfect Victorian lady did not toil within the home but supervised the work of servants. Protected from the trials of the world, women were regarded as the purer, more pious sex, whose special duty was to uphold the family's and society's moral values. If the home failed to exhaust women's time and energy, they could turn their attention to religion, philanthropy or social reform, unleashing their moral authority in the community. Women's little power and influence within society stemmed from their special role as the guardians of virtue.[17]

Not all elite women embraced these Victorian ideals. Among the early repatriates many educated wives had to struggle alongside their husbands to build a place for the family in Yorubaland.[18] Even after the elite became better established, some women rejected economic dependence for financial and other reasons. Abigail Macaulay, daughter of Bishop Samuel Crowther and wife of the Reverend Thomas Babington Macaulay, insisted on trading to supplement her husband's small salary and help support their eleven children, although the Church Missionary Society pressured her to stop.[19] Rebecca Phillips Johnson, sister of merchant Jacob Samuel Leigh and wife of colonial servant G. P. Johnson, traded most of her adult life, dying a wealthy woman in 1907.[20] Government officials periodically complained that wives of African colonial servants traded, violating government regulations.[21] By the 1880s, however, most elite women aspired to the Victorian ideal, and many achieved it. These women devoted themselves to running homes, socializing with friends, and improving the community through good works, not to pursuing independent economic activities. In the press, we read about such women hosting 'soirées', 'conversazioni' and concerts; raising funds for churches, schools and Christian relief; and combating drink and immorality.[22] Lagos marriage registers record the marriages of sixty-seven elite males. The brides in half of these cases describe themselves as 'ladies', reflecting their present status and future expectations. Twenty-two percent gave their occupation as seamstress, 19 percent as schoolmistress, and only 8 percent as trader, the most common economic activity of Lagos women.

As the guardians of moral virtue, it was especially important for elite women to conform to foreign religious and cultural norms. Women had special responsibility for developing and protecting the culture of the elite. Europeans and educated Africans might excuse men who backslid by practicing Yoruba marriage, but they could not treat women so permissively. When an elite woman deviated from Christian teaching, it undermined not only her own reputation and influence but also the respectability of the elite as a whole. If women failed to uphold civilized values, what hope could there be for men?

A double standard based on an assumption of male rights to female sexuality underlay both Victorian and Yoruba attitudes toward women. Probing this phenomenon in English culture, Keith Thomas concluded, 'The double standard . . . is the reflection of the view that men have property in women and that the value of this property is immeasurably diminished if the woman at any time has sexual relations with anyone other than her husband.'[23] N. A. Fadipe explained that the Yoruba believed betrothal gave men exclusive rights to their fiancées' sexual attention, and that men could seek legal remedy in cases of infidelity.[24] Values from these two different cultural traditions reinforced one another among the elite, leaving the group much more tolerant of extra-marital sex for men than for women. The elite welcomed into its innermost circle men who produced children outside Christian marriage, while it ostracized women for such conduct.[25] Referring to a girl who became pregnant outside Christian marriage, Mrs Samuel Crowther advised a friend, 'The sooner Bailey marries her the better. Otherwise she must leave the premises when near her confinement or as soon as you think fit. People will be disgusted when she gets big to go near the shop, hence it would be better she went away to hide.'[26]

This sexual double standard impinged on elite women's marital choices in several ways. Unlike her male counterpart, an elite woman could not form an outside union and then expect to wed someone else in church. Once an educated girl had had sexual relations, she no longer made an attractive ordinance wife for another man. Educated women's only hope lay in protecting their reputations until they could make good Christian matches.[27] Until the very end of the period few elite couples formed customary unions and subsequently married under the ordinance, a practice common in contemporary West African towns.[28] In keeping with this sexual double standard, the elite regarded adultery as a more grievous offense for wives than husbands. Women who broke the family circle were seen as threatening the very social fabric. For this reason Christian wives may have felt greater reluctance than their husbands to form sexual liaisons that might have ended in more permanent unions. Dual marriage was hardly a possibility for women, because husbands rarely tolerated wives who carried on with other men.[29] This is not to say that elite women never formed outside unions, only that they did so more rarely than elite men and that they were severely condemned for such conduct.

Adel Coker's story illustrates the fate of an educated girl who lost her virtue. Daughter of R. A. Coker, an Anglican clergyman, Adel visited her father's relatives in Abeokuta when she was about fourteen. There she had sexual relations with a cousin, all the more shocking because the Yoruba regarded intercourse between such near kin as incest. To make matters worse, Adel bore a child of the liaison. These stains on her reputation unquestionably disqualified her for a respectable ordinance marriage such as her sisters made. Wayward, disappointed or desperate, Adel had another affair and again conceived a child. This time she rebelliously refused to reveal her lover's identity. Following the birth of the second baby, Adel lived in Ebute Metta with her sister and brother-in-law. Her father had taken a church in Ijebu Ode and may not have wanted her in his household. Despite pressure from her sisters and other elite women, Adel continued to live loosely, perhaps because she perceived few other options. In 1904 she became pregnant again, this time by Dr Oguntola Ṣapara, who offered to marry her according to Yoruba custom. Adel demurred, hoping, it seems, for a Christian union. Eager to see Adel married, Rebecca Phillips Johnson urged her to consent to a Yoruba marriage, hinting that if she behaved the doctor might one day wed her in church. Dr Ṣapara approached the Reverend Mr Coker, who rebuked him for mentioning a customary union, but left the door open by adding that his elder brother arranged all family weddings. Customary marriage rituals ensued, in spite of protests from Dr Ṣapara's family and Bishop Isaac Oluwole, who scolded his mother-in-law, Mrs Johnson, for corrupting the morals of the community. Once married, Adel begged to use the name Ṣapara and sit at the head of the doctor's table, as befitted a Christian wife. All went on smoothly until the doctor moved Adel to a new house and announced that he intended to wed another woman in church. Adel told Ṣapara she would not protest if he put the title to the new house in her name. When the doctor refused, she entered a caveat blocking the issue of his marriage license.[30] Perhaps at Adel's behest, Herbert Macaulay objected to Ṣapara's Christian marriage when the banns were read at Christ Church, scoring a point against his political foe Ṣapara Williams, Dr Ṣapara's brother. The doctor retaliated by trying to divorce Adel.[31] What happened next is unclear; however, one thing is certain. Adel's indiscretion with a cousin at age fourteen marked her for life.

The fact that Yoruba culture permitted polygyny but not polyandry also helps explain why elite men and women responded differently to the problem of how to marry. While the church and state held that men who entered Christian unions should practice monogamy, most elite males acknowledged the possibility of plural marriage. Coming from a polygynous tradition, they could imagine having several wives, one of whom they would wed in church and grant a special status. If a man did not make a Christian marriage first, polygyny permitted him to make one later.[32] Yoruba and Western culture both allowed women to have but one husband at a time. When contemplating marriage most educated young women hoped to make a single match.[33] It is not surprising they wanted this to be the kind of union that would bring them greater prestige and new legal rights.

Elite women also had special economic concerns that affected their marriage choices. When these women withdrew from the workplace they sacrificed the autonomy of their illiterate sisters. Their social and economic status depended first on their fathers and later on their husbands.[34] The economic status of even those educated women who worked was low in relation to that of educated men. Most modern occupations did not admit women during this period. Regulations drawn up as late as 1921 reserved to men all posts in the colonial service filled from England, other than positions specifically designated for women.[35] With such restrictive policies at home, it is little wonder Lagos administrators failed to consider women for local appointments. English women entered law and medicine only in tiny numbers well into the twentieth century.[36] In the nineteenth century very few Lagos women received the kind of education needed to train for these professions. The elite regarded trade as unsuitable for young ladies, further narrowing their economic options. Moreover, economic changes in the colonial period made it more difficult for women to compete with men in commerce.[37] Teaching and sewing, the most common employment of elite women, paid very poorly by any standard. Most schools confined women teachers to the lowest grades.[38] Elite women then did not have access to the opportunities that brought elite men wealth and influence.

To secure the status of elite women it was essential for them to wed men who would maintain them in the manner in which they had been raised. Christian marriage rituals, which were expensive and involved a transfer of resources from husbands to wives, tested men's financial position and their willingness to accept new conjugal responsibilities. When men granted their wives real estate, it gave the women a measure of financial security. In the eyes of the public, Christian marriage committed men to support their families. N. A. Fadipe commented, 'It has come to be a generally accepted convention that marriage according to British law commits a man to maintain his wife. Young wives stand on their rights and generally have the support of public opinion.'[39] John Payne Jackson defended Christian wives for demanding of their husbands 'what is yours is mine'. Men knew when they wed, he argued, that these women would not 'hav[e] some visible means of livelihood'.[40] Once educated women's social and economic status depended on their husbands, they had little alternative but to practice Christian marriage. A good Christian marriage provided these women with their only ticket to membership in the elite and the privileges it entailed. The wrong kind of marriage to the wrong kind of man robbed educated Christian women of their status and ruined their life chances. Alluding to this fact, Jacob Kehinde Coker referred to 'brides who inhale a deep and silent breath . . . when the . . . victim that calls himself a bridegroom . . . [is] caught in the trap [of Christian marriage] at last'.[41]

Elite women and their parents also favored ordinance marriage because they believed the new legal rights it gave women would help protect their status. On this subject Jacob Kehinde Coker spoke of parents who 'seek protection under English law in marriage for the security of their daughters'.[42] Ordinance marriage gave wives a legal right to monogamy. Elite women liked this provision for religious reasons. In addition, these women expected enforced monogamy to ensure them and their children exclusive claims to their husbands' resources, and to free them from emotional and sexual competition with other wives.[43] Ordinance marriage also gave women and their children new inheritance rights. In cases of intestacy, it entitled the women to use for life one-third of their husbands' self-acquired property. It entitled ordinance wives' children to the remaining two-thirds of such property. Unless men wrote wills specifying otherwise, Christian marriage effectively disinherited siblings and outside children. Finally, the elite believed that Christian marriage would protect women against divorce, by making unions very difficult to terminate legally.[44]

Some elite women found that Christian marriage lived up to their

The dangers of dependence

expectations. When Emily Cole returned to Lagos in 1871 after two years in England and France completing her education, she married Richard Beale Blaize, a young Saro printer. Soon Blaize began trading and made a fortune. Mrs Blaize assisted her husband in his printing shop as a bride, but withdrew from his affairs as he became more successful, devoting her time to raising six children, teaching music and fine arts at home, and organizing ladies' literary and social clubs. The Blaizes lived in one of the grandest homes in Lagos, travelled regularly to England, and gave their children the best upbringing money could buy. R. B. Blaize remained a faithful and loving husband throughout his life. To most elite women he must have seemed the perfect spouse. Emily sincerely appreciated her good fortune, commenting shortly before she died, 'I have but one study in this world which engrosses my talents and that is my husband.'[45] R. B. Blaize died in 1904 leaving the couple's children the bulk of an estate valued at £60,000.[46]

Anna Sophia Hutchinson was born in Elmina to Robert Hutchinson, who described himself as a 'native of the Gold Coast . . . trained in England'. Hutchinson served as the first mayor of Cape Coast in the late 1850s, and died in Britain's 1863 campaign against the Asante.[47] An aunt took Anna to Edinburgh at age four. There she received her education. In the early 1870s, Anna returned to Cape Coast to become the 'Lady Principal' of the Government School. In September 1888, she married Christopher A. Sapara Williams, Lagos's first African lawyer. Williams fulfilled all the responsibilities of a Christian husband, leaving his wife free to tend her family, teach Sunday school, found the Faji Circuit Ladies' Guild, serve as President of the Ladies' Recreation Club, and establish the Lagos Ladies' League, a charity that ministered to the sick and poor. Anna Williams's obituary remarked, 'In society she was known as a woman of exemplary character and high attainments, possessing the most admirable qualities of a gentlewoman . . . [S]he was an exemplary wife, for she served her husband and family with untiring devotion . . . and genuine motherly sympathy.'[48] Bishop Isaac Oluwole described Mrs Williams as 'a lady of high culture, with character gentle, sweet and pure'.[49]

Other less fortunate elite women found their marital expectations disappointed. Better than half of the elite men who wed in church also formed outside unions. Outside wives and children often deprived Christian wives of their husbands' resources and sometimes embarrassed them. While a few elite women welcomed customary wives into the family, most bitterly resented them.[50] Even in the absence of outside unions, Christian wives frequently found husbands unwilling to support them in the style expected. Articles and letters in the press reveal the bitter conflict couples experienced over maintenance. One writer fumed, 'The result of [the] imperfect education [girls receive] is to leave [them] . . . imbued with the idea that they are above the drudgery of housework, marketing, selling, and other duties which [women] were content to perform before they acquired that "little learning", which is said to be a "dangerous thing".'[51] The man went on to

Marrying well

complain about educated women's insatiable appetite for dress and jewelry. For their part, wives with very indulgent husbands also found dependence untenable at times, facing personal needs or obligations to kin that they would have preferred to meet themselves. An informant commented, 'My mother hated to ask my father each time she needed a shilling.'[52]

While Christian wives and their children stood to inherit all self-acquired property in cases of intestacy, husbands sometimes wrote wills recognizing other heirs.[53] Indeed, elite males occasionally used wills to disinherit their Christian wives. Andrew Wilkinson Thomas, for example, left his widow £5 out of a £9,500 estate, commenting, 'her conduct has compelled me to live apart from her'. Thomas bequeathed his mistress £150.[54] When men died intestate kin sometimes tried to deprive Christian wives and their children of their inheritance. James William Cole died in 1897, survived by a widow, their lunatic son, several outside children and a brother. The brother pressured the widow to grant him and the outside children two-thirds of her husband's estate. When she refused he took the case to court, asking to be declared customary heir and trustee for the lunatic son. The Divisional Court ruled in the brother's favor. Mrs Cole appealed, and the Full Court overturned the lower court's decision.[55] Less resilient women sometimes capitulated to the demands of kin and outside children.[56] To cite one additional disappointment, strict English divorce laws may have discouraged husbands from legally ending Christian unions, but they did not stop men from ceasing to fulfill their conjugal responsibilities. Informants repeatedly told stories about Christian wives whose husbands deserted them.[57]

Court records from the case *Shyngle* v. *Shyngle* reveal how badly elite men sometimes treated Christian wives. Gambian Joseph Egerton Shyngle read law in London, where he wed an English woman named Annie in 1889. In 1890 the couple moved to Lagos and set up housekeeping in Customs Street. Shyngle built a successful law practice, while Annie raised two children and played an active role in the social life of the town. In 1913 Mrs Shyngle visited England and returned to find her husband living with another woman at Tinubu Square. To avoid embarrassment Mrs Shyngle went to stay at her husband's Agege farm. Soon she moved back to Customs Street, where she started a girls' school in 1915, presumably to support herself.[58] In 1918 Shyngle ordered his wife to vacate her residence, which he wished to sell, promising to build her a new house. Mrs Shyngle obeyed, but her husband did not keep his word. After repeatedly begging for assistance, Annie finally rented a house on her own, only to be evicted because she could not pay the rent. Reduced to dependence on the kindness of friends, Mrs Shyngle sued for divorce in 1923.[59] Annie Shyngle may have been particularly vulnerable because she was an Englishwoman and had no kin in Lagos to protect her interests. In many respects, however, her experiences were similar to those of other Christian wives.

When marital disputes arose Christian wives upheld their rights with mixed success. Perhaps most commonly elite women looked to relatives and friends to pressure their husbands to fulfill conjugal responsibilities. If informal sanctions failed, women's kin sometimes called formal meetings where representatives of both families tried to mediate disputes. In Lagos, however, families could not always enforce their decisions. Moreover, relatives did not always share women's ideas about what was right.[60] Within five years of marriage, a serious breach erupted between Victoria (Davies) Randle and Dr John Randle. In 1895 Randle complained to J. P. L. Davies, his father-in-law, that marriage to Victoria made 'every waking hour miserable'.[61] Davies; Stella (Davies) Coker, Victoria's sister; and Dr J. O. Coker, Victoria's brother-in-law and Randle's medical-school friend, all intervened to try to settle the disagreement. Their efforts only provoked Victoria, who in 1898 accused her sister and father of siding with her husband. 'You both joined Randle in an attempt to seize my children', she complained. 'You have laid yourselves at Randle's hands and approved and emulated his cruelties and infidelities and have helped to render him thoroughly unfit to live with. The very Randle who deserted and maltreated me and lives the life of a dog with dozens of women married and unmarried is an honored guest in your dishonored home.'[62] Despite the best efforts of kin, the Randle marriage ended in bitter divorce.

When women deemed family mediation unlikely to succeed, they sometimes took grievances to religious or secular authorities. The identity of the third party varied with the nature of the problem and with women's perceptions of who would make the most effective ally. Some wives reported unfaithfulness to ministers, knowing that churches had mechanisms for punishing adultery.[63] Other wives appealed to Europeans with influence or authority over their husbands. Mrs George Smith, wife of the Chief Clerk in the Customs Department, went straight to the Governor in an effort to obtain a larger allowance. Mrs Smith complained that her husband had deserted his family and sent them only £6 a month maintenance. She begged the Governor to see that she got more money.[64] Third parties, however, had little power to enforce women's rights. When the Reverend James Johnson tried to persuade a deserting husband to return home, the man told him curtly, 'after mature consideration I have come to the conclusion that it is better for us to remain apart. I do not feel that I can live with her as her husband.'[65] Mrs Smith's overture to the Governor succeeded only in getting her husband turned down for an increase in salary.

The colonial courts had jurisdiction in all matrimonial cases involving couples who wed under the ordinance.[66] While a few elite women, such as Mrs Cole and Mrs Shyngle, turned to the colonial courts to uphold their rights, most did not exercise this option. After 1876, a Police Magistrates' court heard all civil cases involving claims of £25 or less. The Supreme Court heard cases involving sums greater than this amount.[67] Until the lower court's records are found it will be impossible to know how important a role this tribunal played in settling domestic disputes. It seems unlikely, however, that many elite women would have taken their cases to the Police

Magistrates' Court, if only because their claims must ordinarily have been for sums greater than £25.[68] Supreme Court records survive, although greatly disordered and little used by historians. A survey of the registers of civil cases for 1885, 1895 and 1905 revealed that only 4 of the roughly 380 cases heard in those years pertained to domestic matters. A check of the judges' notebooks from 1880 to 1915 confirmed that elite women did not often bring marriage disputes before the Supreme Court.[69]

Elite women hesitated to take domestic grievances to the Supreme Court for several reasons. Most simply, taking a case to the Supreme Court required hiring a lawyer, an expensive proposition. Fadipe claimed that prior to 1914 the average divorce cost £60, enough to deter many couples from terminating *de jure* marriages that had ended *de facto*.[70] Elite women, who depended on their husbands economically, may have been especially loath to incur legal fees, which their kin would have had to pay if they lost their cases. To cite a further impediment, family law in Lagos was hopelessly complex. The Supreme Court applied local law to certain categories of persons and types of problems and English law or colonial statutes to others. The jurisdiction of these different bodies of law was vague and subject to the interpretation of individual judges.[71] Moreover, the content of local law was open to debate, because customary norms were changing very rapidly.[72] In these circumstances women and lawyers alike must have been uncertain about the outcome of domestic disputes, heightening reluctance to take them to colonial court. Finally, the Supreme Court was a public tribunal presided over by an influential European and located on a busy thoroughfare in the heart of town. Anyone could stop and listen to testimony. Controversial cases attracted considerable attention, and the press sometimes reported them at length, feeding the fiery tongues of Lagos gossipmongers.[73] Acutely conscious of their public image, many elite women may have refused to air messy domestic disputes in the Supreme Court to spare themselves public embarrassment.

In the eyes of the colonial state, Christian marriage gave women a new status, based on monogamy and assuming new property relations between husbands and wives. The state believed that by prohibiting polygyny and bringing Christian wives within the orbit of English law, it could protect them from African customs contrary to 'justice, equity, and good conscience'.[74] This proved patently untrue. Victorian law gave wives very restricted rights, unsuited to the needs of educated women in Lagos. Under the Marriage Ordinance, men could be fined or imprisoned if they married in church and wed another woman according to Yoruba custom. This law itself proved difficult to enforce. Yet if men left their outside unions vague, practicing *de facto* polygyny, ordinance wives had no legal recourse save divorce, and this only if the adultery was aggravated by desertion, cruelty or some other matrimonial wrong. Moreover, Christian wives could not ask the court for an order for maintenance unless they also asked for divorce.[75]

For many reasons most educated women found divorce an unattractive option. They wanted to protect their status as ordinance wives, not to end their marriages. Even if elite women themselves favored divorce, their kin, on whom they ultimately relied, would rarely have supported them. The Yoruba felt a strong social duty to keep their families out of court.[76] In addition, relatives usually wanted to preserve marriages and did not regard outside wives and children as sufficient reason for divorce. James George Campbell, a minister in an African church, wrote:

> Polygamous life is a part and parcel of our God given nature . . . It is a great shame for a woman [married according to European custom] to seek to divorce her husband because he has a mistress[;] if she does, her own family will resent her and tell her that she is seeking her husband's spoilation . . . Any woman who wishes to keep to the bargain made at church 'and forsake all others cleave to thee and thee only' [*sic*] generally finds herself at the bottom of the ladder and in hot waters and snubbed by society and the affray ends in her downfall.[77]

A relative chided Victoria (Davies) Randle, who bitterly protested her husband's outside wives, '[A]nyone who is stiffnecked shall be humbled to the dust.'[78]

Kin sometimes agreed that Christian marriages should end, but only as a last resort – if husbands abused their wives repeatedly and all efforts to bring them into line failed. Even then, families rarely deemed legal divorce desirable. Women such as Victoria (Davies) Randle, who determined to end their marriages against all opposition, occasionally sought divorce without the support of relatives. These women sometimes used the colonial courts as allies against their families as well as husbands. The social cost of this strategy was high, however, because it drove a wedge between women and their kin.[79]

Contrary to the hopes of elite women and their parents, Christian marriage clearly failed to guarantee women's status. Recognizing this, a local commentator warned, 'It is very much to be feared that [Christian] marriage brings [women] a false sense of security, and it is because of the disaster it has wrought among so many, that we venture to bring this matter to the public notice.'[80] Beginning in the early 1890s the elite grew increasingly preoccupied with the plight of Christian wives. Men first drew attention to the disjunction between educated women's foreign conjugal expectations and the realities of life in Lagos. Women then began discussing their own dilemma. Male and female observers worried about elite women's economic vulnerability and about the disappointment and bitterness they so often experienced after marriage. One writer summarized women's condition: 'The customs of their country have become repugnant to their distorted – but what they erroneously call *refined* – tastes and they are themselves repugnant to their people. Isolated and wretched, they are . . . good for nothing but to be trodden under the [feet] of men.'[81] Wills reflect elite fathers' fears about their daughters' insecurity. Several of these documents instruct sons to take care of their sisters in the event of marital disappointment. Adeyemo Alakija's will established a family house, 'so that if any of my female children needs shelter she can always find accommodation therein'.[82]

Concern about their domestic problems provoked some elite women to begin reconsidering aspects of Christian marriage. Difficult to date precisely, this movement gained momentum around 1900. Most elite women continued to insist that first marriages take place in church, for themselves and their daughters. A few such women, however, began publicly defending Yoruba marriage, even polygyny. Justice Osborne commented in 1904, 'Mrs G. P. Johnson . . . was . . . a leading light of the Wesleyans and [a] highly respected member of the community . . . She was a strong advocate of native marriage, disbelieving in the suitability of monogamy for her own people.'[83] After the turn of the century, respectable widows sometimes formed customary unions or liaisons. Stella Coker, daughter of J. P. L. Davies and Queen Victoria's ward Sarah Forbes Bonetta Davies, a pillar of the Christian community and well-known 'society lady', lived with Herbert Macaulay from 1909 until her death in 1916.[84] Stella's feelings about living with Macaulay outside Christian marriage are lost to memory. Friends hoped the couple would wed in church.[85] Stella may have shared their hopes and accepted an outside union when Macaulay refused. Or she, just as he, may have preferred a customary union. The important point is that Stella consented to live with Macaulay outside Christian marriage, something a woman of her status probably would not have done a generation before.

Most elite women focused their reconsideration on the appropriate roles of Christian wives. Anglican women began counselling young ladies to live more modestly and industriously. Mrs Oluwole warned them that eligible bachelors had begun avoiding Christian marriage because they feared extravagant, lazy wives. She wrote,

> Some men complain that their wives were industrious before marriage, but after they are married they become quite a failure, by thinking that it is below the dignity of a wife to do domestic work . . . Other men say their wives never had any training in domesticity, so there is extravagance in the home through ill-management.[86]

In a related pamphlet Mrs Oluwole argued,

> Our girls are growing up with wrong ideas of a woman's vocation, especially those whose parents happen to be able to give them education in a secondary school . . . Mothers, yours chiefly is the duty to remedy this. Let your girls . . . learn to sweep and dust . . . to cook, to keep house, to do business, to know laundry, and so on . . . Some mothers have the mistaken idea that a girl who has been educated in a secondary school should play the 'lady', which means that she is not to soil her hands with work, but should only be attired in fine dresses and a display of jewellery.[87]

Sabina Johnson, wife of Bishop James Johnson and daughter of merchant Jacob Samuel Leigh, set an example in her own life by cooking, cleaning, sewing and weaving.[88]

The dangers of dependence

Some male and female contemporaries went further than Mrs Oluwole and advocated greater economic independence for elite women. An 1899 article, written by a man, noted 'the precariousness and fallaciousness in our women in starting life and continuing it without a definite and independent means of livelihood'. The author cautioned wives who claimed to be too busy with domestic affairs to work outside the home against 'specious pleading for utter dependence on a husband'. Lest wives become too independent, he added that women's work 'need not be of any magnitude. [It] should be subsidiary but tangible.'[89]

Many observers saw a relationship between elite women's economic dependence and the absence of opportunities for ladies to earn a decent livelihood. A writer 'interested in the employment of women' asserted, 'there is next to nothing for our girls to do besides teaching and sewing'.[90] Realizing that educated women would remain economically vulnerable as long as they were not prepared for the world of work, an 1899 article urged parents, 'In order to enable . . . girls to meet the emergencies of the future . . . set them right at the present. Let them be taught industries so that they may not be mere logs in the hands of their . . . husbands.'[91]

By the early twentieth century leading members of the elite had begun trying to improve educated women's economic opportunities. In 1905 Felicia Ayodele (Benjamin) Wright proposed founding '[a] college [for girls] with an industrial or technical school attached where book learning could be combined with useful occupations' such as farming, nursing, weaving, raising poultry and manufacturing local foodstuffs. A cultural nationalist, Mrs Wright argued, 'There would be real dignity in a native technical school in which African civilization is recognized and developed.' Mrs Wright invited contributions to the school, saying, 'we cannot do better than to provide for the future mothers of our race better education which will enable them to fight their way in the world'.[92]

The elite rallied behind Mrs Wright. In January 1907 the Lagos School for Girls opened at Caxton House, lent by Charlotte O. Obasa, daughter of Emily (Cole) Blaize and Richard Beale Blaize.[93] The school proposed to offer girls 'a sound moral, literary and industrial education' and 'to render [them] fit to cope with any and every emergency [in] . . . life'.[94] In 1910 the Lagos Wesleyan Board took over the school, which became the Wesleyan Girls' High School.[95]

The elite also sponsored other schemes to train and employ women. As early as 1896 Dr Ṣapara proposed a lying-in hospital run by local ladies.[96] Fifteen years later he launched a drive to send two women abroad to become midwives. Ṣapara proposed that the public bear the expense of educating these women, who on their return would serve the community for three years, charging no more than £1 for a nine-day confinement. The doctor called on Lagos churches to build a public maternity home where these midwives could attend poor women free of charge.[97] In 1915 the correspondent 'interested in the employment of women' volunteered 'to get a few young ladies together, have them taught type writing, and open an office', noting that Lagos needed a place where the public could get typing done.[98]

The economic activities of several elite women in the early twentieth century reflect this changing attitude toward women's work. Felicia Ayodele (Benjamin) Wright opened a retail store called Liberty Shop. Then in 1905 she explored starting a fruit trade between England and southwestern Nigeria. When her husband died in 1907, Mrs Wright assumed management of the family's 400-acre farm near Ifako, which produced cocoa, kola, coffee, rubber and cotton.[99] In 1906 Mrs Wright's sister Hannah Matilda Benjamin decided not to close her store after marrying Dr William A. Cole.[100] Carrie Lumpkin, daughter of Dr Charles Jenkins Lumpkin, set up a photography studio in Lagos in 1908.[101] In 1909 Mrs William B. Euba won first prize in rubber preparation at the Calabar Agricultural Show, which suggests that she had entered the rubber trade.[102] Four years later Charlotte O. (Blaize) Obasa established Lagos's first motor transport company. By 1915 she had three taxis, six buses and three lorries on the road.[103] That same year Hope Sarah Adelabu Nelson Cole bought a small farm with money inherited from her father, Jacob Samuel Leigh.[104] After Remilekun Williams married lawyer E. J. Alex Taylor in 1911 she kept a shop on the ground floor of their house. Later she managed two farms, one owned by her husband, one by herself.[105] These women came from the best-educated families in Lagos. All but one attended school in England. With the exception of Miss Lumpkin, who never married, all made excellent matches. Yet these women rejected the European norm of idle dependence in favor of greater economic autonomy, the traditional role of Yoruba women.

A further indication of these changing attitudes: some elite parents in this period began socializing their daughters to have different expectations and ensuring that they received the education needed to fulfill them. Although the numbers remained small and the obstacles to success great, Nigeria's first educated women to seek careers in politics, the professions and the colonial service came from among the daughters of the early-twentieth-century educated elite. These pioneering women included Oyinkan (Ajasa) Abayomi, Stella (Thomas) Marke, Dr E. (Akerele) Awoliyi, Dr Irene Thomas, Ayodele (Oluwole) Manuwa, Ayodele (Taylor) Adeshigbin and Kofoworola (Moore) Ademola. Kofoworola Ademola has told how her father, Eric Olawolu Moore, urged her to study law in the 1920s. He accepted her preference for education only on the condition that she obtain a degree from Oxford or Cambridge.[106] Dr Irene Thomas remembers that her parents, Mr and Mrs P. J. C. Thomas, encouraged their daughters to become doctors and lawyers, just as they did their sons. Mr and Mrs Thomas sent Irene to King's College, a prestigious Lagos boys' school, so she would receive the foundation in mathematics and science necessary to study medicine.[107] Like their mothers, these women expected to make Christian marriages and raise families. Unlike their mothers, they did not see this goal as incompatible with work outside the home.

Europeans and repatriated slaves brought to Lagos Victorian domestic ideology, which undermined the autonomy of educated women and set them on a pedestal. At the same time, changes in the structure of economic and political opportunities wrought by the growth of international trade, the rise of the colonial state and the introduction of Western education prevented educated women from sharing with educated men the rewards of the new socio-cultural order. The colonial state extended to Christian wives new legal rights, which Europeans believed would protect their status. However, these rights were ill suited to the needs of educated women in Lagos and proved difficult to enforce. In these circumstances, elite women embraced Christian marriage for two reasons: because upholding civilized values had become part of their special responsibility as women, and because making a good Christian marriage to an elite man provided their only means of sustaining membership in the elite. Unlike elite men, elite women experienced little tension between their needs and interests and their religious and cultural commitment to Christian marriage. Quite the contrary; elite women found their beliefs and their needs and interests mutually reinforcing.

And yet Christian marriage confronted elite women with a dilemma, just as it did elite men. Elite women had become dependent on elite men, but elite men often failed to fulfill their expectations. After years of disappointment and marital strife, influential elite women began to rethink aspects of Christian marriage. In smaller numbers than elite men and five to ten years later, these women began to dissociate Christian marriage from European conjugal ideals. Elite women continued to want monogamy and the new rights associated with Christian marriage. However, some began to question the wisdom of economic dependence and to advocate greater autonomy for educated women.

Elite women rethought marriage in the context of the larger economic, cultural, religious and political changes discussed in the preceding chapter. These changes clearly affected women's thinking about marriage. By the end of the century, moreover, Western domestic ideology had begun to change, as feminists fought to widen women's sphere.[108] A few girls educated in England returned to Lagos with ideas about the 'new woman', as demonstrated by occasional references to the subject in the local press.[109] Without denying the relevance of these larger historical developments, this chapter has emphasized a different theme: elite women's discovery through personal experience that foreign conjugal ideals glorified by Europeans as a mark of civilization left women dependent, vulnerable and unhappy. Evidence from life histories and written records demonstrates that elite women's reconsideration of their conjugal roles sprang from this realization. Felicia Ayodele (Benjamin) Wright proposed a technical school for girls not to glorify African civilization, but to enable educated women to fight their way in the world.

5

Marriage and the consolidation of status

Marriage can create differences between social strata, or it can break the differences down. In Lagos Christian marriage played a crucial role in the development of a distinctive style of life that defined the educated elite, set it off from the rest of the population, and legitimized its authority and privilege in colonial society. If marriage occurs mainly between members of the same social strata, it can concentrate valuable material and non-material resources within a small number of families and give rise to an hereditary elite. On the other hand, if marriage commonly occurs between members of different social strata, it can open the resources of the elite to outsiders and promote social mobility. To understand the consequences of elite marriage for social stratification in Lagos, we must ask whom elite men and women married and investigate the impact of marriage on the concentration of resources within elite families. We must further inquire whether the concentration of resources within elite families gave their members advantages in the competition for education and elite occupations that ensured the transmission of status and privilege from generation to generation. Here, as throughout, it is necessary to distinguish between the effects of Christian and customary marriage.

Abner Cohen observes that the power of elites is embedded in their total culture. Culture finds expression in what Cohen calls 'symbolic forms', ceremonies, rituals and social institutions, such as marriage. These have implications for the organization of the elite and the distribution of resources within the community. They affect access to opportunity and the effectiveness with which the elite performs those roles that make it an elite.[1] The discussion in this chapter of marriage and social stratification probes the link between the power and privilege of the early Lagos elite and a fundamental aspect of its culture.

When elite men and women made Christian marriages, they chose spouses of the same social and economic status as they. Elite men's Christian wives were predominantly Saro, as Table 5.1 indicates. All professed Christianity; most belonged to the established mission churches. These women had received a high level of education relative to the population as a whole, although they were less well educated than their husbands. Only one Christian wife is known to have been illiterate. At least 48 percent had attended secondary school, 20 percent at private girls' schools in Great

Table 5.1. *Percentage distribution of the origins of elite males' Christian wives*[a]

Saro	80
Brazilian	8
Other	7
Local Yoruba	1
Other Nigerians	5
N	(105)

[a] 'Other' includes Afro-Americans, Ghanaians, Liberians, Gambians and English. 'Other Nigerians' includes Gun and Igbo.

Table 5.2. *Percentage distribution of occupations of fathers of elite males and their Christian wives*[a]

Occupation	Men's fathers	Wives' fathers
Merchants	48	53
Modern	22	25
Traditional	30	22
N	(96)	(81)

[a] 'Modern' includes clerks, teachers, catechists, clergy, doctors, lawyers and planters. 'Traditional' includes farmers, chiefs, medical herbalists, warriors, artisans and slaves.

Britain.[2] Earlier chapters have shown that elite men's Christian wives aspired to be housewives, and that many achieved this status, although attitudes toward work outside the home began to change around 1900.[3]

Elite men's Christian wives came from families as good, if not better, than their own. At least one-third of these women had fathers or brothers who belonged to the Lagos elite or to similar elites in Freetown, Bathurst or Cape Coast. Twenty elite men had illiterate fathers, but only one of their Christian wives is known to have had an illiterate father. Table 5.2 demonstrates that a slightly smaller percentage of men's fathers than the fathers of their Christian wives worked as merchants or in modern occupations. Oral data indicate that fewer wives than husbands came from poor backgrounds, and more had wealthy fathers.

Life histories show that elite women also chose spouses of the same social and economic status as themselves. Zenobia Phillips, educated daughter of Saro catechist Charles Phillips and sister of the Reverend (later Bishop) Charles Phillips, wed Nathaniel Johnson, himself a Saro clergyman.[4] Saro merchant Joseph Samuel Bucknor's accomplished daughters wed a Saro clergyman and a Saro merchant.[5] Harriet Susan Nicol, daughter of the Chief Clerk in the Treasury, married Alfred Latunde Johnson, first an Audit clerk and later a lawyer.[6] While family background mattered when choosing a marriage partner, the characteristics of the spouse counted far more. Young professionals and respectable foreign-educated women would marry well, no matter who their kin. A case in point, Dr Orisadipe Obasa, son of a mechanic, married Charlotte O. Blaize, daughter of Richard Beale Blaize, one of Lagos's richest and best-respected merchants.[7] Religion, education and good career prospects for men, and religion, education and sound reputations for women assured success in the Christian marriage market.

A high degree of symmetry characterized the backgrounds of Christian couples. For example, the best-educated men tended to marry the best-educated women. Of the fifty-four elite men with only a secondary education, 89 percent married women educated in Lagos, and 11 percent married women educated in Great Britain or at Annie Walsh School in Freetown. Of the forty-seven men with advanced education, only 62 percent married women educated in Lagos, and 38 percent married women educated in Great Britain or Freetown. Among younger couples, an even greater percentage of men with advanced education wed foreign-educated women, suggesting that as the period progressed education became an increasingly important criterion in mate selection. A comparison of the occupations of elite men and their Christian wives at the time of marriage shows that colonial servants wed seamstresses and traders slightly more often than did merchants or professionals. This may have been the case because colonial servants had smaller incomes than merchants or professionals and attached greater importance to marrying women who would contribute to the family economically. Or perhaps colonial servants did not enjoy sufficiently high salaries to attract wives of the highest social status. Professionals married schoolmistresses more often than did colonial servants; however, merchants married women who identified themselves as 'ladies' slightly more often than did professionals.

By marrying up and down, merchants deviated from the tendency of like to marry like more commonly than did professionals or colonial servants. Wealth may have permitted little-educated entrepreneurs from non-elite families to attract wives of superior social standing. Grandson of a Nupe slave, Benjamin C. Dawodu attended C.M.S. schools, joined the Anglican church, and entered trade after leaving school. Soon he became a prosperous merchant.[8] In his twenties, Dawodu married three women according to Yoruba custom.[9] At about age thirty, he entered a Christian union with twenty-two-year-old Adeline Hoare, daughter of wealthy Saro merchant Thomas George Hoare.[10] Four years earlier, Adeline had returned from three years at an English girls' school, making her a very attractive Christian marriage partner.[11] No information survives about how or why Benjamin and Adeline decided to wed. Special circumstances in the Hoare family may have helped Dawodu make such a good match. Adeline was the oldest of

Marriage and the consolidation of status

T. G. Hoare's seven children. Her father was sixty-four when she married, and he died less than a year later. Suspecting that his life was ending, Hoare may have permitted or even encouraged his daughter to wed Dawodu to see her taken care of and ease the financial burden on his widow. T. G. Hoare provided in his will for the education and maintenance of his offspring. He stipulated that his two daughters should be excluded from any claim after their marriage.[12] For economic and other reasons, some well-educated merchants from elite families chose non-elite women as Christian wives. For example, Burrell Carter Vaughan, son of merchant James Churchwill Vaughan, married a semi-literate trader whose father was a carpenter.[13] Poor clergymen from humble origins sometimes exchanged respectability and prestige for wealth by marrying daughters of prominent educated merchants. In 1895, the Reverend James Johnson, son of poor, illiterate Sierra Leoneans, married Sabina Leigh, daughter of wealthy, educated Saro merchant Jacob Samuel Leigh.[14] Despite these deviations, the general principle stands. Status divisions demarcated boundaries within which but not between which elite men and women formed Christian marriages.

Over the years, the status endogamy characteristic of the educated elite's Christian marriages created a network of interlocking relations among a small number of educated, Christian and relatively wealthy families in Lagos, Freetown, Bathurst and Cape Coast. The marital histories of two families illustrate the dense web of cousinage that intermarriage created. Cornelius Bartholemew Moore was born in Sierra Leone to William Moore and Mary Ann (Renner) Moore, liberated Egba slaves. Educated by the Church Missionary Society in Freetown, William returned to Abeokuta with his wife and family in the 1850s. There he served as an Anglican catechist and clergyman until his death in 1893. In addition to Cornelius, William fathered two sons and two daughters who survived to adulthood.[15] The youngest daughter married planter Rufus A. Wright, son of the Reverend Thomas B. Wright. Information about the marriages of the middle children would reveal additional alliances between the Moores and influential Abeokuta and Lagos families. Cornelius Moore attended C.M.S. schools and began trading in the 1860s, when commerce was still profitable. During the 1870s, he became a successful merchant with interests in Abeokuta and Lagos. Between June 1882 and June 1883 Moore imported cloth, spirits and hardware worth £2,500.[16]

In 1869, Cornelius married Eliza Sabina Williams, sister of James O'Connor Williams and Zachariah Archibald Williams, later prominent Lagos businessmen. In 1879, Z. A. Williams married Eleanor Cole, daughter of T. F. Cole, a wealthy Saro merchant; sister of Rotimi Alade, a Cape Coast lawyer; and sister-in-law of Richard Beale Blaize, one of the richest men in Lagos. Thus Moore was related by marriage to the Williams family, and through Z. A. Williams he had connections with the Cole and Blaize families.

The marriages of Cornelius and Eliza's five children illustrate the exten-

Marrying well

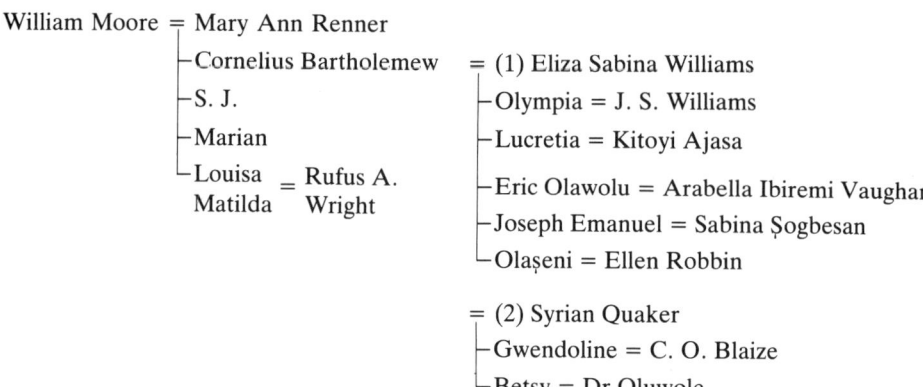

Figure 5.1. Abbreviated genealogy of the William Moore family

sion in the third generation of the web of marriage alliances that bound the elite. The career of their sons and sons-in-law show the movement of this generation away from commerce and into the professions and colonial service. Olympia, their first child, married J. S. Williams, a Saro Anglican and later African Church clergyman, and a younger brother of I. B. Williams, a wealthy Lagos merchant and landowner. Their second child, Lucretia, wed Kitoyi Ajasa, a successful Lagos barrister, who was the son of Thomas B. Macaulay and nephew of David Macaulay, both important traders. Ajasa's two sisters married Daniel Olubi, an Anglican clergyman, and C. J. P. Ibare-Akinsan, a clerk and interpreter in the Governor's office and later the Assistant Chief Clerk in the Colonial Secretariat. Moore's third child, Eric Olawolu, was called to the bar in 1902. In 1904, he married Arabella Ibiremi Vaughan, daughter of James Churchwill Vaughan, who had died in 1893, and sister of James Wilson and Burrell Carter Vaughan, both prosperous merchants. Next among the children came Joseph Emanuel, who wed Sabina Ṣogbesan, about whom no information survives. Last came Olaṣeni, who in 1908 married Ellen Robbin, daughter of Henry Robbin, a prominent Egba merchant, dead since 1887. Olaṣeni traded for a number of years and then qualified as a barrister in 1913. His wife was the sister of J. H. S. Robbin, Chief Registrar in the Judicial Department. Her sisters included Rebecca, wife of merchant J. M. St Anna; Fanny, wife of Anglican clergyman Hugh Stowell Macaulay, himself a grandson of Bishop Samuel Crowther and brother of Herbert Macaulay; Edith, wife of merchant S. A. Wright; Henrietta, wife of Inspector of Schools, Director of Education and later Assistant Colonial Secretary Henry Carr; and Eunice, wife of the Reverend Victor Johnson and daughter-in-law of the Reverend Nathaniel Johnson. Cornelius Moore had two more daughters by Syrian Quaker, whom he wed after his first wife died. The younger, Betsy, married Dr Oluwole, and the older, Gwendoline, wed C. O. Blaize, son of R. B. Blaize, thus creating a direct link between the Moore and the Blaize families.

Charlotte O. (Blaize) Obasa, businesswoman and philanthropist, was one of C. O. Blaize's sisters. His brothers-in-law included Lagos doctor Orisadipe Obasa, Gambian lawyer A. E. M. Gibson and Lagos lawyer M. A. Akinṣemoyin.[17]

Josuah Blackall Benjamin came from Freetown to Lagos, where, after working as a bookkeeper, commercial agent and auctioneer, he founded the *Lagos Observer,* one of the colony's first newspapers.[18] In Lagos Benjamin married Hannah Matilda Williams, daughter of Fanny Barber, one of the town's most successful women traders. Josuah Blackall and Hannah Matilda had five daughters and three sons, all of whom they educated in England. Felicia Ayodele, their vivacious eldest daughter, wed Rufus A. Wright after the death of his first wife, Louisa Matilda Moore. Rufus A. Wright was the son of the Reverend Thomas B. Wright and the brother-in-law of the Reverend R. A. Coker, the Reverend James Okuseyinde and Edith Christiana Robbin, daughter of merchant Henry Robbin. R. A. Wright owned one of the largest farms in Lagos Colony. The Benjamins' second daughter, Henrietta Arabella, married Cape Coast lawyer Gabriel H. Savage, brother of leading Lagos merchant Josiah Alfred Savage. Josuah Begandeji, the couple's eldest son, qualified as a civil engineer and designed many of Lagos's finest buildings. He wed Maybelle George, daughter of Oshoba George, an important trader. Rowland Abiodun, the second son, and Fanny, the third daughter, apparently did not marry. The next daughter, Hannah Matilda, wed Dr William A. Cole, middle son of trader John Theodore Nelson Cole. Dr Cole's elder brother worked as an agent for the European firm Miller Brothers. His younger brother established a successful legal practice and married Hope Adelabu Leigh, daughter of merchant Jacob Samuel Leigh and niece of trader Rebecca Phillips Johnson. The last son, lawyer John Stanley Benjamin, wed Adeyinka Coker, from the large Abeokuta family of Harry O. Coker and James O. Coker. Her cousins included planter Jacob Kehinde Coker and doctor J. O. Coker, husband of Stella (Davies) Coker. Clara, the youngest daughter, also married a doctor, Magnus R. L. Macaulay, son of auctioneer William B. Macaulay, nephew of

```
Josuah Blackall Benjamin = Hannah Matilda Williams
                          ├─ Felicia Ayodele = Rufus A. Wright
                          ├─ Henrietta Arabella = Gabriel H. Savage
                          ├─ Josuah Begandeji = Maybelle George
                          ├─ Rowland Abiodun
                          ├─ Fanny
                          ├─ Hannah Matilda = Dr William A. Cole
                          ├─ John Stanley = Adeyinka Coker
                          └─ Clara = Magnus R. L. Macaulay
```

Figure 5.2. Abbreviated genealogy of the Josuah Blackall Benjamin family

traders David and Thomas B. Macaulay, and cousin of lawyers Kitoyi Ajasa and Sigismund A. Macaulay. Magnus Macaulay's female cousins wed the Reverend Daniel Olubi and colonial servants C. J. P. Ibare-Akinsan and Daniel Taiwo Ṣashegbon.[19]

Some of the connections drawn in these brief sketches of the Moore and Benjamin families were distant and loose. Many of the persons named were related not by but through marriage. For example, Eleanor (Cole) Williams and T. F. Cole were not Cornelius Moore's affines, but the wife and father-in-law of his brother-in-law. In these two networks of relationships, moreover, not all of the links existed at one time. Olaṣeni Moore wed Ellen Robbin and Gwendoline Moore wed C. O. Blaize after Cornelius Moore, Henry Robbin and Richard Beale Blaize had died. A few of the persons mentioned lived in Cape Coast, Bathurst or Freetown, hundreds or thousands of miles from Lagos. Many such persons visited Lagos periodically, to keep alive ties of blood and marriage.[20] Still, absent relatives could not play as active a role in the affairs of kin as could those who lived close by. Finally, affinal relationships carried rights and obligations which had to be met if the relationships were to mean anything. Persons could rarely sustain all the relationships open to them. Inevitably they chose to maintain some and let others die. By scrupulously observing rights and obligations, individuals could strengthen otherwise distant ties. Despite these qualifications, the marital histories of the Moore and Benjamin families demonstrate the extensive network of relationships that intermarriage created. In Lagos ties of friendship formed in school, church and clubs reinforced ties of blood and affinity. Multiply the connections traced here by a hundred or so Lagos families, and it becomes clear that members of the elite could, if they chose, establish personal connections with most other members of the elite. Often these connections extended to Freetown, Cape Coast and Bathurst.[21]

Status endogamy concentrated a broad range of resources among a small number of elite families. It united couples with the best education and greatest familiarity with the culture and institutions of the colonial rulers, merging valuable non-material assets. This proved important not only because education and familiarity with European culture helped to define the elite, but also because they gave couples, their children and their kin concrete social and economic advantages. Elite wives ran homes where their husbands felt comfortable entertaining Europeans and other educated Africans. On these occasions men traded information and advice, building trust and friendships that assured future opportunities.[22] When the Reverend J. H. Harris, Organizing Secretary of the Anti-Slavery and Aborigines Protection Society, visited Lagos in 1911, he stayed in the gracious home of merchant Samuel H. Pearse.[23] Later T. F. Buxton, the Society's President, helped Pearse's daughters obtain admission to an English girls' school. Buxton then acted as the girls' guardian while they were in England.[24] Elite wives' own activities at church, clubs and Government House maintained and extended contacts with influential whites and

Marriage and the consolidation of status

blacks.[25] Still more important, children who grew up in elite homes enjoyed advantages that helped them maintain elite status. Educated parents taught their offspring the English language and European customs and values, easing advancement in school and career. Children of illiterate parents could learn these things at school, but language, customs and values were best taught at home. In addition, elite parents encouraged educational and occupational achievement and could offer assistance and advice when needed. They also provided examples for their children to follow. The eagerness of illiterates to place their children with educated foster parents suggests how seriously contemporaries took these advantages.[26]

Access to opportunities in Lagos often depended on personal contacts, and so the network of relationships built up through intermarriage and reinforced through friendship constituted a valuable resource in itself. The elite drew on this network of alliances to find schools, obtain jobs, secure credit, exert bureaucratic influence and steer litigation through the colonial courts. Elite men and women could turn to someone related by blood or through marriage when they or their children needed assistance in any such matters. The following examples illustrate affinal ties at work. Stella (Davies) Coker let her father-in-law's many descendants attend her school free of charge.[27] Colonial servant Albert E. Carrena asked his 'cousin' Kitoyi Ajasa, a lawyer trusted by whites, to recommend Carrena's brother-in-law for a job with a European firm.[28] The dense web of relationships within the elite was ideally suited to mobilizing resources on behalf of individuals. Often the elite had kin, affines and friends in influential places – schools, churches, clubs and government offices – who would look out for their interests without even being asked.

But the web of relationships among the elite did more than further individual interests. It also helped transform a collection of individuals into a corporate group, conscious of its identity, aware of its interests and able to cooperate in pursuit of its common goals. The elite met regularly at family celebrations and other social events. On these occasions the group enacted the customs and values that defined it as an elite. These performances shaped standards of taste and decorum within the elite and spread them among its members. They reminded the elite what it was and why it enjoyed privileged status. Moreover, at family and other social gatherings the elite talked informally about its concerns. These conversations developed trust and understanding within the group. They built consensus and helped overcome the personality, sub-ethnic and political conflicts that periodically divided the elite.[29] Finally, regular interaction among overlapping sets of kin, affines and friends created networks of communication and cooperation that enabled the elite to coordinate its activities and mobilize to protect its interests. The issues changed, but the elite fought vigorously and often successfully for its causes from the 1860s to the second decade of the twentieth century, when political differences finally split the group.[30] Abner Cohen has shown that the regular interaction of Sierra Leonean Creoles at family and other social occasions enhanced their effectiveness as bureaucrats and professionals.[31] The same can be said of the Lagos elite. By enabling the members of a small number of families better to perform certain elite functions, the network of relationships created by intermarriage helped these families maintain their privileged social status.

Finally, status endogamy concentrated wealth among the elite. Many elite men and women came from prosperous families. Much wealth could be transmitted from generation to generation, because it took the form of self-acquired, privately owned land, houses and luxury goods. Intestate and testate succession favored children and spouses, not siblings or more distant kin. In cases of intestacy male and female children both shared in the estate of the deceased.[32] Men and women who wrote wills made bequests to sons, daughters and sometimes spouses. When such persons owned many parcels of real estate, they commonly left land or houses to individual children. If persons owned too little real estate to divide, or if they wished to keep intact what they did own, the Yoruba institution of family property allowed them to bequeath land and houses to the joint use of all descendants. Even those men and women who made individual bequests often left jointly owned family houses. Wills frequently entailed land and houses, specifying that they could not be sold, mortgaged or otherwise encumbered. This restricted free use of the property, but it also ensured future generations landed wealth, encouraging the development of a local *rentier*.[33]

Elite men channeled economic resources into Christian marriage from what they earned and inherited. Elite women rarely earned substantial incomes or brought dowries into marriage. Property transferred at the time of Christian marriage passed in the other direction, from the man or his kin to the woman. However, elite women sometimes did inherit property from their parents. The colonial state assumed that Christian marriage created a conjugal estate. In keeping with this belief, the government extended new rights to maintenance and property to husbands and wives who married under the ordinance.[34] Many elite couples found the ideal of the conjugal estate difficult to achieve. Christian husbands and wives experienced bitter conflict over the new legal rights, and some took great pains to avoid them. Even so, when both spouses brought property into Christian marriage, the nuclear family benefited as a whole. Wealthy husbands usually helped maintain their wives as well as their children.[35] Well-to-do wives contributed to their own support and that of their offspring, easing the financial burden on their husbands and enhancing the opportunities of their children. Hope Adelabu Nelson Cole inherited a sizeable estate from her father, merchant Jacob Samuel Leigh. Mrs Nelson Cole left her elder son £700 and her younger son the proceeds from the sale of a plot of land. She referred to these bequests as her 'contribution' to the boys' education, implying that she and her husband shared the cost of sending the young men to England for professional training.[36] Hannah Matilda Benjamin, wife of publisher Josuah Blackall Benjamin, inherited property from both of her parents. Mrs

Benjamin, like Mrs Nelson Cole, helped defray the cost of educating her children in England.[37]

The concentration of wealth within families benefited the elite in many ways. Wealth bought luxuries – fine homes, imported clothing, foreign travel and eventually automobiles – enjoyable in themselves and the outward signs of status. This proved highly important, because style of life, expressed in part through consumption, played a vital role in determining status. Moreover, wealth begot still greater wealth through investment in commerce or real estate. Finally, wealth gave the elite and their children leisure and capital to pursue education. Superior education gave men an edge in the competition for high-ranking jobs in the colonial service. Professional education ensured them a position among the elite. Superior education gave women advantages in the competition for elite husbands.[38]

Kinship and monogamy contributed to the concentration of resources among elite families. Elite men and women rarely belonged to big corporate patrilineages in Lagos. They did not have large numbers of less wealthy and influential relatives who had a legitimate right to make social and economic demands on them that drained resources from the nuclear family. Some elite men and women did belong to patrilineages in the interior, but distance made relations with these kin relatively easy to control.[39] The elite had begun to build up sizeable cognatic kin groups. However, these relatives often belonged to the elite or came from backgrounds similar to the elite's. They could give as much as they demanded. Recent discussions of lineage as a principle of social organization stress that kinship is created.[40] Although important in systems of unilineal descent, this fact is fundamental in bilineal systems. The Lagos elite constructed and maintained ties of cognatic kinship by fulfilling mutual obligations. This gave persons latitude to shape their kin groups to their own needs. When educated men and women became highly successful, they often severed ties with less successful relatives who burdened them with frequent demands. The emphasis in Christian marriage on the nuclear family justified such behavior ideologically. It eased pangs of conscience when the elite denied requests of kin or let kin ties lapse altogether.[41] In 1906 Stella (Davies) Coker refused to help a less fortunate 'cousin', explaining that when possible she liked to aid needy relatives, but that she then faced heavy family commitments.[42]

Monogamy limited the number of wives and children who could make claims on elite men's resources. It is true that Christian wives made new kinds of demands. Even so, monogamists with only a few children could do more for their offspring than polygynists with many, assuming the men possessed roughly comparable resources. Inheritance illustrates this simple point. Josiah Henryson Doherty divided an estate valued at £58,000 among more than forty women and children.[43] After generous contributions to charities, Richard Beale Blaize concentrated the bulk of his £60,000 fortune in the hands of only six children.[44] Blaize's individual children clearly received far more than Doherty's. A similar argument holds with respect to education. Blaize trained each of his offspring in England.[45] Doherty could not have done the same without expending vastly greater resources. Indeed, Doherty's will stipulated that only children who showed 'special fitness' should receive prestigious but costly foreign education.[46]

The evidence clearly shows that when elite men and women made Christian marriages they chose spouses of the same social and economic status as themselves. Intermarriage concentrated valuable non-material and material resources among a small number of elite families. Inheritance practices contributed to this process. Kinship and monogamy conserved resources for use by the nuclear family and selected close kin. The concentration of resources among elite families gave individuals and their children advantages in the quest for education and jobs that brought elite status. It ensured that persons learned and could support the distinctive style of life that defined the elite and set it off from the rest of the population. Each of these factors helped transmit status from parents to children and encouraged the development of an hereditary elite. However, a discussion of Christian marriage tells only part of the story. More than half of the elite males in fact made customary or outside marriages.

Data on customary and outside wives proved hard to obtain, making it hard to analyze their origins. The colonial government required registration only in the case of Christian unions. Information of the kind which marriage registers provide about Christian wives is unavailable for customary and outside wives. Oral data only partially fill the gap. Children of polygynists usually refused to talk about wives other than their own mothers, fearing that to do so might provoke misunderstanding within the family. Offspring of Christian unions sometimes tried to hide the fact that their fathers had had relations with other women. Reliable information about customary and outside wives came only from their own descendants. Yet on the average customary and outside wives bore fewer children for elite men than did Christian wives, making their descendants harder to trace.[47] Finally, elite men chose Christian wives from among a small number of interrelated families, so that a single interview with a descendant usually yielded information about several elite men and women. Descendants of customary and outside wives, on the other hand, typically could supply information about those women only.

Despite these difficulties, sufficient information exists to confirm Henry Carr's 1912 assertion that elite men did not choose customary or outside wives from the same 'class of persons' as their Christian wives.[48] A few customary and outside wives were Saro or Amaro, but most were local Yoruba from Lagos or the interior. Some of these women had converted to Christianity, but others had not. Whether Saro or local Yoruba, Christian or non-Christian, customary and outside wives lacked the education of Christian wives. Some had gone to primary school, but few had attended secondary school. Nearly all customary and outside wives worked outside the home, conforming more nearly to Yoruba than to European sex roles.

Most such women traded, but others washed clothes, sold prepared food, or engaged in craft production. Usually customary and outside wives came from illiterate families. Their fathers worked as farmers, traders and artisans, and only rarely as clerks, catechists and merchants. The mothers of customary and outside wives pursued the same kinds of economic activities as the women themselves. Few customary and outside wives had relatives who belonged to the educated elite in Lagos or elsewhere in West Africa. Moreover, few came from title-holding lineages.[49] Individual men occasionally entered customary unions with the daughters or sisters of local chiefs. Merchant Joseph Samuel Bucknor, for example, took wives from the Bajulaiye and Onikoyi families.[50] But the elite as a whole did not use customary marriage to create a far-reaching network of alliances with the traditional elite in Lagos or interior towns. Part of the reason for this may have been that early in the period the traditional elite did not view Christian strangers as attractive husbands for their daughters. Some elite men formed customary or outside unions with the daughters or sisters of wealthy Muslim merchants. The economic status of the kin of customary and outside wives varied widely, however. In general these women did not come from wealthy families.

As a group, customary and outside wives hailed from more traditional backgrounds and lower social and economic status than did elite men or their Christian wives. When elite men took customary or outside wives of their own social status, some disadvantage usually made the women unattractive as Christian wives. Either they had tarnished reputations, as in the case of Adel (Coker) Şapara, or they were separated or divorced.[51] A few elite women made customary marriages once marital attitudes began to change, and parents accepted their choice. In 1913 Jacob Kehinde Coker wrote, 'I desire my daughter to [marry] a polygamist however educated she may be.'[52] But in general, the rule held throughout the period. Elite men chose customary and outside wives from outside the pool of women eligible for Christian marriage.

A comparison of Aminatu Alayo, one of Benjamin C. Dawodu's three customary wives, and Adeline Hoare, his Christian wife, illustrates some of the differences between elite men's customary and Christian wives. The comparison also illustrates the very different quality of these women's lives. Aminatu Alayo came from Abeokuta to Lagos with her mother, a relative of merchants J. A. Williams and Seidu Williams. Aminatu probably grew up very near the Dawodu family home, in the large compound of one of the Williams brothers. Raised a Muslim, Aminatu received no European education and began to trade while still a young girl. In 1886, she married Benjamin C. Dawodu according to Yoruba custom and moved to the Dawodu household, where she lived until her husband died in 1900. Aminatu bore no children, but she raised her deceased sister's three offspring and freed a young female slave. After Dawodu's death, she married a Muslim and remained in Lagos.[53]

Marrying well

Adeline Hoare was born in Lagos to educated Saro parents. She grew up with her mother, father and younger siblings in her parents' comfortable home on Lake Street, in the heart of the Saro quarter. Adeline attended local schools until age fifteen and then went to England to finish her education. She returned three years later, the accomplished daughter of a prosperous merchant.[54] Back home, Adeline opened a private school and busied herself with church activities, ladies' literary and social clubs, and parties with friends.[55] In 1888, she married Dawodu in a society wedding at the Wesleyan Chapel.[56] Afterwards, Adeline apparently went to live in the Dawodu family compound, although this was highly unusual. Elite couples typically established households of their own. Adeline returned to England when Benjamin C. Dawodu died. In 1905 she married I. T. Palmer, a wealthy educated merchant from Sapele, who took her to Eastern Nigeria to live.[57]

Customary and outside wives did not bring to marriage the same resources as Christian wives – wealth, education and contacts with influential Europeans and educated Africans. Husbands enjoyed very restricted rights to what property customary and outside wives did own. And yet some elite men saw clear economic advantages to customary and outside unions. Yoruba marriage rites cost much less than Christian marriage rites. Unions that began informally often cost nothing at all. Moreover, husbands had more limited economic obligations to customary and outside wives than to Christian wives. Customary and outside wives retained a measure of economic independence and contributed to the support of their children. For these reasons customary and outside unions taxed elite men's resources less heavily than did Christian unions, conserving capital for other purposes. When elite merchants married traders, the women sometimes contributed to their husbands' commercial success. Finally, polygyny enabled elite men to construct a wide and flexible network of marriage alliances.[58] In each of these ways, elite men could benefit by making customary and outside marriages.

Of course, customary and outside unions also had certain disadvantages. Europeans disdained them. Yoruba marriage created obligations to less wealthy and influential affines, which could compete for resources with the needs of elite men and their children. Polygyny increased the number of wives, children and affines who could make claims on men's resources. When elite men had to divide their time, attention and wealth among many persons, it limited what they could do for their individual children. However, if elite men could manage relationships with wives, children and affines in such a way as to minimize demands for assistance, then the benefits of customary and outside unions might outweigh the costs.[59] At moments in elite men's lives, customary and outside unions could appear the best domestic strategy for meeting short-term needs and promoting long-term social and economic interests. Dual marriage permitted elite men to eat their cake and have it too. It allowed them to enjoy the benefits of customary or outside unions and good Christian marriages.

Did Yoruba and outside marriage open the resources of the elite to non-elite women and their children, creating for them an avenue of upward mobility and potential movement into the elite? Or did these unions create on the fringe of the elite a group of disadvantaged women and children, reinforcing the barriers between the elite and non-elite? Written records do not permit the historian to reconstruct domestic balance sheets; and informants rarely knew much about the details of domestic arrangements. Moreover, the experiences of customary and outside wives varied greatly. In general, customary wives of elite men who practiced only customary marriage fared better than customary wives of elite men who made Christian and customary marriages. Women whose relations with elite men remained informal or ambiguous suffered the greatest disadvantages. The most fortunate customary and outside wives received regular contributions to the support of their children and substantial gifts of capital or land for their own use. These women could rely on their husbands or lovers for advice and assistance when they needed it. Less fortunate women received only occasional gifts of money or consumer goods and could not count on elite men for aid.[60] Most customary and outside wives ultimately benefited from the advantages to their children discussed below. Successful sons and daughters usually helped support their aging mothers. Wives did not inherit from their husbands according to Yoruba custom, but widows did have the right to remain in their deceased husbands' compounds, usually as the wives of younger brothers or of sons.[61] It is impossible to know how often elite men provided for customary and outside wives in cases of intestacy, although informants insisted that this sometimes occurred.[62] Of the sixty-eight elite males who entered customary or outside unions, twenty-five wrote wills. Of this twenty-five, thirteen bequeathed land, houses or money to their customary or outside wives.[63] Customary wives' kin profited from elite men's resources through bridewealth and gifts and services due affines. In all of these ways, customary and outside wives benefited from their relationships with elite men. These benefits gave women and their kin clear motives for forging unions with elite males.[64]

Despite these advantages, customary and outside wives rarely if ever enjoyed the same privileges as Christian wives. They did not receive marriage settlements of cash, clothing and land; full support for themselves and their children; or expensive luxuries such as trips abroad. Moreover, inheritance practices clearly discriminated against customary and outside wives. Most elite men made no testamentary provisions for such women. In cases of intestacy customary and outside wives enjoyed no legal rights to their husbands' estates.[65] Of the eleven elite men who made Christian and outside marriages and recognized their outside wives in wills, six bequeathed more property to their Christian wives than to their outside wives. In addition to these disabilities, customary and outside unions were very unstable and gave women little security. Elite men could manipulate the status of these unions or terminate them with relative ease. Some customary and outside wives enjoyed life-long relationships with elite men, but others found their unions short-lived.[66] The access of customary and outside wives to elite men's resources depended on the men's own willingness to fulfill conjugal responsibilities, and on the women's ability to enforce their rights alone, with the support of kin, or in Yoruba or colonial courts. If women entered customary unions with men who had already made Christian marriages, then the women had few if any legal rights under colonial law. The same was true of women whose relationships with elite men never acquired the status of customary marriages. Public opinion might support both sorts of women in domestic conflicts, but their only real security lay in obtaining from their husbands or lovers title to a house or other landed property, as Adel (Coker) Şapara tried to do.[67] When men made Christian and outside marriages, the attitude and behavior of the Christian wife and children influenced the treatment of the outside wives and children.[68] These disabilities demonstrate that while customary and outside wives sometimes benefited from their association with elite males, the women did not enjoy the same privileges as Christian wives.

Children of customary and outside wives fared better than their mothers. The Yoruba believed that a child's legitimacy depended on recognition by its father, not on the status of its mother. The Yoruba also held that polygynists should share their resources roughly equally among their offspring. Rules of inheritance specified that a man's estate should be divided *per stirpes,* and that a child born outside wedlock constituted a *stirp* if its father had acknowledged paternity.[69] Each of these norms influenced elite men's treatment of their children. When elite men recognized paternity of children, they usually made efforts to provide for them, even if the men also had children by Christian wives. Moreover, assistance to children often continued after the relationships with their mothers had ended. Children of customary and outside unions benefited from elite men's resources through maintenance, education and inheritance. In addition, fathers used their influence and personal contacts to the advantage of these children.[70] Indeed, several mechanisms enabled elite males to equalize the opportunities of offspring of different kinds of women.

The widespread West African institution of foster parenthood allowed fathers to place children of illiterate or semi-literate women in the homes of educated women for training. Some elite men fostered outside children with relatives in Lagos, Abeokuta or Freetown.[71] Others placed them with prominent elite women in Lagos. Clergymen's wives raised a steady stream of such children.[72] A few elite men even brought outside children home for their Christian wives to train.[73] Fostering exposed children of non-elite women to Western education and to the language, customs and values of the colonial rulers, giving them some of the cultural advantages of children of elite women. Fostering also permitted elite men to improve the material welfare of children of customary and outside wives, without having to support the children's mothers in the style of Christian wives. In addition, fostering enabled fathers to help children establish useful connections with influential educated Africans; connections that sometimes lasted a lifetime. Abigail C. Oluwole bequeathed £25 to one 'adopted' daughter and £10 to each of three others.[74] These sums were not large relative to the size of Mrs Oluwole's estate. However, the bequests illustrate Mrs Oluwole's enduring commitment to these wards.

Education proved the greatest equalizer. Well-educated men could find secure, well-paying clerical jobs in the colonial service or with expatriate firms, no matter what their origins. Well-educated women could marry well. The data do not permit a comparison of the educational and occupational achievements of the children of different kinds of women. Even if they did, such a comparison would remain inconclusive unless it could take into account the talent and initiative of individual children and the role of maternal kin in paying for schooling. Oral data clearly indicate that most elite males helped educate all of their children to the secondary level. Some fathers sent children of customary and outside wives to mission-run boarding schools in hopes of improving their opportunities. At boarding school children received rigorous academic, moral and cultural education. There children of customary and outside wives made friends who could help them in later life.[75] Wealthy fathers sent gifted sons abroad for professional training, regardless of the status of the boys' mothers. A few elite men could afford to educate only one child in England and chose the son of an outside wife for the privilege. Colonial servant Hezekiah Africanus Caulcrick recognized seniority, ability or interest and sent his first son by an outside wife overseas to study medicine, not his second son by his Christian wife.[76] Education provided an avenue into the elite for some children of customary and outside wives.

Wills allowed elite males to make detailed provisions for the distribution of their estates. Of the fifty-four elite men who entered Christian and outside unions, twenty used wills to circumvent the provisions of the Marriage Ordinance and ensure that all of their children inherited. These men left outside children land, houses, money and personal effects, just as they did the children of their Christian wives.

And yet fostering, education and inheritance equalized opportunities imperfectly. Foster parents sometimes treated children no better than domestic servants, leaving little time for schoolwork and minimizing the benefits of growing up in an educated household.[77] Elite men who had offspring by Christian and outside wives usually favored the children of their Christian wives when it came to expensive luxuries and foreign education.[78] The record on inheritance looks no better. Thirty-four elite males who left children by Christian and outside wives did not write wills. What these men intended is hard to interpret. Prior to the highly publicized decision in the

1898 case *Cole* v. *Cole*, a few fathers may not have appreciated the legal implications of intestacy.[79] Other fathers may have provided for their outside children before dying or trusted their Christian wives and children to share their estates.[80] But some fathers undoubtedly chose intestacy as a way of letting colonial law take its course, thereby disinheriting outside children. Of the twenty elite males who left issue by Christian and outside wives and wrote wills, as many bequeathed substantially more property to the offspring of the Christian wife as divided their property roughly equally between the two sets of children.

In sum, customary and outside unions between elite men and non-elite women opened the resources of the elite to the women and their children. This benefited the women and their kin and provided some of the children with an avenue of upward mobility. However, customary and outside wives and children did not enjoy the same advantages as Christian wives and children. When elite men made Christian and outside marriages, the position of the outside wives and children was often decidedly inferior to that of the Christian wives and children. The advantages associated with Christian marriage helped preserve the privileges of the small number of elite families that intermarried under the ordinance.

In certain respects the very existence of customary and outside unions between elite men and non-elite women reinforced status differences and consolidated the identity and exclusiveness of the elite. Edmund Leach has argued that in a fundamental way all of us distinguish those who are of our kind from those who are not of our kind by asking ourselves the question 'Do we intermarry with them?'[81] In Lagos this question became 'How do we intermarry with them?' Addressing this question repeatedly heightened public awareness of the difference between the small number of well-educated men and women who intermarried in Christian unions and the much larger population that did not. Over time this process helped demarcate the boundary of the educated elite. In addition, the distinctive rituals, relationship and roles associated with Christian marriage created cultural barriers to entry into the elite and helped close it to outsiders. Non-elite women might enter customary or outside unions with elite men, but the quality of their domestic lives distinguished them from elite women. Non-elite women could rarely hope to form Christian unions with elite men, because such women did not have the education and cultural background necessary to make them good Christian wives. Illiterate merchants could acquire wealth and influence, but they would not marry like elite men. The barriers that Christian marriage created between the elite and non-elite began to weaken in the mid-1890s, as the elite's marital attitudes and behavior began to change. But the barriers did not disappear. Christian marriage remained an important element in elite status well into the colonial period.[82]

The social base of the Lagos elite had begun to broaden by 1915.[83] This trend accelerated as the twentieth century wore on, so that by the present day the descendants of the early Lagos elite feel they have lost control of the city that their ancestors built.[84] An analysis of intergenerational mobility is beyond the scope of this work. However, interviews with descendants of the early elite made clear that, while some men and women have maintained elite status, others have experienced marked downward social mobility. As Lagos Muslims began attending school and as education spread throughout Nigeria, non-Christians, non-Lagosians and non-Yoruba entered the elite. The roles that brought elite status remained much the same into the 1950s, although they began to change with independence. But new kinds of persons began to perform these roles. The impact of changes in the composition of the elite on the culture of the group and the dynamics of elite formation and maintenance remain open questions. The Creoles of Sierra Leone have been more successful than the early Lagos elite in retaining control of the civil service and the professions. The reasons for this lie in the nature and rapidity of Nigerian economic development and in the size and complexity of the Nigerian state, rather than in differences in the organization of the two elites.[85]

Customary and outside unions between elite men and non-elite women played a small part in opening opportunities to new social groups in Lagos. Other factors proved much more important. The population of the city grew steadily into the middle of the twentieth century. Lagos became the capital and major port of the vast new colony of Nigeria, united in 1914. These developments created new opportunities in commerce and in the professions and colonial service. Education and elite occupations were open and relatively meritocratic. Descendants of the early elite enjoyed advantages that eased educational and occupational success, but they could not monopolize opportunities. Rather, they had to compete for them with members of other social groups determined to get ahead in colonial society. Some talented and industrious children of the elite excelled in school and on the job and retained places among the elite. The rest achieved less than their parents and saw newcomers usurp the status to which they had been born.

6

Economy, society and marriage

Abundant evidence from contemporary sub-Saharan Africa points to radical changes in marriage and in the relationship between the sexes. Marriage has become more unstable than it was in the past. Men and women have seized new opportunities to alter conjugal relationships and roles. Increasing numbers of men and women now avoid permanent conjugal unions and move in and out of a wide range of fluid and flexible domestic and sexual relationships. Many women are remaining single for a greater proportion of their lives, out of choice or necessity. These women do not forgo children and relationships with men, but they choose to have them outside marriage. Similar findings hold for elites and common people and for cities, towns and rural areas, although naturally domestic experience varies with age and social location and with culture and national, regional and local economic and political experience.[1]

A related conclusion emerges from studies of women and marriage. Many African women have come to view relationships with men instrumentally. Women use domestic and sexual relationships as a means of obtaining resources and access to opportunities and of furthering individual social and economic ambitions. If a particular relationship fails to fulfill a woman's goals, she may leave it and seek another more rewarding union.[2] This reality has given rise to an image of African women as aggressive, calculating and manipulative. This image appears in novels, social science literature and media reports written primarily by men, and it has found currency among African males.[3]

The reasons for these changes remain unclear. Some studies indicate that immigration, urbanization and new economic opportunities in trade and wage labor have given men and women greater freedom to assert independence of kin and spouses and to escape or redefine old, restrictive domestic relationships.[4] However, data also demonstrate that in many places deteriorating economic conditions, especially for women, have forced persons to contrive new kinds of domestic and sexual unions and to bargain with spouses or lovers over the division of scarce resources and heavy responsibilities.[5] As yet we have a very incomplete understanding of the impact on domestic life of colonial and post-colonial economic, social and political changes. This chapter analyzes changes in marriage and in the relationship between the sexes in early colonial Lagos and probes the factors

Economy, society and marriage

that contributed to their making. In so doing, it illuminates the link between changes in marriage and the wider economy and society in a particular historical setting. The analysis deepens our understanding of trends in contemporary Africa by uncovering their origins in the past.

Nineteenth-century Lagos underwent a profound social transformation. In mid-century trade in agricultural produce and manufactured goods replaced trade in slaves and firearms. The town became a bustling port and commercial center and grew very rapidly. Trade in imports and exports rested almost entirely on credit, owing to a shortage of capital throughout the economy. Socially defined credit relations began to give way to credit backed by property. Private ownership of land and houses emerged; a market for real estate developed; and land and houses became a major new form of wealth.

In the early stages of this transition, Great Britain annexed Lagos and built a colonial bureaucracy and legal system to promote the development of legitimate commerce and protect the interests of traders. The colonial government quickly replaced the local Yoruba rulers as the supreme political and legal authority in the colony.

Immediately after the annexation, Christian missionaries and repatriated slaves from Sierra Leone and Brazil introduced Christianity and Western education. Christianity justified colonial rule ideologically and eased adaptation to the new economic and political order. The missionaries regarded monogamy as central to conversion and demanded it of converts. They also encouraged the spread of new conjugal relationships and roles. Western education taught skills, information and values increasingly necessary to get ahead in colonial society.

The growth of legitimate commerce, the rise of the colonial state and the spread of Christianity and Western education produced new economic opportunities in trade and, on a much more limited scale, wage labor and salaried employment. These changes widened the gap within the African population between the rich and the poor and, more important, created new processes of social and economic differentiation. Very quickly, economic, political and social changes in the colony gave rise to a new African elite that was Christian, Western-educated and familiar with British language, institutions and culture. These attributes enabled the group to perform roles necessary to the spread of international trade and successful operation of the colonial state. Elite males worked as import–export merchants, colonial servants and professionals; occupations which brought them influence with Europeans, authority over other Africans and wealth in the form of privately owned capital, real estate and luxury goods. For fewer tangible rewards, elite females toiled in the home and community to spread Christianity and civilization. The elite's wealth supported a distinctive style of life learned at church and school and rooted in British manners and customs. This style of life defined the group and gave content and meaning to elite status. Throughout much of the period, it rested on an ideological belief in the moral and cultural superiority of European civilization and legitimized the elite's influence and authority in the colony. Christian marriage played a critical part in the formation and maintenance of the elite. It lay at the heart of the group's distinctive style of life. Moreover, it created a dense web of relationships among the elite that united the group and benefited its members. Finally, Christian marriage concentrated valuable resources among a small number of elite families and facilitated the transmission of status from parents to children.

The economic, political and social changes in late-nineteenth and early-twentieth-century Lagos clearly affected Yoruba marriage. Among the Yoruba, marriage was a kinship affair. It required a transfer of resources and reallocation of labor that affected relatives as well as the couple directly involved. Moreover, marriage created mutual obligations that influenced the welfare of the kin group as a whole. Husbands and wives assumed rights and duties in relation to spouses, children and affines that shaped the life chances of all concerned. In Yoruba marriage, the interests of individuals and kin and husbands and wives often coincided. However, obligations to relatives and spouses for labor and financial assistance sometimes drained persons' resources from their own activities and conflicted with their individual interests. Women remained members of their own kin groups after marriage. This exacerbated conflicts of interest between husbands and wives, as did polygyny. Jane Guyer has pointed out that in Africa domestic relationships consist of explicit and implicit contracts which actors can manipulate and redefine as they shoulder or avoid domestic responsibilities.[6] This was certainly true among the Yoruba.

The economic, social and political changes in the early colonial period created new opportunities for Yoruba men and women to pursue their individual interests in marriage. The authority of kin over marriage weakened. Relatives could not always control the selection of spouses, the terms and timing of unions or the character of conjugal relationships and roles. Simultaneously, spouses became more independent of one another. Many husbands and wives reshaped or ignored basic domestic responsibilities to each other, affines and (in the case of husbands) children. In addition, men and women enjoyed new freedom to move in and out of unions and to manipulate or redefine their status. Contemporary observers commented on the increase in Yoruba divorce during the early colonial period. In 1912 Henry Carr wrote, 'Native marriage is now the loosest tie imaginable.'[7]

By the mid nineteenth century immigrants dominated the population of Lagos, as they have ever since. Many immigrants maintained contacts with relatives back home, although prior to the development of motor transport these were more difficult to sustain than they have since become.[8] Most strangers to the colony established relationships with patrons or earlier immigrants from their home towns, and such persons assumed many of the responsibilities of kin.[9] Even so, many newcomers lived beyond the easy reach of relatives or patrons, and those who wished to could exercise great independence in domestic affairs. Geographical mobility enabled men and women to escape the control of kin by fleeing to different towns during domestic crises.[10]

Economic change also gave men and women greater autonomy in domestic life. Legitimate commerce, which persons could begin on credit or with very limited capital, created opportunities for economic success independent of relatives and the resources they controlled. So did wage labor. Money made from these activities freed men from dependence on kin for bridewealth and other assistance. The 'Report on the Yoruba' concluded that the 'family system [was] breaking down' under the pressure of economic change;[11] and underlined the impact of wage labor: 'In consequence of the rapid opening up of the country . . . [y]oung people easily find employment; they earn considerable wages and emancipate themselves from the control of the family.'[12] Legitimate commerce and wage labor required little if any sustained cooperation beween spouses. Husbands and wives usually pursued these occupations quite independently of one another. This reduced spouses' economic interdependence and increased their autonomy.[13]

Yet marriage and extra-marital sexual liaisons remained important mechanisms for gaining access to resources. Through these relationships men and women obtained capital, credit, land, labor, personal contacts and other forms of assistance. Moreover, obligations to spouses, children and affines still affected how and when persons could use their resources. The continued economic importance of domestic relationships contributed to the changes in Yoruba marriage. At a time of rapid economic change, men and women had to adapt domestic relationships to individual needs if they were to take advantage of new opportunities.[14] This sometimes meant forging unions with particular partners for instrumental reasons; and it sometimes meant avoiding or redefining old, restrictive domestic responsibilities.

Colonialism created new structures of political and legal authority in Lagos, which also affected Yoruba marriage. Power now rested with the colonial government. The state vowed to uphold local laws and customs unless they violated 'justice, equity, and good conscience' or colonial statute.[15] Colonial statutes themselves gradually undermined the authority of kin over marriage and altered the legal rights of husbands and wives. However, the government also established new courts to settle disputes and enforce local and colonial law. These courts gave men and women new authorities to whom they could turn in domestic conflicts with kin or spouses. Colonial magistrates and judges often handed down decisions at odds with Yoruba norms, in the interest of justice and good conscience or out of ignorance of local law.[16] 'Report on the Yoruba' concluded that the growth of the colonial legal system had suppressed 'paternal power'.[17] An article in a local newspaper lamented that it had undermined 'the safeguards provided by native law'.[18]

Marrying well

Men and women quickly took advantage of the colonial legal system to assert new independence in marriage. Men formed liaisons with betrothed and married women; women terminated betrothals and marriages that they did not like. A colonial official described the changes he observed. '[D]isturbing elements are at work where European ways meet African ways . . . [G]irls find that they can with some degree of safety be guided by their inclinations: summary punishment for seduction and adultery is becoming difficult or impossible, and these practices are consequently on the increase.'[19] Governor William MacGregor commented on these developments:

> There is no doubt . . . that the chief cause of these seductions is the native custom of early engagements without the possibility of the girl's consent. The evil of this custom was not so apparent formerly when a check was kept by the severe punishment it was then possible for the Kings . . . to inflict, but since the country has been taken over the greater part of the King's authority has gone . . . young men . . . set all moral and customary law at defiance and . . . women too have become less dependent upon their husbands.[20]

Fadipe described similar changes in the interior. He emphasized the role of economic as well as legal factors in their making.

> Rapid changes in customs and practices have been steadily going on since the establishment of British rule over the whole country . . . The opening . . . of the interior to trade . . . by the building of a railway . . . accelerated these changes. The railway construction camps and later on, the railway stations . . . attracted women and girls, chiefly for trade. Their contacts with clerks and artisans born or trained in Lagos led to some, who were already married, leaving their husbands to become the mistresses of the men from Lagos. Beautiful girls who had already been betrothed, almost invariably without their consent, could defy both their parents and public opinion and become attached to . . . clerks or artisans as mistresses. Women who wanted to renounce their husbands simply went up the hill to the office or court of the Resident Commissioner to sue for divorce. The husband filed his claim for the total amount he spent in payment of brideprice . . . and when the amount was paid, the wife received her freedom.[21]

Lagos men felt very bitter about the new autonomy that colonial legal changes gave women. In a letter to the *Lagos Standard* one man complained, 'It costs a woman nothing to exchange her husband for another man; there is no law made to protect the husband from losing his wife, so long as the wife can say to the law, "I don't want him again."' The man continued, 'It is our present law that has given our women so much freedom that they would not like to make themselves subordinate to their husbands.' He concluded, 'We live under a law that gives women too much freedom.'[22]

New values brought by Europeans legitimized changes in marriage. 'Report on the Yoruba' observed, 'The family system is breaking down, owing to the gradual destruction of native social and domestic control by infiltrations of the idea of personal independence and freedom.' The report argued, '[T]he spread of enlightenment . . . has resulted in a greatly increased sense of individuality and personality.'²³ Men and women sometimes turned to Christianity for moral and institutional support in marital conflicts with kin or spouses. Memoirs and diaries reveal that converts often sought refuge at missionary stations during domestic crises.²⁴ Christian faith helped men and women justify domestic behavior at odds with customary norms.

Old ways did not collapse under the pressure of economic, political and social change. Much survived in domestic life, even to the present.²⁵ Yoruba marriage remained a union of kin groups, and relatives continued to exercise authority over it. Yoruba conjugal ideals retained great moral force, and many couples adhered to them by choice. After the 1890s, moreover, a cultural nationalist movement emerged among educated Africans. This movement aroused new appreciation of Yoruba marriage and deep-felt concern that contact with Europe had wrought widespread moral, social and physical decay. Among some men and women, cultural nationalism awakened a desire for conservative reform in domestic life. While visiting Lagos, Liberian Edward W. Blyden implored his friends, 'We must go back above all to the marriage customs of our fathers. This is . . . a *sine qua non*. We must abandon the promiscuous sexual relations and the polyandry introduced with European civilization which are disgracing and destroying the life of the people and go back to the chaste, clean, sanitary marriage customs of our fathers.'²⁶ Lagosians who shared Blyden's beliefs sought to stem the tide of change in marriage by upholding precolonial norms and values. Despite much continuity, however, the growth of legitimate commerce, the rise of the colonial state and the spread of Christianity and Western education deeply affected Yoruba marriage.

Christian marriage also changed after its introduction into West Africa. The origins of these changes lay in the problems that monogamy and Victorian conjugal relationships and roles created for early educated Africans, such as the Lagos elite. The domestic experiences of the Lagos elite help explain the behavior of contemporary educated West Africans.

Christian teaching about marriage conflicted sharply with Yoruba marital norms. In spite of this fact, some of the elite conformed to Christian precepts. Indeed, as Peter C. Lloyd has shown, a few educated Nigerians upheld Victorian ideals of marriage and family life into the middle of the twentieth century, long after they had changed in Britain.²⁷ About two-fifths of the elite males in this study succeeded in making marriage a life-long union of one man and one woman. Some couples achieved a close companionate relationship and new sexual division of labor. Colonial servant J. A. O. Payne wrote to his Christian wife's brother shortly after she died, 'My jewel is gone – she is no more – the Flower of my house is asleep in Jesus.'²⁸ Payne's lament captures the grief he felt at the loss of a treasured helpmate and friend. Merchant J. P. L. Davies wrote regularly to his wife Sarah Forbes Bonetta Davies when she visited England in the 1870s. His letters reveal the love and intimacy between the couple. In December 1875

Davies confided in Sarah, 'I value my life especially when I have you and the children to look after.'[29] Davies's letters also show that he wanted to provide for his wife and children in the manner of a good Victorian father. Even on the verge of bankruptcy, he urged his wife not to scrimp, but to see that she and their children had everything they needed. He wrote, 'You should not hesitate to carry out my orders with regard to *money* as it is my desire to keep you well supplied.'[30] On another occasion he scolded, 'I take notice of your finances from time to time. I must say you are too careful.'[31] Couples such as J. A. O. and Martha Payne and J. P. L. and Sarah Davies realized Christian conjugal ideals. They founded in Nigeria a new kind of marriage based on monogamy, a close companionate relationship and a new sexual division of labor.

Christian marriage was not well suited to local social and economic conditions. From the beginning a few elite males rejected the new form of marriage. Like many less-educated converts, these men made no effort to conform to foreign conjugal ideals. But many, perhaps most, elite men and women could neither reject Christian marriage nor live by its rules. These persons experienced deep-seated tension between Christian and Yoruba marital norms. Elite males saw advantages to polygyny and Yoruba conjugal relationships and roles. Elite females embraced Christian ideology more enthusiastically than did elite males; but the new sexual division of labor left women dependent on their husbands. When husbands failed to fulfill their conjugal responsibilities, Christian wives suffered disappointment and hardship. In time, some elite women began to want greater economic autonomy, which required working outside the home. The tension that elite men and women felt between Yoruba and Christian conjugal ideals made marriage a burning issue fraught with moral and social difficulties. It created crises in the lives of individuals and brought marriage to the forefront of group consciousness. The tension in marriage may have eased or changed focus after the mid-1890s. The rise of cultural nationalism and the African churches enabled some elite men to resolve their fears about the religious and cultural inferiority of Yoruba marriage. But the tension itself did not disappear.

Elite men and women responded differently to Christian marriage, and this generated conflict between husbands and wives. Couples fought bitterly over monogamy, domestic relationships and roles, and legal rights and duties. Elite men pushed for flexibility in their domestic lives so that they could cope with the conflicting pressures they felt. Elite women pressed men to live up to their responsibilities as Christian husbands.[32] The on-going conflict between Christian husbands and wives created much domestic unhappiness and exacerbated the marriage dilemma. In 1895 the *Lagos Standard* referred to the 'disastrous effect of European marriage on our home and social life'.[33] In 1901 the *Lagos Weekly Record* charged, '[Christian marriage] offers a minimum of domestic happiness if any at all.'[34] In 1907 a clergyman in an African church said, '[Christian marriage] has ruined the homes of many a convert.'[35]

Among the educated elite marriage and status were intimately linked. The importance of marriage to status made instrumental considerations critically important in domestic decision-making. Elite men and women had to make careful domestic calculations and pay close attention to their interests in marriage if they were to maximize their life chances. This was particularly true of women. Elite women had been shut out of most of the new opportunities created during the early colonial period. Moreover, they had embraced an ideology which put them on a pedestal and undermined their autonomy. All but a tiny number of the most wealthy women depended on their husbands for their livelihood and status. Elite men's and women's beliefs and needs and interests changed during their lives and with changes in local economic, political and social conditions. But no matter what persons' values or circumstances, they could rarely separate decisions about marriage from considerations of its wider implications. Elite men and women wed to advance certain life goals, and they expected marriage to further these ends.

The importance of instrumental considerations in Christian marriage raised the stakes in these unions and heightened the conflict between husbands and wives. Spouses jockeyed to get what they needed and wanted in Christian marriage. As they did so, elite men and women grew to suspect and mistrust one another. Many elite men came to view elite women as manipulative gold-diggers, greedy and deceitful.[36] Elite women, on the other hand, began to see elite men as selfish and untrustworthy. These women came to believe that they could not rely on their husbands and would have to take care of themselves.[37] The negative attitudes which elite men and women developed toward one another compounded the problems in Christian marriage. Once husbands and wives expected the worst of one another, it became all the more likely that the worst would occur. By the end of the nineteenth century friends and foes of Christian marriage regarded it as an institution in crisis.

The abundant problems in Christian marriage made these unions highly unstable. Few couples who wed in church took their grievances to the colonial courts and sued for divorce.[38] Many Christian marriages ended without legal sanction when couples separated and ceased to fulfill conjugal obligations. One man ended his Christian marriage by announcing, 'I do not feel I can live with her as her husband' and then leaving his wife.[39] A 1901 article in the local press questioned how many couples who had made Christian marriages continued to live together as man and wife.[40]

By 1915 the serious difficulties in Christian unions had produced changes in that form of marriage. Elite men and women began reshaping conjugal relationships and roles. Elite women started to work outside the home in larger numbers to regain their economic autonomy and better provide for themselves and their children. Many such women saw building or buying a house of their own as the ultimate goal. Houses gave women a place to go should they need or want to leave their husbands. In the meantime, real estate generated rent.[41] An increasing number of elite husbands and wives kept financial and other affairs secret and minimized joint activities.[42] Effectively, such men and women were retreating from marriage and distancing themselves from their spouses. They had in effect abandoned the idea of joint interest in marriage and seemed to believe that the less spouses knew about each other's resources and commitments, the less they would have to fight over and the better off they would be. Ironically, the emphasis in Christian marriage on a close companionate relationship and a novel sexual division of labor produced antagonisms that drove spouses apart and cast them back upon the Yoruba tradition of separate conjugal relationships and roles. Ultimately, the problems in Christian marriage gave rise to a new kind of union among educated men and women, one characterized by distant conjugal relations, separate conjugal roles and carefully circumscribed and clearly defined areas of domestic interaction.[43] By the early twentieth century, elite husbands and wives sometimes chose to live in separate residences, physically demonstrating the changes in Christian marriage.

The marriage of a prominent elite couple, the son and younger sister of members of the turn-of-the-century elite, typified this new kind of union. The man and woman married in church, set up house together, and had several children. Initially the couple discussed financial affairs and domestic matters and tried to reach mutually acceptable decisions. But soon the man and woman fell to quarreling over fundamental issues. Gradually they began to handle more and more of their affairs separately and privately. Matters came to a head when the husband announced he wanted to bring an outside wife into the home. This the Christian wife refused to tolerate. Soon the man moved out and set up house with the other woman. After the separation the Christian husband and wife continued to regard themselves as married; indeed, their marriage long survived the outside union. They lived quite independently day by day and never again shared a residence, but they cooperated in matters which concerned their children and attended public occasions as husband and wife. The woman hosted a lavish party for her husband's retirement and presided over the head table. She played a leading role in his funeral. When asked why she and her husband wanted so much autonomy the woman replied, 'We found it better not to meddle in each other's lives.' The woman enjoyed considerable wealth and influence in her own right, and this made the new domestic arrangement much easier for her than it would otherwise have been.

Studies of marriage among contemporary West African educated elites show that tensions between old and new marital norms persist to this day. As in nineteenth-century Lagos, the tensions are less acute among second- and third-generation educated Africans than among first-generation educated

Africans.[44] Studies of contemporary elites emphasize the problems that changing marital norms have created between couples and their kin, as well as between husbands and wives. They show that educated husbands and wives fight with their relatives over the allocation of resources and the structure of power and authority within the family. Struggles between couples and kin are particularly acute among the Akan senior civil servants studied by Christine Oppong. The Akan practice matrilineal descent. Men are responsible first as brothers and uncles to their matrikin and second as husbands and fathers to their conjugal families. The conflicting expectations of these groups create tension between matrilinies and their male members. This tension has risen sharply as educated Akan have begun to invest in their wives and children, because this new pattern of expenditure transfers resources out of the lineage and fundamentally threatens its interests.[45] Problems between couples and kin also exist among patrilineal elites, but they are less severe than among the matrilineal Akan.[46]

Conflicts with relatives provoke serious disagreements between spouses, and aggravate the tensions between them.[47] Couples cope with these difficulties in different ways. They may draw closer together and carefully manage relationships with relatives to minimize the demands of kin, resorting to what Christine Oppong calls 'conjugal solidarity'. She writes, 'In this case neither spouse is intensely involved in relationships with kin. They are therefore not subject to expectations, nor involved in transactions, at variance with the expectations of their spouses.'[48] Alternatively, husbands and wives may distance themselves from one another and keep their affairs private in hopes of eliminating marital discord. Barbara E. Harrell-Bond observes, 'Economic obligations to relatives are a source of serious conflicts of interest between husband and wife and so . . . the spouses' finances are kept strictly secret.'[49] She quotes an informant who said, 'It is better to keep finances separate because if you don't it becomes almost like competition in marriage.'[50] Kenneth Little and Anne Price rightly note that financial independence affects other aspects of the conjugal relationship: 'The result of this situation is that familial activities tend to be organized on the basis of the husband's and the wife's respective social networks. Some of these activities complement each other, but in the main man and wife have a considerable number of separate interests.'[51]

Research on educated women in Accra and other African towns demonstrates that some have experienced sufficient emotional and financial disappointment in marriage to prefer to remain single. These women believe they can do better on their own than with husbands, although they continue to want children and to have sexual relationships with men.[52] The data on early colonial Lagos suggest two things about the experiences of contemporary educated elites. First, modern men and women who respond to domestic problems by seeking greater autonomy are following a much older pattern. Second, educated couples who marry under the ordinance may well anticipate domestic conflict and eventual autonomy because of what they have observed in their parents' and grandparents' generations. Anticipation undoubtedly increases the likelihood that marital problems will occur.

Little evidence from late-nineteenth and early-twentieth-century Lagos points to serious and repeated conflicts over marriage between elite couples and their kin. The tensions in marriage among the Lagos elite arose primarily from the difficulties that couples themselves experienced over changing marital norms. Cognatic descent explains why the early Lagos elite differed in this respect from contemporary West African elites.

Most members of the Lagos elite were repatriated slaves or their descendants. Unlike modern elites in Lagos and most other West African towns, these men and women rarely belonged to large, corporate patrilineal or matrilineal descent groups. The early Lagos elite traced descent cognatically, through both the male and female lines. Cognatic descent minimized conflicts of interest between couples and their kin. When elite men and women invested in children, it sometimes diverted resources from other relatives, but ultimately both sides of the family would benefit. Equally important, the Lagos elite had to construct its cognatic kinship relations by fulfilling mutual obligations. Kinship did not rest on a clearly articulated ideology or set of legally defined norms. This gave elite men and women great latitude to shape their kin groups to their own ends. It allowed them to avoid close ties with relatives who made troublesome demands or did not share their values. Among the Lagos elite, relatives' claims may have carried less moral weight than among patrilineal or matrilineal elites, because kinship rested on reciprocal obligation rather than on law or ideology. Unlike elites in most contemporary West African towns, the early Lagos elite did not have to contend with large, diverse and tightly organized groups of kin who could make demands backed by the weight of custom and then sustain social pressure until the demands were met.

Elite women in early colonial Lagos could not avoid marriage. To do so became a real option only when women had made sufficient gains in education, trade and modern occupations to dispense with husbands. However, the domestic experiences of elite women in the early colonial period certainly motivated subsequent generations of educated women to reclaim their economic independence and assert new autonomy in private and public life. Modern elite women who reject or redefine marriage are responding to the disappointment and vulnerability of their educated forebears as well as to contemporary realities.

The continued appeal of polygyny and Yoruba conjugal relationships and roles to elite men gave rise to a new kind of domestic arrangement; one that set a precedent for the future and has subsequently become very common in West African towns.[53] Almost half of the two hundred elite men in this study married one woman in church and also entered one or more outside unions. In some cases these outside unions began with customary rituals and had the status of Yoruba marriages. In others they began informally and later acquired formal status. Still other outside unions remained extra-marital liaisons. Sometimes the status of outside unions was left deliberately ambiguous so that it could be manipulated and redefined. Contemporaries claimed that extra-marital liaisons became more prevalent among the elite after the turn of the century. At that time men of such different outlook as Jacob Kehinde Coker and Henry Carr decried the painfully low standard of sexual morality among educated Africans.[54]

Christian and outside wives came from different social and economic backgrounds and had different conjugal expectations. They and their offspring enjoyed different social status and legal rights. Occasionally Christian and outside wives and their children lived in the same household and related as members of a polygynous family. Merchant C. A. Oni dwelled with his Christian wife, two outside wives and at least ten children in the large, fine two-story house that still stands at the center of Garber Square. Oni's wives pursued independent economic activities and maintained and cared for their own offspring, but the women sometimes helped one another with domestic chores.[55] More commonly Christian and outside wives lived in separate residences and saw each other rarely, if ever. This was certainly the case when the outside unions remained extra-marital liaisons. Elite men hoped that by maintaining distance between the women they could minimize strife and keep up the appearance of monogamy.[56] Most elite men lived with one of their wives, usually the Christian wife if that union survived. However, some such men preferred to reside with one or more of their outside wives. Colonial servant Hezekiah Africanus Caulcrick provided in his will for several customary wives who lived with him at the time of his death. He then stipulated that his Christian wife 'though now away from my premises under mutual separation should share in such maintenance and support during her widowhood or lifetime'.[57] A few elite males thought it best to live with none of their wives. These men invited sisters or other female relatives to dwell in their households and look after their domestic affairs.[58]

Christian and outside wives sometimes maintained good relations. Burrel Carter Vaughan's several wives and children did not live together, but they gathered for a family dinner most Sundays after church.[59] When amicable relations existed among the women, children sometimes linked the households of their mother and father by moving regularly between them. Francis Olatunde Sogunro, son of colonial servant Edward Sogunro, lived with his mother, an outside wife, a short distance from where his father dwelled with the Christian wife. Each day after school, the boy visited his father, sometimes taking food that his mother had prepared. Later in the evening Francis returned home, occasionally accompanied by his father.[60] Typically relations among different wives and children were distant, if cordial. Informants commonly said of their half-siblings, 'We knew one another and might meet at weddings, funerals or other family gatherings, but we had little to do with one another.'[61] Too often relations between Christian wives and children and outside wives and children were openly hostile and competitive. In such cases men discreetly played the roles of lover, husband and father with autonomous groups of women and children.[62]

Elite men liked outside unions because they allowed them to enjoy the benefits of Christian and Yoruba marriage and to adapt domestic circumstances to changing personal needs. Through these unions men could deal with, if not reconcile, the conflicting domestic pressures that they felt. Non-elite women liked outside unions because such relationships gave them access to elite men and the resources at their disposal. But outside unions created their own problems. Amicable relations among the different women and children easily deteriorated into rivalry and animosity. Men who maintained Christian and outside unions usually had to devote considerable time and attention to juggling domestic responsibilities and managing complex and volatile family relationships. Moreover, helping to support multiple households taxed men's financial resources and diverted funds from other uses.[63] Elite males became more open about their outside unions after the mid-1890s, but some men still performed social gymnastics to keep these relationships from Europeans, educated Africans and their Christian wives and children. The Reverend James George Campbell described how men tried to deceive religious authorities about outside unions. 'To avoid church discipline the Mr and Mrs so and so are members of a certain church. Then the other mistresses distribute themselves in the other churches and the civilized Native African lives happily in his hypocritical life thinking . . . that he has deceived others.'[64] As Campbell's remark suggests, elite men who entered Christian and outside unions often led two lives. Publicly they pretended to live with their Christian wives and children in homes dedicated to upholding Victorian conjugal ideals. Privately they maintained relationships with other women and children and worked out much more complicated domestic arrangements. Outside unions placed women and children in a position inferior to that of Christian wives and children and gave them a status that was at best second-class.

In time outside unions themselves affected Yoruba and Christian marriage and the relationship between the sexes. This new domestic arrangement also altered the relationship among Lagos women. As this study has shown, the status of customary unions was sometimes ambiguous and could change as the partners assumed or neglected conjugal and affinal responsibilities. This greatly facilitated outside unions, and outside unions reinforced this characteristic of Yoruba marriage. When men and women chose, they could remain vague or be deliberately misleading about their marital standing. Men could take customary wives and maintain that the women were only mistresses. In effect, they could practice polygyny and pretend that they were not doing so. Mistresses could assert that they were really customary wives, and customary wives that they were in fact only mistresses. Men and women could present one face on one occasion and another on the next.[65] The fact that outside marriage violated the laws of church and state and invited public censure encouraged elite males to leave the status of these unions ill defined. This permitted them to practice polygyny and enjoy the benefits of Christian and customary unions without arousing public indignation or violating the letter of the Marriage Ordinance. As contemporaries pointed out repeatedly, Europeans and many elite men and women found concubinage and prostitution more acceptable than polygyny.[66]

Outside marriage heightened the conflict, suspicion and mistrust between Christian husbands and wives and between elite men and women. It strengthened the trend toward greater autonomy in Christian marriage. Outside wives and children created an additional and very serious cause of misunderstanding between Christian spouses. Outside wives threatened not only the interests of Christian wives but even their very identity. The possibility of husbands' forming such unions strengthened elite women's determination to protect themselves and their children. It led them to anticipate trouble and to watch their husbands' activities vigilantly. Outside marriage gave elite men an excellent reason to keep their financial and personal affairs private and to maintain distance between themselves and their Christian wives.[67]

Not surprisingly, outside unions proved highly unstable. Many lasted only a few years. The instability, ambiguity and fluidity of such unions gave their partners little security and soured the relationship between elite men and non-elite women. Easily and at almost any time, persons could alter the status of outside unions or the division of domestic responsibility within them. This aroused suspicion and mistrust between men and women and predisposed them to protect their interests in domestic and sexual relationships. Elite men and non-elite women often wanted different things from outside unions. Many elite men preferred to leave the status of such unions informal and preserve their ambiguity. Non-elite women often hoped to affirm basic conjugal and affinal responsibilities and formalize their status as customary wives.[68] In these circumstances, cooperation and complementarity of interests between men and women gave way to competition and conflict.

Finally, outside marriage divided women and children and set them at odds with one another. The different status, expectations and legal rights of Christian and outside wives and their offspring heightened the tensions that normally existed in polygynous families. Outside unions made elite women suspicious of their illiterate sisters. The privileged status of Christian wives and children led outside wives and children to resent their inferior position.[69]

Some contemporaries recognized the toll that outside marriage took of domestic life. Critics charged that it rested on hypocrisy, and that this hypocrisy itself had undermined domestic relationships. An article in the *Lagos Weekly Record* in 1897 stated succinctly, '[T]his seeming to be what we are not and seeming not to be what we are, this simulation and dissimulation, is poisoning all the springs of society and undermining all the relations of life.'[70]

The far-reaching economic, social and political changes in early colonial Lagos deeply affected domestic life. They undermined the stability of marriage and altered conjugal relationships and roles, whether Yoruba or Christian. They also gave rise to new kinds of domestic arrangements. By the end of the nineteenth century, contemporaries believed that the coming of Europeans had transformed the way men and women thought about marriage and sexual relationships. Commentators lamented that Yoruba and Christian marriage had lost all sanctity.[71] An article in 1897 complained that 'men of loose habits . . . take to themselves women without care or understanding',[72] while in 1915 a writer worried about men and women who made marriage vows without intending to keep them.[73] Contemporaries asserted that too many persons now viewed relationships with the opposite sex instrumentally and cared only about what they could get out of them. A story of 1910 condemned the 'prostitution of marriage into a money-bidding concern'.[74] Moreover, social critics charged that men and women thought solely about their individual interests in domestic relationships. Literates and illiterates alike felt free to move in and out of unions and to ignore or redefine basic conjugal responsibilities, without regard for the interests of kin or the fundamental inviolability of Yoruba and Christian marriage.[75] When unions ceased to satisfy individuals, they left them in quest of more rewarding relationships. Diagnosing the problem, if not prescribing the cure, a 1912 article called for 'some legal provision which will impart greater validity and binding power to the marriage contract in the case of Christians, Mohammedans and Pagans all, and ensure for marriage more respect and a stricter observance of its obligations'.[76]

Writers, mostly male, saved their most biting criticism for women. Men accused elite women of using their wiles to entrap men into Christian marriage and then of nagging and manipulating their husbands to get money, clothes, jewelry and even land and houses.[77] Men complained that non-elite women aggressively pursued extra-marital sexual relationships for what they could get out of them and as a means to formal, longer-term unions with particular men.[78] Contemporaries charged that chastity and fidelity were rapidly disappearing among non-elite women. They argued that girls engaged in pre-marital sex openly and with impunity and excoriated wives for committing adultery.[79] In early references to the 'femmes libres' who have so preoccupied Western social scientists, observers claimed that concubinage and prostitution had become a way of life among non-elite women. On this subject Fadipe wrote,

> [I]n th[e] good old days, there was no room in society for a class of girls now very familiar in Lagos and the big towns. These girls, without being professional prostitutes, consider themselves in the height of fashion if they enjoy extra-marital association with men, especially men of fashion or means. At the same time they turn their association to good account for themselves by demanding money of their paramours.[80]

Frequent references in newspapers to polyandry indicate that women sometimes maintained more than one sexual relationship at a time.[81] Some women horrified men by choosing to leave domestic and sexual unions informal.[82]

The magnitude of change in sexual behavior is difficult to assess. Fornication and adultery clearly occurred in precolonial Yorubaland, as did concubinage and prostitution. Just as clearly, these practices violated Yoruba norms, and persons who engaged in them sometimes received severe punishment.[83] In late-nineteenth-century Lagos, widespread concern about fornication, adultery, concubinage and prostitution, and popular belief that these forms of deviance had become more common, suggest that they were indeed on the increase.[84] Men certainly experienced new difficulty controlling women's sexuality.

The growth of new economic opportunities, the establishment of new legal authorities and the introduction of new religious institutions created opportunities for individuals in early colonial Lagos to assert independence of kin and spouses in domestic life. Men and women seized these opportunities to escape or redefine domestic relationships that they found restrictive or otherwise undesirable. They sought greater individual freedom and the emotional and material rewards that new domestic arrangements could bring. Lest we judge turn-of-the-century Lagosians too harshly, as they sometimes judged one another, we should remember that changing conditions in Lagos often put great pressure on persons to reshape domestic relationships and roles to their particular needs. Yoruba and Christian marriage had clear economic and social implications. In different ways, these unions defined social identity and status and affected the mobilization and management of valuable resources. Moreover, domestic arrangements were one of the few aspects of their lives over which the many Lagosians who lacked capital, land, education and skills exercised much control. Given the overwhelming economic and social importance of domestic relationships, both men and women had to take them into account when devising strategies for mobility and deciding how to respond to changing opportunities.

This was especially true of women, for reasons that most men failed to grasp. Women faced serious disadvantages in commerce and wage labor, as well as in education and modern occupations. Moreover, in the colony male relatives sometimes tried to deprive women of their rights to land and houses.[85] Many women could obtain access to opportunities and resources only through relationships with men. As we have seen, elite women depended first on their fathers and then on their husbands for food and housing and for the symbolic trappings of elite status. Non-elite women bore much of the burden of supporting themselves and their children. Through husbands and lovers these women could sometimes acquire capital, credit, information, advice and even land and houses that would otherwise have remained beyond their reach.[86] Non-elite women who were ambitious for themselves and their offspring enjoyed few opportunities with as much promise as liaisons and potential long-term unions with elite males. They were compelled to pay close attention to their interests in domestic and sexual relationships and to use whatever means they could to establish and preserve advantageous unions. If a particular union failed to meet a woman's needs, she probably enjoyed few alternatives as attractive as leaving it in pursuit of another.

For this reason, some women turned to adultery as a way out of unsatisfactory marriages. Women had limited options when husbands disappointed them or ceased to fulfill conjugal responsibilities. They could try to enforce their rights. But if this failed they would have to return to live with kin, assuming their relatives would have them back. Alternatively, women could set up housekeeping on their own in rented quarters or the households of patrons and eke out a living as teachers and seamstresses if educated, and petty traders if uneducated. Court records attest to the thousands of women and men in Lagos who shared dismal, crowded rooms with strangers.[87] Women who had not passed childbearing age could seek to improve their domestic circumstances through relationships with other men. This last option often offered wives the best opportunity to maintain or improve their status.

Yoruba marriage carried obligations to husbands, affines and children that drained women's limited resources from their own activities. If women could minimize these obligations, they stood to gain. For this reason, some non-elite women sought to redefine domestic relationships so as to reduce commitments to others. A few women pursued a strategy that has become more common in the present day. They eschewed marriage in favor of informal unions to minimize obligations to husbands and affines and maximize personal freedom.[88]

In the most dire cases, declining opportunity pushed women to prostitution. Henry Carr clearly saw this, showing rare insight for a man of his generation. He wrote,

> [T]he introduction of the agencies of civilization had a tendency to abridge the sphere of women's labours . . . The petty trading . . . and other occupations, by means of which they had been able to provide for themselves in former days, eventually passed into the hands of men who, in addition, had available such new occupations as . . . shop-boy, clerk or schoolteacher. In such a way, a large number of unemployed and unemployable women were thrown upon these communities, and it was not a matter of surprise if they took to undesirable means of getting their livelihood and satisfying their wants. A very difficult social problem was the outcome of this state of things – a social problem resulting from the changes in the economic conditions of native communities.[89]

Women who could support themselves and their children in no other way turned to selling domestic and sexual services.

The changes in Yoruba and Christian marriage were not universal. Some husbands and wives continued to live up to Yoruba ideals; others, to Christian teaching. Moreover, the emphasis in this chapter on the tensions in marriage and the basic conflicts of interest between the sexes should not obscure the fact that many husbands and wives worked out harmonious and complementary relationships. But the history of marriage in early colonial Lagos illustrates the origins of trends in domestic life that dominate contemporary Africa. The story is important for what it reveals about the domestic experiences of men, women and children. It is of additional academic interest because it diverges so fundamentally from the history of marriage and the family in the West. The economic, social and political changes in modern Africa have given individuals greater freedom from kin in domestic life, although kin ties have certainly remained very important. These changes have not given rise simultaneously to companionate marriage and the nuclear family. In Africa marriage and sexual relationships remain an important mechanism for adapting resources to needs, and hence of responding to changing circumstances. Marriage and the family have not become a haven in which persons can find shelter from the demands of the wider world.

Appendix: Educated elite males in Lagos Colony, 1880–1915

Adeniyi-Jones, Curtis Crispin	Doctor	1876–1957
Adeshigbin, Akintunde	Publisher	1880–1952
Adeshigbin, Moses Dada	Merchant	1865–1925
Agbebi, George Debanyo	Surveyor/engineer	1886–1926
Agbebi, Mojola (alias David Brown Vincent)	Minister	1860–1917
Ajasa, Kitoyi (alias Edmund Macaulay)	Lawyer	1866–1937
Akerele, David Evaristo	Merchant	1876–1943
Akinṣemoyin, Mobolaji Adeyemi (alias Samuel V. Davies)	Lawyer	1885–1938
Akitoye, Daniel	Colonial servant	–1919
Alakija, Adeyemo (alias Placido Maclean Assumpcao)	Lawyer	1884–1952
Alakija, Olayimika (alias Honorio Assumpcao)	Lawyer	1884–1940
Barnes, Charles Arthur Albert	Colonial servant	
Benjamin, Josuah Begandeji	Surveyor/engineer	–1950s
Benjamin, Josuah Blackall	Publisher	1854–1919
Benka-Coker, Ambrose	Colonial servant	1864–1962
Bennett, Charles Kaye	Colonial servant	
Blaize, Richard Beale	Merchant	1845–1904
Branco, Joaquim Francisco Devode	Merchant	1852–1924
Britto, Benedicto Antonio	Merchant	1845–1910
Bucknor, Joseph Samuel	Merchant	1840–90
Buko, Thomas Bankole	Colonial servant	
Campbell, James George	Minister	1876–1944
Campbell, Robert	Publisher	–1884
Campos, Juan A.	Merchant	–1904
Campos, Ramon	Merchant	–1887
Cardoso, Lourenzo Antonio	Merchant	1885/6–1940
Carew, Thomas Josephus	Colonial servant	1868–1939
Carr, Henry	Colonial servant	1863–1945
Caulcrick, Emmanuel Alpheus	Pharmacist	1864–1911
Caulcrick, Hezekiah Africanus	Colonial servant	1851–1908
Caulcrick, John Akilade	Doctor	1879–1952
Coates, Charles Dandeson	Minister	1856–1903
Coker, Alfonso Thomas	Colonial servant	1866–1927
Coker, Daniel	Minister	–1913
Coker, Jacob Kehinde	Merchant/planter	1866–1945

Coker, Jonathan Koṣimo	Colonial servant	
Coker, Samuel A.	Minister	
Coker, Samuel Alfred Akiwande	Merchant	1865–1917
Coker, Victor Leopold	Colonial servant	1883–1950
Cole, Amos Nathan	Minister	1853–1932
Cole, Charles Randall	Colonial servant	1854–1910
Cole, George Josephus	Colonial servant	c. 1855–1901
Cole, James William	Merchant	1834/40–97
Cole, John Theodore Nelson	Lawyer	1874–1952
Cole, Rotimi Alade (alias Rotimi Alade)	Lawyer	1863–1921
Cole, Thomas Frederick (alias Daddy Alade)	Merchant	1841–90
Cole, William Alexander	Doctor	1871–1919
Cole, William Edwin	Colonial servant	1841–91
Collins, Ebenezer Ephraim (alias Tella Adebiyi)	Minister	1849–
Costa, P. F. da	Merchant	
Crowther, Josiah	Merchant	1839–1910
Crowther, Samuel, Jr	Merchant	
Daniel, John	Colonial servant	
Davies, Charles Bright	Colonial servant	
Davies, James Bright	Publisher	1848–1920
Davies, James Pinson Labulo	Merchant/planter	1827–1906
Davies, Samuel Sogunro	Merchant	1855–1911
Davis, Solomon Samuel	Colonial servant	
Dawodu, Benjamin Charles	Merchant	1858–1900
Dawodu, Thomas Bankunbi	Colonial servant	1872–1920
Dawodu, William Akinola	Merchant	1879–1930
Doherty, Ithiel Kolayo	Lawyer	1883–
Doherty, Josiah Henryson	Merchant	1866–1928
Edun, Agegboyega (alias Jacob H. Samuel)	Minister	1860–1930
Euba, William B.	Headmaster	1857–1933
Euler-Ajayi, M.	Minister	–1913
Faderin, Kubolaji (alias Sutton)	Doctor	1873–1942
Fafunwa, William Kudehinbu	Colonial servant	c. 1867–1937
Faminokum, Joseph Suberu	Headmaster	c. 1867–1920
Foresythe, Charles	Colonial servant/ locally trained lawyer	–1889
Foresythe, Charles Albert	Lawyer	1866–1918
Franklin, A. E.	Minister	
George, Charles Joseph	Merchant	1841–1906
George, Jacob Sylvanus	Colonial servant	1849–1914
George, James	Locally trained lawyer	1849–1945
George, John Olawunmi	Merchant	c. 1850–1915
Gilpin, Benjamin Josiah/Jonah	Colonial servant	1846–
Glover, Henry (alias Oshodi Glover/Ọmọ Glover)	Merchant	1853–1923

Marrying well

Green, Francis Colley	Colonial servant	1846–1908
Haastrup, Ajimoku Kumokun (alias Frederick Haastrup)	Merchant	–1901
Haastrup, Joseph Pathagorus (alias Prince Ademuyiwa)	Merchant	1852–1903
Harding, William Richmond	Colonial servant	–1927
Harrison, Thomas Lloyd	Locally trained lawyer	–1922
Hethersett, Andrew L.	Colonial servant	–1896
Hoare, Benjamin Jonathan Odunmbaku	Doctor	1881–
Hoare, Thomas George	Merchant	1824–89
Howells, Adolphus Williamson	Bishop	1866–
Ibare-Akinsan, Cornelius Josephus Phelps	Colonial servant	1867–1947
Ijaoye, A. O.	Minister	
Jackson, John Payne	Publisher	1847–1915
Joaquim, Henrique	Merchant	–1895
Johnson, Alfred Latunde	Colonial servant	1885–1956
Johnson, Chris Kumolu	Publisher	1875–
Johnson, James	Bishop	1836–1917
Johnson, Josuah Ebinezer	Publisher	–1916
Johnson, Nathaniel	Minister	1843–1921
Johnson, Obadiah	Doctor	1849–1920
Johnson, Simeon P.	Minister	
Jones, David A.	Minister	1849–1918
Jones, Samuel Theophilus	Colonial servant	
Jones, Thomas	Minister	1852–1917
King, Nathaniel Thomas	Doctor	1847–84
King, Samuel Frederick	Colonial servant	
King, Thomas Alfred	Pharmacist/merchant	1851–98
Lawson, William Thomas George	Colonial servant	1841/3–1913
Leigh, Jacob Samuel	Merchant	1837–1907
Leigh, Jacob T.	Colonial servant	–1901
Leigh, Joseph	Colonial servant	–1908
Leigh-Ṣodipe, Ṣodeinde Akisiku (alias Alfred C. Leigh)	Doctor	1865–1901
Libert, Henry	Colonial servant	–1918
Lumpkin, Charles Jenkins	Doctor	1851–1919
Macaulay, Charles Buxton	Minister	1828–95
Macaulay, David	Merchant	1842–1914
Macaulay, Herbert Samuel Heelas	Colonial servant/ surveyor	1864–1946
Macaulay, Magnus Raikes Leverson	Doctor	1879–1940
Macaulay, Owen Emeric	Publisher	–1909
Macaulay, Sigismund Adolphus	Lawyer	1878–
Macaulay, Thomas Benjamin (alias Smart Macaulay)	Merchant	–1899
McEwen, Jack R. P.	Colonial servant	1890–1946
Marke, Peter Adolphus	Publisher	
Martins, F. J.	Minister	c. 1840–1915
Martins, Frederick Germano	Colonial servant	1866–1931
Martins, George Nicholas	Colonial servant	1871–1934
Martins, Pedro Josiah	Colonial servant	1864–1900

Mensah, J. A.	Colonial servant	
Moore, Cornelius Bartholemew	Merchant	1841–1906
Moore, Eric Olawolu	Lawyer	1878–1944
Moore, Olaṣeni	Lawyer	1882–1944
Morgan, William	Minister	–1892
Nicol, Alfred Josiah Lanfear	Colonial servant	1857–1931
Nylander, Africanus Gustavus Reinhold	Colonial servant	1872–1959
Obasa, Orisadipe	Doctor	1863–1940
Ogunbiyi, James	Merchant	1858–1933
Ogunbiyi, Thomas A. J.	Minister	1867–1952
Ologundudu, J. M.	Minister	1859–1926
Oluwole, Isaac	Bishop	1852–1932
Oni, Claudius Ayodele	Merchant	c. 1870–1932
Oshodi, Alfred Ade	Merchant	1869–1931
Oyejola, Ayodeji	Doctor	1874–1960
Payne, John Augustus Otonba	Colonial servant	1839–1906
Pearse, Samuel	Minister	c. 1827–1902
Pearse, Samuel Herbert	Merchant	1865–1955
Phillips, A. E.	Colonial servant	
Pike, Charles	Colonial servant	1849–
Porter, Cornelius Josephus	Colonial servant	1858–1903
Pratt, Adolphus	Colonial servant	c. 1850–1921
Randle, John	Doctor	1855–1928
Reffell, Joseph Nicholas	Colonial servant	
Reffell, Samuel Metzger	Colonial servant	1868–1931
Robbin, Claudius Adenekan	Colonial servant	1869–1916
Robbin, Henry	Merchant	1835–87
Robbin, John Henry Stanley	Colonial servant	1879–1930
Rocha, Candido da	Merchant	1867–1959
Rocha, João da	Merchant	1821–91
Ṣapara, Oguntola	Doctor	c. 1860–1935
Ṣapara Williams, Christopher Alexander	Lawyer	1855–1915
Ṣaṣegbon, Daniel Taiwo	Colonial servant	–1958
Savage, Josiah Alfred	Merchant	c. 1850–1920
Shaw, Sigismund Daniel Turner	Colonial servant	1876–1928
Shepherd, Nathaniel Thomas Babington	Merchant	1830–1909
Shyngle, Joseph Egerton	Lawyer	1862–1926
Siffre, Walter Paul	Merchant	–1923
Smith, George	Colonial servant	1849–1914
Sogunro, Edward (alias Edward Roper)	Colonial servant	1865–1948
Solomon, John Elijah	Colonial servant	
Souza, Simon Izidro da	Colonial servant	1864–1939
Stone, Moses Ladejo	Minister	c. 1850–1913
Taylor, David Augustus	Merchant	1865/8–1932
Taylor, E. J. Alexander	Lawyer	1876–1947
Taylor, Josephus Samuel, Sr	Colonial servant	c. 1850–1920
Thomas, Akedeko M.	Publisher	
Thomas, Andrew Wilkinson	Merchant	1857–1924

Marrying well.

Thomas, Horatio Wilson	Colonial servant	
Thomas, James Bright	Minister	c. 1830–1904
Thomas, James Jonathan	Merchant	1850–1919
Thomas, Peter John Claudius	Colonial servant/ merchant	1872–1947
Turner, James Moses	Merchant	c. 1830–1909
Vaughan, Burrel Carter	Merchant	1871–1926
Vaughan, James Churchwill	Merchant	1828–1893
Vaughan, James Wilson	Merchant	1866–1923
Wey, Francis Theodore	Colonial servant	1876–1928
White, James	Minister	c. 1810–90
Williams, Christian Eardly	Colonial servant	
Williams, Edwin Oshonko	Merchant	–1899
Williams, Evan Euthymius (alias Aganga Williams)	Minister	1878–1955
Williams, Frederick Ephram	Merchant/planter	c. 1867–1918
Williams, George Alfred	Publisher	1833–1919
Williams, Isaac Benjamin	Merchant	1845–1925
Williams, Jacob Sylvanus	Minister	1848–1933
Williams, James O'Connor	Merchant	1843–1906
Williams, Julius Augustus	Colonial servant	–1914
Williams, Nash Hamilton	Lawyer	–1893
Williams, Phillip Henryson	Merchant	1872–1946
Williams, Zachariah Archibald	Merchant	1851–1912
Willoughby, Abraham Claudius	Colonial servant	–1890
Willoughby, Isaac Humphrey	Colonial servant/ merchant	1832–90
Wilson, Michael Nathan Bright	Lawyer	1874–
Wright, James Emanuel	Minister	–1928
Wright, Rufus Alexander	Merchant/planter	1856–1907
Wright, Thomas Benjamin	Minister	–1892

Notes

INTRODUCTION

1 On the history of West Africa's educated elites see J. F. Ade Ajayi, *Christian Missions in Nigeria, 1841–1891: The Making of a New Elite* (Harlow, Longman, 1965); Jean Herskovits Kopytoff, *A Preface to Modern Nigeria: The 'Sierra Leonians' in Yoruba, 1830–1890* (Madison, University of Wisconsin Press, 1965); E. A. Ayandele, *The Educated Elite in the Nigerian Society* (Ibadan, Ibadan University Press, 1974); Patrick Cole, *Modern and Traditional Elites in the Politics of Lagos, 1884–1938* (Cambridge, Cambridge University Press, 1975); Robert W. July, *The Origins of Modern African Thought* (New York, Praeger, 1967); Philip D. Curtin (ed.), *Africa and the West* (Madison, University of Wisconsin Press, 1972); Christopher Fyfe, *A History of Sierra Leone* (London, Oxford University Press, 1962); Arthur T. Porter, *Creoledom: A Study of the Development of Freetown Society* (London, Oxford University Press, 1963); John Peterson, *Province of Freedom: A History of Sierra Leone, 1787–1870* (London, Faber and Faber, 1969); Leo Spitzer, *The Creoles of Sierra Leone: Responses to Colonialism, 1870–1945* (Madison, University of Wisconsin Press, 1974); Barbara E. Harrell-Bond, Allen M. Howard and David E. Skinner, *Community Leadership and the Transformation of Freetown (1801–1976)* (The Hague, Mouton, 1978); David Kimble, *A Political History of Ghana: The Rise of Gold Coast Nationalism, 1850–1928* (Oxford, Clarendon Press, 1963); Margaret Priestley, *West African Trade and Coast Society: A Family Study* (London, Oxford University Press, 1969); Edward Reynolds, *Trade and Economic Change on the Gold Coast, 1807–1874* (Harlow, Longman, 1974); Adu Boahen, *Ghana: Evolution and Change in the Nineteenth and Twentieth Centuries* (Harlow, Longman, 1974); and G. Wesley Johnson, *The Emergence of Black Politics in Senegal: The Struggle for Power in the Four Communes, 1900–1920* (Stanford, Stanford University Press, 1971).
2 Kopytoff, *Preface to Modern Nigeria*, pp. 252 and 273–6, July, *The Origins of Modern African Thought*, pp. 66, 261, 269, 283–6, 294–5 and 425–6, Peterson, *Province of Freedom*, p. 274, and Spitzer, *The Creoles of Sierra Leone*, pp. 18 and 29–33, refer in passing to the importance of marriage among the early educated Africans, but no study investigates this subject in detail.
3 See for example Keyinde Okoro, *Views of Some Native Christians of West Africa on the Subject of Polygamy* (Lagos, General Printing Press, 1887); 'The Debate on the European Marriage Custom, 2 November 1888' in Mojola Agbebi, *Africa and the Gospel* (Lagos, T. A. King, n.d.), pp. 19–22; Henry Carr, *Diocesan Synod of Western Equatorial Africa, Report of Speeches Delivered in Synod, May 1907 . . .* (Exeter, Townsend and Sons, 1907), and *Diocesan Synod of Western Equatorial Africa, Report of Speeches Delivered in Synod, May 1912 . . .* (Newcastle-upon-Tyne, Mawson, Swan, and Morgan, 1912); Jacob Kehinde Coker, *Polygamy Defended* (Lagos, 1915); and Samuel A. Coker, *The Rights of Africans to Organize and Establish Indigenous Churches Unattached to and Uncontrolled by Foreign Church Organizations* (Lagos, Tika Tore Press, 1917).

For examples of newspaper articles see *LWR*, 1 May 1897, p. 4, c. 3; 27 February 1904,

p. 4, c. 2; 13 March 1909, p. 4, c. 2; and 17 February 1912, p. 4, c. 1; and *LS*, 31 January 1900, p. 5, c. 1; 13 August 1913, p. 4, c. 3; and 1 September 1915, p. 4, c. 2. The Lagos press frequently reprinted articles on marriage from Freetown and Cape Coast newspapers.

4 With the coming of African independence in the 1950s and 60s, educated Africans received much scholarly attention. Most studies treated their subjects as elites, many without explicitly discussing the theoretical implications of 'elite' as an analytical category. Historians documented the origins of these groups at the end of the nineteenth century. Other social scientists discussed their rise to political power in the late colonial period and their role as leaders in new African nations. Early elite studies paid little attention to the processes of economic and political change on the international, regional and local levels that produced educated elites. They often failed to locate these groups in relation to changing structures of economic and political opportunity, and hence to explain the basis of their power and influence. (In addition to the works cited in note 1 see J. E. Goldthorpe, 'An African Elite: A Sample Survey of Fifty two Former Students of Makerere College in East Africa', *British Journal of Sociology*, 6 (1955), pp. 31–47; Symposium on African Elites, *International Social Science Bulletin*, 8 (1956), pp. 413–98; James S. Coleman, *Nigeria: Background to Nationalism* (Berkeley, University of California Press, 1958), pp. 63–166; and Peter C. Lloyd (ed.), *The New Elites of Tropical Africa* (London, Oxford University Press, 1966).)

In the 1970s, educated elites received little attention. Recently a study of the Creoles of contemporary Sierra Leone has analyzed the causal relationship between the political power of an elite and the symbols underlying its culture. This work has been criticized for failing to examine the relationship of the elite to the post-colonial state and to foreign capital and domestic production. Abner Cohen, *The Politics of Elite Culture: Explorations in the Dramaturgy of Power in a Modern African Society* (Berkeley, University of California Press, 1981); and the review of Cohen's book by John Dunn in the *International Journal of African Historical Studies*, 15 (1982), pp. 715–18.

In the last decade, Marxists have applied class analysis to Africa with mixed results. The best historical studies have examined changes in the ownership of the means of production and the organization of labor that have followed the incorporation of agricultural or mining areas into the world economy. (See for example Charles Van Onselen, *Chibaro: African Mine Labour in Southern Rhodesia, 1900–1933* (London, Pluto Press, 1976); Gavin Kitching, *Class and Economic Change in Kenya: The Making of an African Petite-Bourgeoisie* (New Haven, Yale University Press, 1980); and Frederick Cooper, *From Slaves to Squatters: Plantation Labor and Agriculture in Zanzibar and Coastal Kenya, 1890–1925* (New Haven, Yale University Press, 1980).) Such works have significantly advanced our understanding of African social and economic change. Not surprising given Marx's emphasis on production rather than exchange, few Marxists have examined the social transformation of commercial and administrative cities such as Lagos.

5 'Class, Status, Party' in H. H. Gerth and C. Wright Mills (eds.), *From Max Weber: Essays in Sociology* (New York, Oxford University Press, 1958), p. 185.

6 Reinhard Bendix and Seymour Martin Lipset, 'Karl Marx's Theory of Social Classes' in Bendix and Lipset (eds.), *Class, Status, and Power: Social Stratification in Comparative Perspective* (New York, Free Press, 1966), pp. 6–12; T. B. Bottomore, *Classes in Modern Society* (New York, Allen and Unwin, 1966), pp. 9–35; and Edward P. Thompson, *The Making of the English Working Class* (New York, Pantheon Books, 1963), pp. 9–11.

7 'Class, Status, Party', pp. 186–8 and 190–4.

8 S. F. Nadel, 'The Concept of Social Elites', *International Social Science Bulletin*, 8 (1956), pp. 413–24, remains a useful introduction to elites. See also T. B. Bottomore, *Elites and Society* (Harmondsworth, Penguin, 1966).

9 As part of a larger study of the social transformation of nineteenth-century Lagos, I am currently comparing the careers of early Christian and Muslim merchants. I believe this

Notes to pp. 5–8

research will illuminate the role of religion and culture in shaping processes of economic accumulation and strategies about how to use resources.
10 Vilfredo Pareto, *The Mind and Society*, 4 vols. (London, Jonathan Cape, 1935), vol. 3, pp. 1427–30. See also Gaetano Mosca, *The Ruling Class* (New York, McGraw Hill, 1939), p. 474.
11 Karl Mannheim, *Man and Society in an Age of Reconstruction* (London, Kegan Paul and Co., 1940), pp. 199–236.
12 For the classic examples of this method see Floyd Hunter, *Top Leadership, U.S.A.* (Chapel Hill, University of North Carolina Press, 1959), and *Community Power Structure* (Garden City, Anchor Books, 1963).
13 The Appendix lists the men investigated in this study.

Medical Directories and *Law Lists* for Great Britain name African doctors and lawyers who practiced in Lagos Colony. The 'Return of Churches' in the *Blue Books* for Lagos Colony and Southern Nigeria gives the pastors of Lagos churches, while the 'Civil Establishment' lists in the *Blue Books* include African colonial servants by rank. Anthony G. Hopkins, 'An Economic History of Lagos, 1880–1914', unpublished Ph.D. thesis, University of London, 1964, identifies leading African import–export merchants.
14 Several recent works use life histories as a method of studying African social and economic change. See for example Marcia Wright, 'Women in Peril: A Commentary upon the Life Stories of Captives in Nineteenth-Century East-Central Africa', *African Social Research*, 20 (1975), pp. 800–19; Kristin Mann, 'Women's Rights in Law and Practice: Marriage and Dispute Settlement in Colonial Lagos' in Margaret Jean Hay and Marcia Wright (eds.), *African Women and the Law: Historical Perspectives*, Boston University Papers on Africa, vol. 7 (1982), pp. 151–71; Edward A. Alpers, 'The Story of Swema: A Note on Female Vulnerability in Nineteenth Century East Africa' in Claire C. Robertson and Martin A. Klein (eds.), *Women and Slavery in Africa* (Madison, University of Wisconsin Press, 1983), pp. 185–201; and Sara S. Berry, *Fathers Work for their Sons* (Berkeley, University of California Press, forthcoming).

This book departs from these previous studies by analyzing the life histories of an entire social group. European and American historians have long used a similar method which they call collective biography or prosopography. Lawrence Stone, 'Prosopography', *Daedalus*, 100 (1971), pp. 46–79.
15 Cohen, *The Politics of Elite Culture*, pp. xiii–xvii and 9–10.

For historical studies of the role of marriage in the consolidation of class or status see Elinor G. Barber, *The Bourgeoisie in Eighteenth Century France* (Princeton, Princeton University Press, 1955), pp. 99–105; Bernard Bailyn, *The New England Merchants in the Seventeenth Century* (Cambridge, Harvard University Press, 1955), pp. 135–8; Verena Martinez-Alier, *Marriage, Class and Colour in Nineteenth-Century Cuba* (Cambridge, Cambridge University Press, 1974), pp. 99–105; Michael B. Katz, *The People of Hamilton, Canada West: Family and Class in a Nineteenth Century City* (Cambridge, Harvard University Press, 1975), pp. 18–19, 32–3, 40–2, 124–5 and 241–92; and Susan M. Socolow, *The Merchants of Buenos Aires, 1778–1810* (Cambridge, Cambridge University Press, 1978), pp. 34–53.
16 Ayandele, *The Educated Elite in Nigerian Society*, pp. 9–93, and Michael J. C. Echeruo, *Victorian Lagos: Aspects of Nineteenth Century Lagos Life* (London, Macmillan, 1977), pp. 25–50, express different opinions on this subject. Other contributions to the debate include Kopytoff, *Preface to Modern Nigeria*, pp. 272–80; Cole, *Modern and Traditional Elites*, pp. 46 and 48–9; and Fred I. A. Omu, *Press and Politics in Nigeria, 1880–1937* (Atlantic Highlands, Humanities Press, 1978), pp. 100–70.
17 In addition to the works cited in note 1 see the following biographies and studies of professional groups: John D. Hargreaves, *A Life of Sir Samuel Lewis* (London, Oxford University Press, 1958); Hollis Ralph Lynch, *Edward Wilmot Blyden: Pan-Negro Patriot*,

1832–1912 (London, Oxford University Press, 1967); E. A. Ayandele, *Holy Johnson: Pioneer of African Nationalism, 1836–1917* (London, Frank Cass, 1970), and *A Visionary of the African Church: Mojola Agbebi, 1860–1917* (Nairobi, East African Publishing House, 1971); David E. Skinner, *Thomas George Lawson: African Historian and Administrator in Sierra Leone* (Stanford, Hoover Institution Press, 1980); A. Adeloye, *Nigerian Pioneers of Modern Medicine: Selected Writings* (Ibadan, Ibadan University Press, 1975); Omoniyi Adewoye, *The Legal Profession in Nigeria, 1865–1962* (Ikeja, Longman Nigeria, 1977); and Bjorn M. Edsman, *Lawyers in Gold Coast Politics, c. 1900–1945* (Uppsala, University of Uppsala Press, 1979).

18 E. A. Ayandele calls for just this kind of study in *The Educated Elite in Nigerian Society*, pp. 4–5. He argues, 'I am of the opinion that . . . the best way to understand the educated elite is through . . . a collective study of the lives and characteristics of the main leaders . . . For all we have now is a series of uncoordinated biographical insights.'

19 Jane I. Guyer, 'Household and Community in African Studies', paper commissioned by the Social Science Research Council, June 1981, pp. 44–53, draws attention to this important problem.

20 A. R. Radcliffe-Brown, 'Introduction' in Radcliffe-Brown and Daryll Forde (eds.), *African Systems of Kinship and Marriage* (London, Oxford University Press, 1950), p. 2, predicted that we would never have a history of African social institutions, because of the shortage of reliable historical sources. Until recently we have had no history of the African family, because historians have not used the sources available to them and because they have treated kinship and marriage as background to other subjects.

The *Journal of African History*, 24, 2 (1983), devotes a special issue to the history of the family in Africa. Shula Marks and Richard Rathbone comment in the introduction (p. 145), 'the history of the family . . . so lively and important an area of study in Europe and America since the 1960s, [has been] almost totally neglected in Africa'. Karen Tranberg Hansen and Margaret Strobel, 'Family History in Africa' (forthcoming), review recent periodical literature relevant to African family history. Luise White, 'Women and the Changing African Family' in Margaret Jean Hay and Sharon Stricter (eds.), *Women in Africa* (New York, Longman, forthcoming), surveys the subject from the perspective of women.

21 Mary Bird, 'Urbanization, Family and Marriage in Western Nigeria' in *Urbanization and African Social Change*, Proceedings of the Inaugural Seminar Held at the Centre for African Studies, University of Edinburgh, 1963, pp. 66–72; Peter C. Lloyd, 'The Elite' in Lloyd, Akin Mabogunje and Bolanle Awe (eds.), *The City of Ibadan* (Cambridge, Cambridge University Press, 1967), pp. 138–44; Kenneth Little and Anne Price, 'Some Trends in Modern Marriage among West Africans' in Colin Turnbull (ed.), *Africa and Change* (New York, Knopf, 1973), pp. 185–207; Christine Oppong, *Marriage among a Matrilineal Elite: A Family Study of Ghanaian Senior Civil Servants* (Cambridge, Cambridge University Press, 1974), pp. 28–160; and Barbara E. Harrell-Bond, *Modern Marriage in Sierra Leone: A Study of the Professional Group* (The Hague, Mouton, 1975), pp. 67–81 and 157–223.

22 Elizabeth Bott, *Family and Social Network: Roles, Norms, and External Relationships in Ordinary Urban Families* (London, Tavistock Publications, 1955), pp. 216–30; and Oppong, *Marriage among a Matrilineal Elite*, pp. 20–5.

23 Peter T. Omari, 'Changing Attitudes of Students in West African Society towards Marriage and Family Relationships', *British Journal of Sociology*, 2 (1960), pp. 197–210; Little and Price, 'Some Trends in Modern Marriage among West Africans', pp. 190 and 194; Kenneth Little, *African Women in Towns: An Aspect of Africa's Social Revolution* (Cambridge, Cambridge University Press, 1973), pp. 147–8; and Harrell-Bond, *Modern Marriage in Sierra Leone*, pp. 3, 34, 64 and 286–8.

24 Bird, 'Urbanization, Family and Marriage', pp. 59 and 64–72; Lloyd, 'The Elite', pp. 138–

45; Little and Price, 'Some Trends in Modern Marriage among West Africans', pp. 195–200; Little, *African Women in Towns*, pp. 49–60 and 145–78; Oppong, *Marriage among a Matrilineal Elite*, pp. 85–160; and Harrell-Bond, *Modern Marriage in Sierra Leone*, pp. 196–249 and 279–95.

25 See for example Lloyd, 'Introduction' in Lloyd (ed.), *The New Elites of Tropical Africa*, pp. 28–31; John C. Caldwell, *Population Growth and Family Change in Africa: The New Urban Elite in Ghana* (Canberra, Australian National University Press, 1968), pp. 52–72; Harrell-Bond, *Modern Marriage in Sierra Leone*, pp. 196–249 and 279–95; and Oppong, *Marriage among a Matrilineal Elite*, pp. 1–27 and 153–60.

26 Essays in Christine Oppong's stimulating collection *Female and Male in West Africa* (London, Allen and Unwin, 1983) provide a welcome exception. Unfortunately, Oppong's anthology appeared after the completion of this work.

27 For other studies of the impact of colonialism on African women see Mona Etienne and Eleanor Leacock (eds.), *Women and Colonialism: Anthropological Perspectives* (New York, Praeger, 1980); Nancy J. Hafkin and Edna G. Bay (eds.), *Women in Africa: Studies in Social and Economic Change* (Stanford, Stanford University Press, 1976); Hay and Wright, *African Women and the Law*; Edna G. Bay (ed.), *Women and Work in Africa* (Boulder, Colo., Westview Press, 1982); and Hay and Stricter, *Women in Africa*. Margaret Strobel, 'African Women', *Signs*, 8 (1982), pp. 109–31, reviews the literature on African women.

28 See the introductions and articles in Michelle Zimbalist Rosaldo and Louise Lamphere (eds.), *Woman, Culture and Society* (Stanford, Stanford University Press, 1974); and Hafkin and Bay, *Women in Africa*. See also Caroline H. Bledsoe, *Women and Marriage in Kpelle Society* (Stanford, Stanford University Press, 1980), pp. 10–12 and 179–88.

I THE MAKING OF THE EDUCATED AFRICAN ELITE

1 On the early history of Lagos see Alan Burns, *History of Nigeria* (London, Allen and Unwin, 1969), pp. 38–40; Robert S. Smith, *Kingdoms of the Yoruba* (London, Methuen, 1969), pp. 91–2; A. B. Aderibigbe, 'Early History of Lagos to about 1850' in Aderibigbe (ed.), *Lagos: The Development of an African City* (Ikeja, Longman Nigeria, 1975), pp. 1–5 and 9; Robert S. Smith, *The Lagos Consulate, 1851–1861* (Berkeley, University of California Press, 1979), pp. 2–5. John B. Loşi, *History of Lagos* (Lagos, Tika Tore Press, 1914), pp. 1–4, records traditions of origin. A recent article by Robin Law, 'Trade and Politics behind the Slave Coast: The Lagoon Traffic and the Rise of Lagos, 1500–1800', *Journal of African History*, 24 (1983), pp. 321–48, emphasizes the importance of trade in the political development of Lagos.

2 John Adams, *Remarks on the Country Extending from Cape Palmas to the River Congo* (London, Whittaker, 1823), p. 100.

3 Smith, *The Lagos Consulate*, p. 4; T. Olawale Elias, *Nigerian Land Law and Custom* (London, Routledge and Kegan Paul, 1962), pp. 9–15; G. B. A. Coker, *Family Property among the Yorubas* (London, Sweet and Maxwell, 1958), pp. 183–5; and Anthony G. Hopkins, 'Property Rights and Empire Building: Britain's Annexation of Lagos, 1861', *Journal of Economic History*, 40 (1980), p. 784.

4 The following works discuss rights in people as an economic resource in Africa: Claude Meillassoux, 'Essai d'interprétation du phénomène économique dans les sociétés traditionnelles d'autosubsistance', *Cahiers d'Etudes Africaines*, 4 (1960), pp. 38–67; Lloyd A. Fallers, *Inequality: Social Stratification Reconsidered* (Chicago, University of Chicago Press, 1973), p. 74; Anthony G. Hopkins, *An Economic History of West Africa* (Harlow, Longman, 1973), pp. 14–27; Jack Goody, *Production and Reproduction: A Comparative Study of the Domestic Domain* (Cambridge, Cambridge University Press, 1976), pp. 31–40 and 99–114; Caroline H. Bledsoe, *Women and Marriage in Kpelle Society*

(Stanford, Stanford University Press, 1980), pp. 46–80; and Igor Kopytoff and Suzanne Miers, 'African "Slavery" as an Institution of Marginality' in Miers and Kopytoff (eds.), *Slavery in Africa: Historical and Anthropological Perspectives* (Madison, University of Wisconsin Press, 1977), pp. 7–11. For a critical review of this literature see Jane I. Guyer, 'Household and Community in African Studies', paper commissioned by the Social Science Research Council, 1981, pp. 13–21 and 23–35.

5. Lagos Chiefs to Glover, 8 September 1863, C.O. 147/4. Quoted in Hopkins, 'Property Rights and Empire Building', p. 794.
6. Law, 'Trade and Politics Behind the Slave Coast', pp. 327–31; Smith, *Kingdoms of the Yoruba*, pp. 92–3; Aderibigbe, 'Early History of Lagos', pp. 5–8; and Smith, *The Lagos Consulate*, p. 4.
7. H. L. Ward-Price, *Notes of Evidence Regarding the House of Docemo* (Lagos, Government Printer, 1933); Patrick Cole, *Modern and Traditional Elites in the Politics of Lagos, 1884–1938* (Cambridge, Cambridge University Press, 1975), pp. 16–18; Smith, *The Lagos Consulate*, pp. 5–7; Aderibigbe, 'Early History of Lagos', pp. 8–9; and 'Oshodi Chieftaincy Family', pamphlet prepared for the installation of Chief Durojaiye Olajuwon Oshodi as the seventh Chief Oshodi of Lagos, 26 September 1970, pp. 1 and 10.
8. Cole, *Modern and Traditional Elites*, pp. 18–20; and Smith, *The Lagos Consulate*, p. 42. Peter C. Lloyd, 'Conflict Theory and Yoruba Kingdoms' in I. M. Lewis (ed.), *History and Social Anthropology* (London, Tavistock Publications, 1968), pp. 56–7, argues that conflict among titled officials and between titled officials and the king characterized nineteenth-century Yoruba kingdoms. At issue, he maintains, was the degree of power attributed to different offices, not succession. Elias, *Nigerian Land Law*, pp. 7–12, asserts that in the mid nineteenth century conflict over land rights emerged between the Idẹjọ and the Ọba.
9. Hopkins, 'Property Rights and Empire Building', p. 782. On the development of Lagos as a center of the slave trade see Law, 'Trade and Politics behind the Slave Coast', pp. 343–8.
10. Saburi O. Biobaku, 'Madame Tinubu' in *Eminent Nigerians of the Nineteenth Century* (Cambridge, Cambridge University Press, 1960), pp. 34–5; and Cheryl Jeffries Johnson, 'Nigerian Women and British Colonialism: The Yoruba Example with Selected Biographies', unpublished Ph.D. thesis, Northwestern University, 1978, pp. 77–82.
11. Cole, *Modern and Traditional Elites*, p. 19; Aderibigbe, 'Early History of Lagos', pp. 10–16; and Smith, *The Lagos Consulate*, p. 11.
12. E. Adeniyi Oroge, 'The Institution of Slavery in Yorubaland with Particular Reference to the Nineteenth Century', unpublished Ph.D. thesis, Birmingham University, 1971, pp. 171–4. Smith, *The Lagos Consulate*, chronicles this rivalry.
13. Christopher Lloyd, *The Navy and the Slave Trade: The Suppression of the African Slave Trade in the Nineteenth Century* (London, Longman, Green and Co., 1949), pp. 39–183 passim.
14. Colin W. Newbury, *The Western Slave Coast and its Rulers* (Oxford, Clarendon Press, 1961), pp. 42–3; and Hopkins, *An Economic History of West Africa*, p. 128.
15. Smith, *The Lagos Consulate*, p. 2.
16. Ibid. pp. 18–33.
17. For the debate over the causes of British annexation see Newbury, *The Western Slave Coast*, pp. 49–76; J. F. Ade Ajayi, 'The British Occupation of Lagos, 1851–1861: A Critical Review', *Nigeria*, 69 (1961), 96–105; and Smith, *The Lagos Consulate*, pp. 18–33 and 111–27. Hopkins, 'Property Rights and Empire Building', cites other relevant literature and offers a provocative new interpretation of this event.
18. On the administrative history of the colony see Smith, *The Lagos Consulate*, pp. 126–7; Newbury, *The Western Slave Coast*, pp. 79–95; Ian F. Nicolson, *The Administration of Nigeria, 1900–1960* (Oxford, Clarendon Press, 1969), pp. 46–81 and 100–23; and T. N. Tamuno, *The Evolution of the Nigerian State: the Southern Phase, 1898–1914* (Harlow, Longman, 1972), pp. 64–95 and 122–222.

19 T. Olawale Elias, *The Nigerian Legal System* (London, Routledge and Kegan Paul, 1963), pp. 17 and 40–57.
20 'Ordinance No. 4, Lagos, 1876' in Edward Harrison Richards, *Ordinances, Orders and Rules in Force in the Colony of Lagos, 1893* (London, Stevens and Sons, 1894). For discussions of the development of the colonial legal system see Elias, *The Nigerian Legal System*; A. E. W. Park, *The Sources of Nigerian Law* (London, Sweet and Maxwell, 1963); E. A. Keay and S. S. Richardson, *The Native and Customary Courts of Nigeria* (London, Sweet and Maxwell, 1966); and Omoniyi Adewoye, *The Judicial System in Southern Nigeria, 1854–1954* (Atlantic Highlands, Humanities Press, 1977).
21 *Census, Lagos Colony*, 1881.
22 John D. Hargreaves, *Prelude to the Partition of West Africa* (London, Macmillan, 1973), pp. 28–90.
23 'Report of the Select Committee of the House of Commons on British Establishments in West Africa, 26 June 1865' in Colin W. Newbury, *British Policy towards West Africa: Selected Documents, 1786–1874* (Oxford, Clarendon Press, 1965), pp. 529–30.
24 Hargreaves, *Prelude to the Partition*, pp. 31–2; and Anthony G. Hopkins, 'An Economic History of Lagos, 1880–1914', unpublished Ph.D. thesis, University of London, 1964, pp. 126–30 and 155–66. For a discussion of the role of the Treasury in colonial policy-making see John W. Cell, *British Colonial Administration in the Mid-Nineteenth Century: The Policy-Making Process* (New Haven, Yale University Press, 1970), pp. 220–53.
25 Most Europeans in Lagos in the 1880s were males in the prime of life. At that time, Lagos's mean annual death rate for Europeans was 71 per 1,000. In England in 1881, death rates for males aged 25 to 34 and 45 to 54 were 7 per 1,000 and 18 per 1,000, respectively. William N. M. Geary, *Nigeria under British Rule* (London, Methuen, 1927), p. 67; and Thomas McKeown and R. G. Record, 'Reasons for the Decline in Mortality in England and Wales during the Nineteenth Century', *Population Studies*, 16 (1962), p. 100.
26 Anthony G. Hopkins, 'Economic Imperialism in West Africa: Lagos, 1880–1892', *Economic History Review*, 21 (1968), p. 604.
27 J. F. Ade Ajayi and Ralph A. Austen, 'Hopkins on Economic Imperialism in West Africa', *Economic History Review*, 25 (1972), pp. 303–6. Robin Law, *The Oyọ Empire, c. 1600–c. 1836: A West African Imperialism in the Era of the Atlantic Slave Trade* (Oxford, Clarendon Press, 1977), discusses the importance of trade in the rise and fall of the Oyo empire.
28 Sara S. Berry, *Cocoa, Custom and Socio-Economic Change in Rural Western Nigeria* (Oxford, Clarendon Press, 1975), pp. 25–6.
29 Newbury, *The Western Slave Coast*, pp. 54–62; and Hopkins, 'Property Rights and Empire Building', pp. 782–4.
30 Hopkins, 'Property Rights and Empire Building', pp. 785–9.
31 Newbury, *The Western Slave Coast*, pp. 57–60; Hopkins, 'An Economic History of Lagos', pp. 45–9 and 79–82; and Berry, *Cocoa, Custom and Socio-Economic Change*, p. 27.
32 Interviews in Lagos with Sufianu Braimah Affini, July 1974; Abdul Wuhabi Animashaun, February 1974; Işmaila Lawal Apatira, December 1973; Abimbola Ali Balogun, February 1974; Durojaiye Olajuwon Oshodi, January 1974; Daniel Akinola Ogunbiyi, May 1974; Iya Onigari, March 1974; and Percy Savage, January 1974.
33 According to the 1881 *Census, Lagos Colony*, 30 percent of the population traded. Hopkins, 'An Economic History of Lagos', p. 26, argues that half of all Lagosians engaged in some kind of commercial activity.
34 Richard Beale Blaize began trading in the 1860s with £20 capital, and died in 1904 leaving an estate valued at £60,000. Josiah Henryson Doherty commenced trade in 1891 with £47 capital, and died in 1928 leaving an estate worth £58,000. Braimah Igbo and Ali Balogun, illiterate merchants, began life as slaves. Anthony G. Hopkins, 'Richard Beale Blaize, 1854–1904: Merchant Prince of West Africa', *Tarikh*, 1 (1966), pp. 70–8; *LWR*, 24

September 1904, p. 3, c. 2; and Hopkins, *Economic History of West Africa*, p. 240. Will, R. B. Blaize, Wills, vol. 2, pp. 341–6; and Will, J. H. Doherty, Wills, vol. 7, pp. 188–96, Lagos Probate Registry. 'Positions of *Ibigas* in Lagos Chieftaincy', Macaulay Papers, 10/2. Further evidence comes from interviews in Lagos with T. A. Doherty, April 1974; Dr Abiodun Pearse, March 1974; Sulamon Alabi B. I. Forrest, January 1974; Abimbola Ali Balogun, February 1974; Işmaila Lawal Apatira, December 1973; and N. E. S. Adewale, July 1974.

35 Between 1881 and 1885 European firms paid 80 percent of the customs duties, while a few large African firms paid the remaining 20 percent. Hopkins, 'An Economic History of Lagos', p. 69.

36 For references to hostilities encountered by Lagos traders *en route* to interior markets see Moloney to Stanhope, 6 August 1886, C.O. 147/56; Moloney to Knutsford, 19 October 1888, C.O. 146/66; Moloney to Knutsford, 1 October 1889, C.O. 147/72; Carter to Ripon, 4 October 1892 and 29 December 1892, C.O. 147/86; and McCallum to Chamberlain, 29 April 1898, C.O. 147/131.

37 Hopkins, 'An Economic History of Lagos', pp. 49–53.

38 Ibid. p. 58 lists thirty-two leading African merchants in Lagos in the 1880s. Oral information on their life histories reveals that fewer than one-third participated in the slave trade or owned large numbers of slaves.

39 Hopkins, 'Property Rights and Empire Building', pp. 785–94, discusses the significance of land ownership for commercial success.

40 Pauline H. Baker, *Urbanization and Political Change: The Politics of Lagos, 1917-1967* (Berkeley, University of California Press, 1974), p. 33; and Newbury, *The Western Slave Coast*, p. 80.

41 Christopher Fyfe, *A History of Sierra Leone* (London, Oxford University Press, 1962); Jean Herskovits Kopytoff, *A Preface to Modern Nigeria: the 'Sierra Leonians' in Yoruba, 1830–1890* (Madison, University of Wisconsin Press, 1965), pp. 3–60; and T. G. O. Gbadamoşi, *The Growth of Islam among the Yoruba, 1841–1908* (Harlow, Longman, 1978), pp. 27–32.

42 Lees to Beach, 28 February 1879, C.O. 806/130.

43 On the history of the Brazilian repatriates see A. B. Laotan, *The Torch Bearers of the Old Brazilian Community* (Lagos, Ile-Olu Printing Works, 1943), and 'Brazilian Influence on Lagos', *Nigeria*, 69 (1961), pp. 157–65; Pierre Verger, *Flux et reflux de la traite de Nègres entre le Golfe de Bénin et Bahia de Todos os Santos du dix-septième au dix-neuvième siècle* (Paris, Mouton, 1968), pp. 573–630; and Jerry Michael Turner, 'Les Brésiliens – The Impact of Former Brazilian Slaves upon Dahomey', unpublished Ph.D. thesis, Boston University, 1975, pp. 55–85.

44 Campbell to Clarendon, 28 December 1853, F.O. 84/920.

45 Kristin Mann, 'A Social History of the New African Elite in Lagos Colony, 1880–1913', unpublished Ph.D. thesis, Stanford University, 1977, pp. 34–5; Newbury, *The Western Slave Coast*, p. 56; and Gbadamoşi, *The Growth of Islam*, pp. 26–30.

46 Geary, *Nigeria*, pp. 30–2; Kopytoff, *Preface to Modern Nigeria*, pp. 59–60 and 87–8; J. F. Ade Ajayi, *Christian Missions in Nigeria, 1841–1891: The Making of New Elite* (Harlow, Longman, 1965), pp. 51–90; Verger, *Flux et Reflux*, pp. 612–32; Cole, *Modern and Traditional Elites*, pp. 45–50; and Turner, 'Les Brésiliens', pp. 140–54 and 171–8.

47 Interviews in Lagos with Percy Savage, January and July 1974; W. R. Shitta, July 1974; and S. E. da Silva, July 1974.

48 James Bertin Webster, *African Churches among the Yoruba, 1888–1922* (Oxford, Clarendon Press, 1964), Ajayi, *Christian Missions*, and E. A. Ayandele, *The Missionary Impact on Modern Nigeria, 1842–1914: A Political and Social Analysis* (Harlow, Longman, 1966), discuss the spread of Christianity into Yorubaland.

49 Disu Ige, James Ogunbiyi and Taiwo Olowo, prominent illiterate merchants, converted to

Notes to pp. 18–20

Christianity. *LS*, 12 April 1911, p. 6, c. 2; Loṣi, *History of Lagos*, p. 85; and interview with Daniel Akinola Ogunbiyi, Lagos, May 1974.
50 *Blue Book, Lagos Colony*, 1886.
51 'General Educational Statistics', *Blue Book, Lagos Colony*, 1884; and *Blue Book, Southern Nigeria*, 1912. In 1912 one Catholic secondary school and ten Catholic primary schools failed to report their enrollments. The number of students on the books undoubtedly exceeded the number in attendance.
52 Hopkins, 'Property Rights and Empire Building', pp. 777–82 and 786–92.
53 Ibid. pp. 789–93. See also McCallum to Chamberlain, 23 August 1897, C.O. 147/114; McCallum to Chamberlain, 10 August 1897, C.O. 147/116; and McCallum to Chamberlain, 23 September 1897, C.O. 147/118.
54 I am currently analyzing these documents for information about inheritance among the educated elite.
55 Maps showing land ownership in central Lagos illustrate this point. See for example MR 1805, MPG 987, MR 813 and MR 1810 in the map collection at the Public Record Office. Cole, *Modern and Traditional Elites*, p. 22, asserts that in the twentieth century *Idẹjọ* have reasserted their rights to land in Lagos suburbs. For the landmark decision upholding the *Idẹjọ*'s title to land see *Tijani* v. *Secretary, Southern Provinces*, 1921, 2AA, the Privy Council, pp. 295–302.

Hopkins, 'Property Rights and Empire Building', p. 790, rightly notes that land and court records might be used for a study of changing land tenure and land ownership. While records in the Lagos Land Registry are well organized and in good condition, records in the High Court Archives are very disorganized. In 1973–4 and in 1980, I found the Civil and Criminal Court Records for the 1860s through the 1930s strewn on the floor and thickly covered with dust. Many volumes were missing and others had been torn apart. In the summer of 1980, I began cleaning and organizing these documents. In 1983, after the completion of *Marrying Well*, I began a systematic study of the Civil Court Records from the Lagos Supreme Court. At that time I also began tracing individuals through Crown Grants, Conveyances, Mortgages and other legal documents in the Lagos Land Registry.
56 Spencer H. Brown, 'A History of the People of Lagos, 1852–1886', unpublished Ph.D. thesis, Northwestern University, 1964, pp. 101 and 127–9; and Hopkins, 'Property Rights and Empire Building', p. 791. See also McCallum to Chamberlain, 10 August 1897, C.O. 147/116; J. A. O. Payne to Sir John H. Kennany, 5 August 1897, C.O. 147/128; and McCallum to Chamberlain, 26 May 1898, C.O. 147/132.
57 Fyfe, *A History of Sierra Leone*, pp. 142–4, 231 and 376. See also the wills of Joaquim d'Almeida and Domingo José Martins in Verger, *Flux et reflux*, pp. 540–1 and 483–5.
58 Hopkins, 'Property Rights and Empire Building', pp. 786 and 789–94.
59 Moloney to Knutsford, 26 January 1889, C.O. 147/69.
60 Carter to Chamberlain, 18 June 1896, C.O. 147/105.
61 Interviews with T. A. Doherty, Lagos, April 1974; and Dr Abiodun Pearse, Lagos, March 1974. In *Halliday* v. *Apatira*, 1 N.L.R., p. 1, the defendant, an illiterate merchant, testified that he frequently asked literate acquaintances to read trade documents. This case nicely illustrates a disadvantage facing illiterate traders. Apatira paid J. P. L. Davies £725 but failed to obtain a receipt because he did not keep written records. Davies's trustee in bankruptcy later sued Apatira for the amount, and Apatira had difficulty proving he had paid it.
62 These figures include the churches at Iddo, Ebute Metta and Yaba, but not those at Badagry, Palma and Lekkie. *Blue Book, Lagos Colony*, 1881. Ajayi, *Christian Missions*, pp. 206–33, discusses Crowther's episcopacy.
63 *Blue Books, Lagos Colony*, 1863–81.
64 Omoniyi Adewoye, *The Legal Profession in Nigeria, 1865–1962* (Ikeja, Longman Nigeria, 1977), pp. 14–36.

65 T. Olawale Elias, *Law in a Developing Society* (Benin City, Ethiope Publishing Co., 1973), pp. 45–6; and Omoniyi Adewoye, 'Ṣapara Williams: The Lawyer and Public Servant', *Journal of the Historical Society of Nigeria*, 6 (1971), pp. 47–65. A list of lawyers admitted to practice before the Supreme Court can be found in the Supreme Court Archives, the Nigerian Supreme Court, Lagos.

66 Ralph Schram, *A History of the Nigerian Health Services* (Ibadan, Ibadan University Press, 1971), pp. 66 and 413–14.

67 Interviews in Lagos with Mrs C. O. Blaize, January 1974; and E. M. Willoughby, January 1974. See also Hopkins, 'Richard Beale Blaize', pp. 70–9.

68 Interviews in Lagos with Mrs Ayodele Ṣapara-Peragrino, January 1974; Dr Afolabi Alakija, February 1974; Dr Mobolaji Alakija, January 1974; and Mrs Ebun Lucas, February 1974. It is possible to trace colonial servants' careers through the 'List of Officers', *Blue Books, Lagos Colony*.

69 Ajayi, *Christian Missions*, p. 235, correctly sees the 1880s as a period of transition in racial attitudes.

70 See for example Moloney to Stanhope, 27 February 1886, C.O. 147/54; Moloney to Knutsford, 16 June 1888, C.O. 147/64; Moloney to Knutsford, 9 October 1888, C.O. 147/66; Denton to Knutsford, 7 February 1891, C.O. 147/79; and Denton to Ripon, 21 April 1893, C.O. 147/89.

71 Notes dated 11 May 1886, C.S.O. 8/2, vol. 11.

72 Evans to Holland, 12 May 1887, C.O. 147/59.

73 MacGregor to Chamberlain, 15 September 1901, C.O. 147/157.

74 McCallum to Chamberlain, 23 September 1897, C.O. 147/118; McCallum to Chamberlain, 10 August 1897, C.O. 147/116; and Denton to Chamberlain, 4 October 1898, C.O. 147/135.

75 Newbury, *The Western Slave Coast*, pp. 46 and 86–7; and Hopkins, 'An Economic History of Lagos', pp. 49–59, 250 and 299–300.

76 Hopkins, 'An Economic History of Lagos', pp. 88–9, and *Economic History of West Africa*, pp. 148–54; Anthony G. Hopkins, 'The Currency Revolution in South-Western Nigeria in the Late Nineteenth Century', *Journal of the Historical Society of Nigeria*, 3 (1965), pp. 241–8. See also 'Report of the Commission on Trade', Denton to Chamberlain, 25 May 1898, C.O. 147/132; and 'Evidence Presented to the Commission on Trade', Denton to Chamberlain, 4 June 1898, C.O. 147/133.

77 Interviews in Lagos with T. A. Doherty, April 1974; Mrs E. I. Oni, August 1974; Iya Onigari, March 1974; and Akin Adeshigbin, April 1974 and July 1980.

78 Hopkins, 'Economic Imperialism in West Africa', pp. 590–1.

79 See the petition from the Lagos Chamber of Commerce enclosed with Moloney to Knutsford, 10 December 1890, C.O. 147/77; and 'Memorial from Lagos Traders Objecting to the Obstruction of Trade by the Ijebu', Confidential Prints, West Africa (428).

80 *LWR*, 29 August 1891. The local press regularly demanded intervention in the interior wars. *E & LC*, 11 April 1885; 27 February 1886 and 13 March 1886; *LO*, 20 February 1886, 17 March 1886, 3 April 1886, 1 May 1886, 22 May 1886 and 7 August 1886; and *LWR*, 5 December 1891 and 20 February 1892.

81 A. B. Aderibigbe, 'The Ijebu Expedition, 1892: An Episode in the British Penetration of Nigeria Reconsidered' in *Historians in Tropical Africa*, proceedings of the Leverhulme Inter-Collegiate History Conference (Salisbury, Southern Rhodesia, 1962), pp. 267–82; O. O. Ayantuga, 'Ijebu and its Neighbours, 1851–1914', unpublished Ph.D. thesis, University of London, 1965; and Robert S. Smith, 'Nigeria – Ijebu' in Michael Crowder (ed.), *West African Resistance: The Military Response to Colonial Occupation* (London, Hutchinson, 1971), pp. 170–204.

82 'Evidence Presented to the Commission on Trade', Denton to Chamberlain, 4 June 1898, C.O. 147/133.

83 Hopkins, 'An Economic History of Lagos', p. 166.
84 Nicolson, *The Administration of Nigeria*, pp. 1–19; Tamuno, *The Evolution of the Nigerian State*, pp. 48 and 52; Peter Fraser, *Joseph Chamberlain: Radicalism and Empire* (London, Cassell, 1966), pp. xiv-xv; and Robert V. Kubicek, *The Administration of Imperialism: Joseph Chamberlain at the Colonial Office* (Durham, Duke University Press, 1969), pp. 11–12 and 174–6.
85 Geary, *Nigeria*, p. 67; and McKeown and Record, 'Reasons for the Decline in Mortality', p. 100. See also Raymond E. Dumett, 'The Campaign against Malaria and the Expansion of Scientific Medical and Sanitary Services in British West Africa, 1898–1910', *African Historical Studies*, 1 (1968), p. 1.
86 *Census, Lagos Colony*, 1891, and *Census, Southern Nigeria*, 1911; and 'List of Officers', *Blue Book, Lagos Colony*, 1891, and *Blue Book, Southern Nigeria*, 1911.
87 In 1898 Captain G. C. Denton celebrated his tenth anniversary as a colonial servant in Lagos and wrote a memo describing the changes he had witnessed. 'Report on Ten Years of Service in Lagos', Denton to Chamberlain, 11 June 1898, C.O. 147/133.
88 F. D. Lugard, *The Dual Mandate in British Tropical Africa* (Edinburgh, W. Blackwood and Son, 1922), pp. 9–16, vividly expresses this new point of view. See also Nicolson, *The Administration of Nigeria*, pp. 1–81.
89 See for example Moloney to Stanhope, 27 February 1886, C.O. 147/54; Moloney to Knutsford, 10 December 1890, C.O. 147/77; and Carter to Chamberlain, 6 December 1895, C.O. 147/100. Articles in the Lagos press also called for greater British involvement in Yorubaland. *E & LC*, 11 April 1885, 27 February 1886 and 13 March 1886; *L.O.*, 17 March 1886, 22 May 1886 and 1 January 1887; and *LWR*, 15 August 1891, 5 December 1891 and 26 December 1891.
90 Mann, 'A Social History of the New African Elite', pp. 46–7. Popular wisdom attributes worsening race relations to the arrival of European wives in the colony. Insufficient attention has been paid to the simultaneous arrival of working-class white males who resented subordination to better-educated blacks. In 1896, for example, white railroad employees refused to be treated by African doctors. Rohrweger to Chamberlain, 11 November 1896, C.O. 147/107; and McCallum to Chamberlain, 13 July 1897, C.O. 147/115.
91 Ajayi, *Christian Missions*, pp. 250–4 and 260–5; and Webster, *African Churches among the Yoruba*, pp. 8–20. On Fanimokun's dismissal see J. O. Lucas, 'Short Historical Notes' in Souvenir Programme of the Centenary Celebration of the C.M.S. Grammar School, Lagos, 1959; and Coker to Melville-Jones, 11 August 1915, Coker 2/1.
92 Mann, 'A Social History of the New African Elite', pp. 37, 69 and 93–4; Tamuno, *The Evolution of the Nigerian State*, pp. 191–9; Leo Spitzer, *The Creoles of Sierra Leone: Responses to Colonialism, 1870–1945* (Madison, University of Wisconsin Press, 1974), pp. 66–9; *Parliamentary Papers*, LXI, *Report of the Departmental Committee on the West African Medical Staff*, 1909; Rohrweger to Chamberlain, 11 November 1896, C.O. 147/107; and Rowland to Under Secretary of State for the Colonies, 24 July 1897, C.O. 147/128.
93 Anthony G. Hopkins, 'The Lagos Chamber of Commerce, 1888–1903', *Journal of the Historical Society of Nigeria*, 3 (1965), pp. 247–8.
94 E. A. Ayandele, 'The Colonial Church Question in Lagos Politics, 1905–1911', *Odu*, 4 (1968), pp. 53–73.
95 'Report on Lord Onslow's Committee on Malaria', MacGregor to Chamberlain, 8 July 1901, C.O. 147/155; and MacGregor to Chamberlain, 10 March 1902, C.O. 147/160.
96 Mann, 'A Social History of the New African Elite', pp. 46–7; and Ayandele, 'The Colonial Church Question', pp. 60–3.
97 Hopkins, 'An Economic History of Lagos', pp. 377–413, and *Economic History of West Africa*, pp. 203–4; and Anthony G. Hopkins, 'Peter Thomas: un commerçant nigérian à

Notes to pp. 24–9

l'épreuve d'une économie colonial en crise' in Charles André Julien et al. (eds.), *Les africains*, 10 vols. (Paris, Editions J.A., 1977), vol. 9, pp. 309–18.
98 Interview in Lagos with Dr Irene Thomas, July 1974.
99 Denton to Ripon, 8 March 1895, C.O. 147/98.
100 Abner Cohen, *The Politics of Elite Culture: Explorations in the Dramaturgy of Power in a Modern African Society* (Berkeley, University of California Press, 1981), pp. 48–9, discusses the retreat of the Sierra Leonean Creoles from business in the 1920s and 1930s. This process began much earlier in Lagos.
101 T. A. Doherty recalled that his father, Josiah Henryson Doherty, regarded education as 'capital invested in the brain'. Interviews with T. A. Doherty, Lagos, April 1974; Lady Ademola, Lagos, July 1974; Mrs Jack McEwen, Lagos, July 1974 and July 1980; Mrs Kwao Sagoe, Lagos, February 1974; Mrs R. A. Wright, Lagos, March and April 1974; Mrs Layinka, Ibadan, May 1974; and Mrs J. J. Marinho, Lagos, January 1974. Peter C. Lloyd (ed.), *The New Elites of Tropical Africa* (London, Oxford University Press, 1966), p. 28, also notes the emphasis placed on higher education as an investment for the future.
102 Kristin Mann, 'The Dangers of Dependence: Christian Marriage among Elite Women in Lagos Colony, 1880–1915', *Journal of African History*, 24 (1983), pp. 37–57.
103 Interviews in Lagos with Mrs J. T. A. Williams, January 1974; Mrs Ebun Lucas, February 1974; and Mrs Ayo Manuwa, May 1974.
104 Moloney to Knutsford, 9 October 1888, C.O. 147/66; and Moloney to Knutsford, 12 March 1889, C.O. 147/70.
105 According to the 1911 *Census, Southern Nigeria*, only 16.5 percent of Lagos's population was literate. This figure is probably too high, because more illiterates than literates must have remained uncounted.
106 *Medical Directories* and *Law Lists* for Great Britain include information about the education of Lagos's early doctors and lawyers.
107 Fyfe, *A History of Sierra Leone*, p. 498; and Gbadamọṣi, *The Growth of Islam*, pp. 135–7 and 164–71. See also Correspondence Relative to the Appointment of Edward Wilmot Blyden as Agent for Native Affairs in the Colony of Lagos, 1895–7, Africana Collection, University of Ibadan Library.
108 Ajayi, *Christian Missions,* pp. 218 and 270; Gbadamọṣi, *The Growth of Islam*, pp. 137–9; and 'The School Report for 1892', Denton to Ripon, 1 May 1893, C.O. 147/90.
109 *Census, Southern Nigeria,* 1911.
110 Webster, *African Churches*, pp. 42–89, discusses the history of Lagos's African churches.
111 Baker, *Urbanization and Political Change*, pp. 49–73, 116–18 and 148–50, demonstrates that local Yoruba did not displace Saro in public life until the 1940s.
112 Cole, *Modern and Traditional Elites*, pp. 45–8; and E. A. Ayandele, *The Educated Elite in Nigerian Society* (Ibadan, Ibadan University Press, 1974), pp. 9–14.
113 Kopytoff, *Preface to Modern Nigeria*, p. 283; Cole, *Modern and Traditional Elites*, pp. 45–8; Baker, *Urbanization and Political Change*, pp. 286–7.
114 Interviews in Lagos with Ajayi Coker, February 1974 and July 1980; Mrs R. A. Wright, March and April 1974; and Percy Savage, January 1974 and August 1980. Interview in Abeokuta with Abner Coker, June 1974.
115 Mann, 'A Social History of the New Educated Elite', pp. 60–3. Interviews in Lagos with Dr Akinola Maja, May 1974; Mrs Ayodele Ṣapara-Peragrino, January 1974; Miss Ibironke Ṣapara, April 1974; and Mrs Oyejola Turner, January 1974. For discussions of this phenomenon in modern West Africa see Lloyd, *New Elites*, pp. 28–30; Christine Oppong, *Marriage among a Matrilineal Elite: A Family Study of Ghanaian Senior Civil Servants* (Cambridge, Cambridge University Press, 1974), pp. 22, 55 and 90–9; and Barbara E. Harrell-Bond, *Modern Marriage in Sierra Leone: A Study of the Professional Group* (The Hague, Mouton, 1975), pp. 43, 120 and 209–11.

Notes to pp. 29–32

116 As part of my research on the educated elite, I built up profiles of their families. See for example pp. 95–8 above.
117 Interviews in Lagos with Mrs C. O. Blaize, January 1974; and Archdeacon J. O. Lucas, April 1974.
118 Interview with Mrs Oyejola Turner, Lagos, January 1974.
119 *LWR*, 13 May 1905, p. 3, c. 3; and *LS*, 27 December 1905, p. 3, c. 2.
120 Interviews in Lagos with Mrs Kwao Sagoe, February 1974; Lady Ademola, July 1974; Mrs Jack McEwen, July 1974 and July 1980; Dr da Rocha-Afodu, April 1974; and Mrs Afolabi Johnson, March 1974. Most elite women dropped their maiden names and took their husbands' names after Christian marriage. When the elite wished to designate a woman's family of origin they wrote '(née [maiden name])' after the married name. For greater felicity of style, I give women's maiden names in parentheses before their married names when I want to designate family of origin.
121 Letters of Administration granted in the estate of João da Rocha, Wills, vol. 2, p. 193, Lagos Probate Registry; and interview with Dr da Rocha-Afodu, Lagos, April 1974. Letters of Administration granted in the estate of H. T. Doherty, Wills, vol. 4, p. 89, Lagos Probate Registry. Interviews with T. A. Doherty, Lagos, April and May 1974.
122 Will, Richard Beale Blaize, Wills, vol. 2, pp. 341–6; and Will, Hannah Matilda Benjamin, Wills, vol. 4, pp. 200–2, Lagos Probate Registry.
123 Interviews in Lagos with J. A. Akitoye, November 1973; Kunle Akinşemoyin, January 1974; Idowu Ola Fafunwa, July 1974; and J. A. Oshodi, January 1974. Loşi, *History of Lagos*, pp. 80–2. Raised by J. P. L. Davies, Samuel Sogunro Davies may have benefited little from his family's position.
124 MacGregor to Chamberlain, 22 June 1899, C.O. 147/143; and Phillips to Harding, 7 September 1896, Phillips Papers 1/1/4. See also Anthony G. Hopkins, 'The Lagos Strike of 1897: An Exploration in Nigerian Labour History', *Past and Present*, 35 (1968), p. 136; and Brown, 'A History of the People of Lagos', p. 118.
125 Hopkins, 'An Economic History of Lagos', p. 78.
126 Hopkins, 'The Lagos Strike', pp. 144–8, discusses the government's difficulty in attracting unskilled laborers.
127 Deprived of his right to collect tolls, Ọba Dosunmu received £2,000 a year from the British when he died in 1885. The Colonial Office granted Oyekan, his successor, only £200 a year, increasing this amount to £300 in 1894 and £400 in 1898. Moloney to Stanhope, 13 April 1886, C.O. 147/55; Carter to Ripon, 6 March 1894, C.O. 147/94; and Denton to Chamberlain, 23 December 1898, C.O. 147/136. See also Newbury, *The Western Slave Coast*, pp. 60–1.
128 *Blue Books* for Lagos Colony and Southern Nigeria contain information about the salaries of clergy, headmasters and colonial servants.
129 McCallum to Chamberlain, 10 March 1896, C.O. 147/104; McCallum to Chamberlain, 15 August 1896, C.O. 147/106; MacGregor to Chamberlain, 20 September 1899, C.O. 147/144.
130 Egerton to Lyttelton, 2 January 1905, C.O. 147/174. Adewoye, 'Şapara Williams', p. 51. Adewoye, *The Judicial System in Southern Nigeria*, pp. 52, 75–8, 143–59, 180–200 and 230–46, notes that in Lagos lawyers' fees were high enough to deter many persons from taking cases to court.
131 Carter to Ripon, 22 November 1893, C.O. 147/91.
132 Moloney to Knutsford, 26 January 1889, C.O. 147/69.
133 *LS*, 7 August 1895, p. 2, c. 3.
134 Hopkins, 'An Economic History of Lagos', pp. 75 and 305. Hopkins, *Economic History of West Africa*, p. 240, notes that 'during the three years 1899–1901 Doherty's average net receipt from sales amounted to nearly £50,000 per annum'.

135 'Evidence Presented to the Commission on Trade', Denton to Chamberlain, 4 June 1898, C.O. 147/133.
136 'Return of . . . Schools', *Blue Books, Lagos Colony*, 1880–9.
137 *LS*, 5 February 1913, p. 6, c. 3.
138 McCallum to Chamberlain, 23 August 1897, C.O. 147/114; McCallum to Chamberlain, 10 August 1897, C.O. 147/116; and McCallum to Chamberlain, 23 September 1897, C.O. 147/118. See also 'Report of the Commission on Trade', Denton to Chamberlain, 4 June 1898, C.O. 147/133.
139 Wills, vols. 1–15, Lagos Probate Registry.
140 Interview with A. K. Lamilisa, Lagos, January 1974; and Will, I. B. Williams, Wills, vol. 6, pp. 346–54, Lagos Probate Registry.
141 *LS*, 7 August 1895, p. 2, c. 3.
142 Will, Adeyemo Alakija, Wills, vol. 12, pp. 289–96, Lagos Probate Registry.
143 *Olowu v. Miller Bros.*, 1 N.L.R., p. 110.
144 Hopkins, 'Property Rights and Empire Building', p. 792.
145 Hopkins, 'Peter Thomas', pp. 309–10.
146 Macaulay Papers, 57/6.
147 Several authors point to the economic and political importance of land for the Creoles of Sierra Leone. See Fyfe, *A History of Sierra Leone*, pp. 117–18, 175 and 361; John Peterson, *Province of Freedom: A History of Sierra Leone, 1787–1870* (London, Faber and Faber, 1969), pp. 271–8; and Cohen, *The Politics of Elite Culture*, pp. 51–6.
148 The elite sometimes bought real estate in the names of wives or children. Such property did not always appear in wills. Many parents transmitted property to children through education. McCallum to Chamberlain, 10 August 1897, C.O. 147/116.
149 P. J. C. Thomas and Kitoyi Ajasa wrote wills in mid-life; by the time they died they had lost much of the property listed in these documents. Will, P. J. C. Thomas, Wills, vol. 11, pp. 230–42; and Will, Kitoyi Ajasa, Wills, vol. 9, pp. 199–201, Lagos Probate Registry.
150 This figure is based on a 20 percent sample of all estates probated.
151 Elite men's estates ranged in value from £5 to £60,000, with a standard deviation of 9,776.
152 Elite women's estates ranged in value from £7 to £4,500, with a standard deviation of 1,164.

2 YORUBA AND CHRISTIAN MARRIAGE

1 Anthony G. Hopkins, 'A Report on the Yoruba, 1910', *Journal of the Historical Society of Nigeria*, 5 (1969), pp. 77–8; and Adebesin Folarin, *The Laws and Customs of Egbaland* (Abeokuta, E. N. A. Press, 1939), p. 6. For the debate over Yoruba descent see Peter C. Lloyd, 'The Yoruba Lineage', *Africa*, 25 (1955), pp. 235–51; William B. Schwab, 'Kinship and Lineage among the Yoruba', *Africa*, 25 (1955), pp. 352–74; Peter C. Lloyd, 'Agnatic and Cognatic Descent among the Yoruba', *Man* (NS), 1 (1966), pp. 484–500; Donald R. Bender, 'Agnatic or Cognatic? A Re-evaluation of Ondo Descent', *Man* (NS), 5 (1970), pp. 71–87; and J. S. Eades, *The Yoruba Today* (Cambridge, Cambridge University Press, 1980), pp. 45–9 and 51–5.
2 Samuel Johnson, *The History of the Yorubas* (London, Church Missionary Society, 1921), pp. 98–100, and N. A. Fadipe, *The Sociology of the Yoruba* (Ibadan, Ibadan University Press, 1970), pp. 97–118, discuss Yoruba residence. Many nineteenth-century missionaries and travellers describe compounds in Lagos and other Yoruba towns, including William H. Clarke, *Travels and Explorations in Yorubaland* (Ibadan, Ibadan University Press, 1972), p. 23; Thomas Jefferson Bowen, *Adventures and Missionary Labours in Several Countries in the Interior of Africa from 1849 to 1856* (London, Frank Cass, 1968), pp. 297–9; Richard Francis Burton, *Abeokuta and the Camaroons Mountains*, 2 vols.

(London, Tinsley Brothers, 1863), vol. 1, pp. 80–2; and Anna Hinderer, *Seventeen Years in Yoruba Country* (London, Religious Tract Society, 1877), p. 60. Eades, *The Yoruba Today*, pp. 45–9 and 51–3, reviews the anthropological literature on Yoruba residence.

3 Interviews in Lagos with T. A. Doherty, April 1974; and in Ikeja with Akin Adeshigbin, April 1974 and August 1980.

4 Hopkins, 'Report on the Yoruba', p. 78; Ajayi Kolawole Ajisafe, *The Laws and Customs of the Yoruba People* (Lagos, Church Missionary Society Bookshop, 1924), p.1; Fadipe, *Sociology of the Yoruba*, pp. 119, 126–7 and 134; and Eades, *The Yoruba Today*, pp. 49–51. For evidence on the role of women in lineage affairs see *Lewis v Bankole*, 2 N.L.R., pp. 81–106.

5 Hopkins, 'Report on the Yoruba', p. 84; Johnson, *History of the Yorubas*, pp. 95–7; and Ajisafe, *Laws and Customs of the Yoruba*, pp. 9–11 and 12–18. See also Peter C. Lloyd, *Yoruba Land Law* (London, Oxford University Press, 1962), pp. 60–70 and 73–7; Eades, *The Yoruba Today*, pp. 55–6 and 73–7; T. Olawale Elias, *Nigerian Land Law and Custom* (London, Routledge and Kegan Paul, 1962), pp. 6–15 and 92–8; and G. B. A. Coker, *Family Property among the Yorubas* (London, Sweet and Maxwell, 1958), pp. 16–31 and 182–216.

6 Anthony G. Hopkins, 'Property Rights and Empire Building: Britain's Annexation of Lagos, 1861', *Journal of Economic History*, 41 (1980), pp. 777–98; and Coker, *Family Property among the Yorubas*, pp. 182–204. Wills often turned privately owned property into family property for the joint use of all descendants.

7 Fadipe, *Sociology of the Yoruba*, pp. 135–46; Ajisafe, *Laws and Customs of the Yoruba*, pp. 11 and 18; Hopkins, 'Report on the Yoruba', pp. 86–8; Peter C. Lloyd, 'Yoruba Inheritance and Succession' in John Duncan Derrett (ed.), *Studies in the Laws of Succession in Nigeria* (London, Oxford University Press, 1965), pp. 139–73; Eades, *The Yoruba Today*, pp. 55–6; and Coker, *Family Property among the Yorubas*, pp. 219–83.

8 Coker, *Family Property among the Yorubas*, pp. 219–83.

9 Hopkins, 'Report on the Yoruba', p. 81. For a useful review of the literature on the meaning of marriage payments see John L. Comaroff, 'Introduction' in Comaroff (ed.), *The Meaning of Marriage Payments* (New York, Academic Press, 1980), pp. 1–47.

10 *LWR*, 21 January 1911, p. 4, c. 1.

11 See for example articles in *LWR*, 2 June 1900, p. 3, c. 1; 19 January 1907, p. 6, c. 2; and 21 January 1911, p. 4, c. 1. See also Johnson, *History of the Yorubas*, p. 113; Fadipe, *Sociology of the Yoruba*, pp. 69–70; and Hopkins, 'Report on the Yoruba', p. 81.

12 *LWR*, 19 January 1907, p. 6, c. 1. See also *LWR*, 26 January 1907, p. 6, c. 2; and *LS*, 18 October 1911. On infant betrothal see Ajisafe, *Laws and Customs of the Yoruba*, p. 47; Folarin, *Laws and Customs of Egbaland*, pp. 17–18; Bowen, *Adventures and Missionary Labours*, p. 303; and R. H. Stone, *In Afric's Forest or Jungle; or Six Years among the Yorubans* (Edinburgh, Oliphant, Anderson, and Ferrier, 1900), pp. 98 and 125.

13 Jacob Kehinde Coker, 'Is Native Marriage Advisable or Not Advisable?', 26 July 1904, Coker 4/2/53.

14 Jacob Kehinde Coker, *Polygamy Defended* (Lagos, 1915), p. 3.

15 Kristin Mann, 'Women's Rights in Law and Practice: Marriage and Dispute Settlement in Colonial Lagos' in Margaret Jean Hay and Marcia Wright (eds.), *African Women and the Law: Historical Perspectives*, Boston University Papers on Africa, vol. 7 (1982), pp. 151–71.

16 Johnson, *History of the Yorubas*, p. 113; Fadipe, *Sociology of the Yoruba*, pp. 69–71 and 92; Ajisafe, *Laws and Customs of the Yoruba*, pp. 47–8; and Hopkins, 'Report on the Yoruba', p. 81.

17 *LWR*, 21 January 1911, p. 4, c. 1.

18 Fadipe, *Sociology of the Yoruba*, p. 71. An article in a Lagos newspaper commented, 'The heathen . . . looks upon marriage as chiefly intended to propagate the human species

rather than designated to promote some fanciful relationship between the husband and wife.' *LWR*, 21 March 1908, p. 4, c. 2.
19 Interview with Archdeacon J. O. Lucas, Lagos, April 1974.
20 Interview with Atanda Balogun, Lagos, July 1974.
21 Johnson, *History of the Yorubas*; p. 113; and Ajisafe, *Laws and Customs of the Yoruba*, p. 48.
22 Hopkins, 'Report on the Yoruba', p. 82; Fadipe, *Sociology of the Yoruba*, p. 78; and Folarin, *The Laws and Customs of Egbaland*, p. 17.
23 Interview with Archdeacon J. O. Lucas, Lagos, April 1974.
24 For contemporary descriptions of these rituals see Alfred Burdon Ellis, *The Yoruba-Speaking People of the Slave Coast of West Africa* (London, Chapman and Hall, 1894), p. 185; Hopkins, 'Report on the Yoruba', pp. 80–1; C. Partridge, 'Native Law and Custom in Egbaland', *Journal of the African Society*, 10 (1910–11), p. 425; Johnson, *History of the Yorubas*, p. 114; Ajisafe, *Laws and Customs of the Yoruba*, pp. 47–9; Percy Amaury Talbot, *The Peoples of Southern Nigeria*, 4 vols. (London, Oxford University Press, 1926), vol. 3, pp. 431–2; Fadipe, *Sociology of the Yoruba*, pp. 69–73; Folarin, *Laws and Customs of Egbaland*, pp. 17–20; Isaac O. Delano, *The Soul of Nigeria* (London, Frank Cass, 1978), pp. 44–52; and *LS*, 7 April 1915, p. ?, c. 1.
25 *LS*, 7 April 1915, p. ?, c. 1.
26 Delano, *Soul of Nigeria*, pp. 122–5; and interview with Archdeacon J. O. Lucas, Lagos, April 1974. The Bible and gold wedding band also formed part of the bridewealth of Creoles in Sierra Leone. Leo Spitzer, *The Creoles of Sierra Leone: Responses to Colonialism, 1870–1945* (Madison, University of Wisconsin Press, 1974), p. 31; and Olumbe Bassir, 'Marriage Rites among the Aku (Yoruba) of Freetown', *Africa*, 24 (1954), pp. 351–2.
27 Interview with Archdeacon J. O. Lucas, Lagos, April 1974. See also Peter Awoonor Renner, *Reports, Notes of Cases and Proceedings and Judgments in Appeal . . . Relating to the Cape Coast Colony and Colony of Nigeria from 1861 to 1914*, 2 vols. (London, Sweet and Maxwell, 1915), vol. 1, p. 608; and Fadipe, *Sociology of the Yoruba*, pp. 83–4.
28 MacGregor to Chamberlain, 18 October 1899, and 17 November 1899, C.O. 147/145.
29 *LS*, 11 March 1914, p. 4, c. 2. See also *LWR*, 26 January 1907, p. 6, c. 2.
30 Kola symbolized the value of the bride, bitter kola the unity and longevity of the marriage, alligator pepper the fertility of the bride and honey the happiness of the marriage. *LS*, 11 March 1914, p. 4, c. 2; and interview in Lagos with Mrs Oluremi Onosanya, July 1980.
31 Interview with Seidu Olowu at Government House, 27 November 1889, C.S.O. 8/7, v. 2; and *LS*, 11 March 1914, p. 4, c. 2. For information on the value of bridewealth in Yorubaland see Kristin Mann, 'A Social History of the New African Elite in Lagos Colony, 1880–1913', unpublished Ph.D. thesis, Stanford University, 1977, p. 221.
32 Ellis, *The Yoruba-Speaking People*, p. 154; Ajisafe, *Laws and Customs of the Yoruba*, pp. 50–1; Fadipe, *Sociology of the Yoruba*, p. 81; and Delano, *Soul of Nigeria*, pp. 133–9.
33 In the eighteenth and nineteenth centuries the growth of the slave trade and the palm-produce trade led to innovations in production and the development of slave estates owned by powerful war chiefs. These estates may have dominated the production and trade of palm produce for export. However, the bulk of the free population certainly engaged in domestic production. Anthony G. Hopkins, *An Economic History of West Africa* (Harlow, Longman, 1973), pp. 154–7; Sara S. Berry, *Cocoa, Custom and Socio-Economic Change in Rural Western Nigeria* (Oxford, Clarendon Press, 1975), pp. 25–6.
34 On the organization of economic production in Yorubaland and the sexual division of labor see Bowen, *Adventures and Missionary Labours*, p. 308; Robert Campbell and Martin Robinson Delaney, *Search for a Place* (Ann Arbor, University of Michigan Press, 1969), p. 39; Hopkins, 'Report on the Yoruba', p. 82; *LWR*, 22 March 1913, p. 4, c. 10;

Notes to p. 40

Johnson, *History of the Yorubas*, pp. 102 and 117–18; Fadipe, *Sociology of the Yoruba*, pp. 87, 147–9 and 150–5; Folarin, *Laws and Customs of Egbaland*, pp. 21 and 29; and Jane I. Guyer, 'Food, Cocoa, and the Division of Labour by Sex in Two West African Societies', *Comparative Studies in Society and History*, 22 (1980), pp. 361–4 and 368. Eades, *The Yoruba Today*, pp. 67–9, reviews recent literature on the subject. For a study of Yoruba slavery see E. A. Oroge, 'The Institution of Slavery in Yorubaland, with Particular Reference to the Nineteenth Century', unpublished Ph.D. thesis, University of Birmingham, 1971.

35 Beginning with Claude Meillassoux's important work on the Guro, Marxist anthropologists have explored the relationship in Africa among bridewealth, marriage, and social and economic differentiation. Meillassoux argues that Guro elders enjoyed a monopoly over bridewealth, which enabled them to control the labor of younger men by manipulating the terms and timing of their marriages. Because Guro elders had limited control over production, Meillassoux sees their control over labor as the source of their economic and political dominance. Following Meillassoux, Emmanuel Terray argues that control over women and bridewealth reproduced social structures that sanctioned the supremacy of elders. While the Yoruba regarded the labor of wives and children as a valuable asset, bridewealth, marriage, and social and economic differentiation stood in a more complex relationship in Yorubaland than Meillassoux's model would suggest. Yoruba elders did not monopolize bridewealth, which was in any case low relative to the ability of men to accumulate resources. Until the advent of cash payments, readily available goods made up Yoruba marriage prestations. Moreover, in Yorubaland a wide circle of cognates rather than a small group of elders contributed bridewealth. In addition, the Yoruba regarded the timing of marriage as the business of the lineage, and they believed elders had a social responsibility to help young men marry. Fathers encountered severe pressure from kin when they postponed marriages unduly to retain the labor of their sons or to delay the division of productive resources necessary to establish new domestic groups. Finally, Yoruba fathers derived certain benefits from seeing sons married. Claude Meillassoux, *Anthropologie économique des Guro de Côte d'Ivoire: De l'économie de subsistance à l'agriculture commerciale* (Paris, Mouton, 1964), pp. 90, 204, 217, 223–4 and 233; and Emmanuel Terray, *Marxism and 'Primitive' Societies* (New York, Monthly Review Press, 1972), pp. 164 and 176. For fuller discussions of Marxist perspectives on this subject see Comaroff, *The Meaning of Marriage Payments*, pp. 22–6; and Jane I. Guyer, 'Household and Community in African Studies', paper commissioned by the Social Science Research Council, June 1981, pp. 14–21 and 24–7.

36 Hopkins, 'Report on the Yoruba', p. 80; Johnson, *History of the Yoruba*, p. 113; and Jacob Kehinde Coker, *Polygamy Defended*, p. 2.

37 The following works discuss the rights and duties of husbands and wives in late-nineteenth and early-twentieth-century Yorubaland: *LWR*, 22 March 1913, p. 4, c. 1; Ajisafe, *Laws and Customs of the Yoruba*, pp. 57–8; Fadipe, *Sociology of the Yoruba*, pp. 88–9, 148–9, 151 and 155–6; and Folarin, *Laws and Customs of Egbaland*, pp. 21–2 and 29. For discussions of the subject in more recent times see Niara Sudarkasa, *Where Women Work: A Study of Yoruba Women in the Market Place and in the Home* (Ann Arbor, University of Michigan Press, 1973); Peter C. Lloyd, 'The Status of the Yoruba Wife', *Sudan Studies*, 2 (1963), pp. 37–9; Jean Comhaire, 'Enseignement féminin et mariage à Lagos, Nigéria', *Zaire*, 9 (1955), pp. 261–77; S. Comhaire-Sylvain, 'Le travail des femmes à Lagos', *Zaire*, 5 (1951), pp. 169–87 and 475–502; H. U. Beier, 'The Position of Yoruba Women', *Présence Africaine* (NS), 1–2 (1955), pp. 39–46; and Eades, *The Yoruba Today*, pp. 67–8.

38 *LWR*, 22 March 1913, p. 4, c. 1.

39 Hopkins, 'Report on the Yoruba', p. 81.

40 Burton commented that in polygynous families each wife was a 'free dealer'. Burton,

Abeokuta and the Camaroons Mountains, vol. 1, p. 81. See also Fadipe, *Sociology of the Yoruba*, p. 118; and Eva Krapf-Askari, *Yoruba Towns and Cities: An Enquiry into the Nature of Urban Social Phenomena* (Oxford, Clarendon Press, 1969), p. 65.

41 Comaroff, *The Meaning of Marriage Payments*, pp. 33–4.
42 Guyer, 'Household and Community in African Studies', p. 13; and Fredrik Barth, *Models of Social Organization*, Royal Anthropological Institute Occasional Paper No. 23 (1966), pp. 1–2.
43 See testimony in the case *In re Ṣapara, LS*, 25 October 1911, p. 7, c. 1.
44 *LS*, 11 October 1911, p. 7, c. 2.
45 *LS*, 25 October 1911, p. 7, c. 1. The 'Report of the Committee on Infant Mortality' stated, 'Parents do not seem to have as much control over their sons and daughters and this leads to a lowering of the moral tone and a looser way of living amongst young people. Native marriage laws are not respected.' MacGregor to Chamberlain, 20 April 1901, C.O. 147/155.
46 *LWR*, 19 January 1907, p. 6, c. 1. See also *LWR*, 7 March 1908, p. 4, c. 1; 16 May 1908, p. 4, c. 2; and 9 September 1911, p. 4, c. 1.
47 *LS*, 11 October 1911, p. 7, c. 2; 25 October 1911, p. 7, c. 1; and 1 November 1911, p. 7, c. 2.
48 Interviews in Lagos with Mrs R. A. Wright, March 1974; Mrs Comfort Maja, August 1974; and Archdeacon J. O. Lucas, April 1974.
49 Interviews in Ikeja with Akin Adeshigbin, April 1974 and July 1980; and in Lagos with T. A. Doherty, April 1974; and Archdeacon J. O. Lucas, April 1974.
50 Comaroff, *The Meaning of Marriage Payments*, p. 36.
51 *LS*, 15 March 1911, p. 5, c. 3. See also *LS*, 23 August 1911, p. 5, c. 3.
52 *LS*, 18 October 1911, p. 7, c. 2; 25 October 1911, p. 7, c. 1; 1 November 1911, p. 7, c. 2; and 8 November 1911, p. 6, c. 2.
53 Fadipe, *Sociology of the Yoruba*, p. 68. An informant who fell to talking about contemporary marriage said, 'We now have seven kinds of marriage', and went on to distinguish among them. Interview with O. A. Ṣobande, Lagos, July 1980.
54 *LS*, 11 October 1911, p. 7, c. 1.
55 *LS*, 25 October 1911, p. 7, c. 2.
56 *LS*, 11 October 1911, p. 7, c. 2.
57 *In re Ṣapara*, in Renner, *Reports, Notes of Cases and Proceedings*, vol. 1, pp. 605 and 608. Caroline H. Bledsoe, *Women and Marriage in Kpelle Society* (Stanford, Stanford University Press, 1980), p. 7, makes a similar point.
58 *LWR*, 5 January 1907, p. 3, c. 2. See also *LS*, 27 November 1895, p. 3, c. 3; and *LWR*, 25 April 1908, p. 4, c. 2.
59 *LWR*, 21 January 1911, p. 4, c. 1.
60 Fadipe, *Sociology of the Yoruba*, p. 91.
61 For the debate over the origins of English marriage see Lawrence Stone, *The Family, Sex and Marriage in England, 1500–1800* (New York, Harper and Row, 1977); E. P. Thompson, 'Happy Families', *New Society*, 41, 779 (8 September 1977), pp. 499–501; Christopher Hill, 'Sex, Marriage and the Family in England', *Economic History Review*, 31 (1978), pp. 450–63; and Alan Macfarlane, review of Stone, *History and Theory*, 18 (1979), pp. 103–26.
62 J. F. Ade Ajayi, *Christian Missions in Nigeria, 1841–1891: The Making of a New Elite* (Harlow, Longman, 1965), pp. 14–18.
63 *LWR*, 4 July 1908, p. 5, c. 1.
64 *LWR*, 22 April 1905, p. 3, c. 1.
65 *Annual Reports, Lagos Colony*, 1880–1907; *Census, Lagos Colony*, 1891; and *Census, Southern Nigeria*, 1911.
66 'Notes on Polygamy', 1902, Phillips 1/2/1. See also Henry Carr, *Diocesan Synod of*

Notes to pp. 44–6

Western Equatorial Africa, Report of Speeches Delivered in Synod, May 1907 . . . (Exeter, Townsend and Sons, 1907), pp. 8–13; the Rev. M. O. Dada, 'The Problem of Polygamy and Allied Evils', Minutes of the Marriage Conference, 1930, Macaulay 21/8; *LS*, 15 February 1905, p. 4, c. 1; *LWR*, 29 May 1909, p. 4, c. 2; and *LS*, 27 May 1914, p. 5, c. 1. Lyndon Harries, 'Christian Marriage in African Society' in Arthur Phillips (ed.), *Survey of African Marriage and Family Life* (London, Oxford University Press, 1953), pp. 335–59, discusses the history of missionary attitudes toward polygyny.

67 'Ordinance No. 10, Lagos, 1863' and 'Ordinance No. 21, Lagos, 1863' in J. Algernon Montagu, *Ordinances of the Settlement of Lagos* (London, G. E. Eyre and W. Spottiswoode, 1874).
68 'Ordinance No. 14, Lagos, 1884' in Edward Harrison Richards, *Ordinances, Orders, and Rules in Force in the Colony of Lagos, 1893* (London, Stevens and Sons, 1894), pp. 443–57.
69 Abigail C. Oluwoli[e], *Christian Marriage* (Coventry, Curtis and Beamish, n.d.), pp. 5, 7 and 12–13 (emphasis Mrs Oluwole's). See also Carr, *Diocesan Synod . . . May 1907*, pp. 8–13; and 'Christian Marriage' in C. O. Taiwo (ed.), *Henry Carr: Lectures and Speeches* (Ibadan, Oxford University Press, 1969), p. 24.
70 Williams to Carrena, 25 March 1924, Carrena, Letters (9).
71 Daniel John Sorinolu, 'Paper on Polygamy', 1883, C.M.S.-Y.M. G3A2-03. Contrary to expectation, the Church Missionary Society Yoruba Mission Papers contain little correspondence or other manuscript material relevant to marriage. Several important pamphlets on marriage, otherwise difficult to locate, do survive in these records.
72 *Report of the Proceedings of the First and Second Sessions of the First Synod of the Diocese of Western Equatorial Africa* (Exeter, Townsend and Sons, 1907), p. 135.
73 Oluwoli, *Christian Marriage*, p. 19. See also *LWR*, 29 May 1897, p. 4, c. 2; and *LS*, 31 August 1910, p. 6, c. 1. On Victorian conjugal ideals see Martha Vicinus (ed.), *Suffer and Be Still: Women in the Victorian Age* (Bloomington, University of Indiana Press, 1972), pp. ix–xii; and Patricia Branca, *Silent Sisterhood: Middle Class Women in the Victorian Home* (Pittsburgh, Carnegie-Mellon University Press, 1975), pp. 6–8.
74 Oluwoli, *Christian Marriage*, pp. 14–15 and 22–3.
75 John Augustus Otonba Payne, *Lagos and West African Almanack and Diary* (London, J. S. Phillips, 1894), pp. 71–2. See also 'Bonetta Davies Memorial Ladies School', Oke 3/7/4; and *LWR*, 25 March 1905, p. 6, c. 2.
76 *LS*, 22 June 1904, p. 2, c. 2. See also *LWR*, 22 May 1897, p. ?, c. 1; and 'Education of Women' in Taiwo (ed.), *Henry Carr*, pp. 33–4.
77 Interview with Mrs. C. O. Blaize, Lagos, January 1974.
78 Victor to Coker, 25 June 1907, Coker 1/4/3. The language in this letter is very similar to that used in the West to describe the ideal Victorian woman. Barbara Welter, 'The Cult of True Womanhood: 1820–1860' in Michael Gordon (ed.), *The American Family in Social–Historical Perspective* (New York, St Martin Press, 1973), pp. 224–50.
79 *LS*, 6 October 1915, p. 6, c. 2.
80 *LWR*, 10 October 1896, p. 3, c. 3. *LS*, 2 June 1897, p. 3, c. 2, expresses a similar point of view.
81 Such events constituted a regular feature of life among the elite. Payne, *Lagos and West African Almanack and Diary, 1877–94*, and Lagos newspapers chronicle these gatherings in great detail.
82 Interview with Mrs C. O. Blaize, Lagos, January 1974.
83 Olympio to Coker, 19 April 1906, Coker 1/4/3.
84 Interviews in Lagos with Mrs Ayo Manuwa and Mrs. C. O. Blaize, January and May 1974. Oral information from Professor Gabriel O. Olusanya, Director, Correspondence and Open Studies Institute, University of Lagos.
85 Fadipe, *Sociology of the Yoruba*, p. 70.

Notes to pp. 47–50

86 Davies to Davies, 6 June 1890; and Randle to Davies, 21 October 1898, Coker 1/4/2.
87 Oluwoli, *Christian Marriage*, pp. 10–11. Interview with Archdeacon J. O. Lucas, Lagos, April 1974.
88 Davies to Davies, 12 December 1875, Coker 6/2. E. A. Ayandele, *Holy Johnson: Pioneer of African Nationalism, 1836–1917* (London, Frank Cass, 1970), p. 251, discusses Johnson's difficulty in finding a wife.
89 Phillips to Johnson, 14 March 1874, Phillips 1/1/6.
90 Interviews in Lagos with Mrs C. O. Blaize, Archdeacon J. O. Lucas and Mrs R. A. Wright, January, March and April 1974; and *LS*, 17 July 1901, p. 3, c. 1. Spitzer, *The Creoles of Sierra Leone*, p. 29, notes similar concerns among educated Africans in colonial Freetown.
91 Interviews in Lagos with Mrs C. O. Blaize, Archdeacon J. O. Lucas and Mrs R. A. Wright, January, March and April 1974. See also correspondence in Carrena, Letters (9), especially Randall to Carrena, 10 July 1923.
92 Bishop Charles Phillips's papers contain documents that discuss his marriage and that of his sister, Zenobia (Phillips) Johnson. Zenobia's suitors spoke to Charles Phillips because her parents had died, and she had no other close relatives in Abeokuta where she lived. 'Memoirs' and 'Notes on Zenobia Phillips', Phillips 1/1/6.
93 Carrena to Nogueira, 18 September 1913, Carrena, Letters (9).
94 Martins to Carrena, 20 October 1913, Carrena, Letters (9).
95 For additional letters of proposal and consent see Carrena, Letters (9).
96 Randall to Carrena, 10 July 1923, Carrena, Letters (9).
97 Ajisafe, *Laws and Customs of the Yoruba*, p. 48.
98 For references to the Christian betrothal see ? to Coker, 24 October 1890, Coker 6/1; Carrena to Savage, 13 July 1923, Carrena, Letters (9); *Savage* v. *Macfoy* and *In re Ṣapara*, in Renner, *Reports, Notes of Cases and Proceedings*, vol. 1, pp. 508 and 609; and *LS*, 11 March 1914, p. 4, c. 2. Also interviews in Lagos with Mrs Edith Harrison and Mrs Oluremi Onosanya, July 1980.
99 Among the elite, men made Christian marriages at an average age of 30.1 years and women at 22.6 years. Marriage registers at the Lagos Marriage Registry and St Paul's Church, Christ Church Cathedral and Holy Cross Cathedral contain information on age of marriage.
100 Fadipe, *Sociology of the Yoruba*, p. 95. Interviews in Lagos with Mrs C. O. Blaize and Archdeacon J. O. Lucas, January and April 1974.
101 Thomas to Coker, 5 March 1907, Coker 1/4/3.
102 Interview with Mrs Oyejola Turner, Lagos, July 1974.
103 Interviews in Lagos with Mrs C. O. Blaize and Archdeacon J. O. Lucas, January and April 1974. See also 'Notes on Zenobia Phillips', Phillips 1/1/6; and Fadipe, *Sociology of the Yoruba*, p. 95.
104 Ayandele, *Holy Johnson*, p. 28; and interview with Mrs Oyejola Turner, Lagos, July 1974.
105 Evans to Stanhope, 1 January 1887, and Moloney to Holland, 3 May 1887, C.O. 147/78; Will, Thomas George Hoare, Wills, vol. 1, pp. 35–8, Lagos Probate Registry; and interview with Mrs Ayo Smith, Ibadan, May 1974. A marriage settlement transferring property from a husband to his wife survives in the possession of Dr J. T. Nelson Cole, Iju, Lagos State. I am grateful to Dr Nelson Cole for permission to consult this document.
106 Undated document, Phillips, 1/1/6. See also Tytler to Carrena, 1 July 1915, Carrena, Letters (9); and Fadipe, *Sociology of the Yoruba*, pp. 95–6. Creoles in Freetown gave similar gifts of money and clothing. Spitzer, *The Creoles of Sierra Leone*, pp. 29–30.
107 *LS*, 18 March 1914, p. 4, c. 2.
108 Interviews in Lagos with Mrs C. O. Blaize, Mrs R. A. Wright, and Archdeacon J. O. Lucas, January, March and May 1974; and Mrs Edith Harrison, July 1980.
109 Interviews in Lagos with Archdeacon J. O. Lucas and Mrs Tinuola Dedeke, April 1974.

Notes to pp. 50–2

Comaroff, *The Meaning of Marriage Payments*, p. 35, emphasizes the role of marriage payments in defining social identity and kinship.
110 Jack Goody and S. J. Tambiah, *Bridewealth and Dowry* (Cambridge, Cambridge University Press, 1973), pp. 1–2 and 61–2.
111 *LS*, 4 March 1914, p. 4, c. 3.
112 *LO*, 21 January 1888. The press of the period contains numerous lengthy descriptions of Christian weddings. See also 'Fashionable Marriage', *LS*, 4 September 1895, p. 3, c. 1; and the description of the wedding of Dr J. O. Coker and Stella Davies, *LWR*, 26 November 1898, p. 6, c. 2.
113 Studies of marriage in contemporary West African towns have found that Christian couples commonly engage in pre-marital sex. Girls' parents do not necessarily approve of this behavior, but they are unable to control the activities of their daughters. These studies also have shown that during the last several decades many couples have cohabited or married according to local custom prior to marrying under the Marriage Ordinance. This enables the man to take a wife before he can afford an expensive church wedding, and to ensure that the woman can conceive before he invests heavily in the union. In nineteenth-century Lagos, few elite couples who married in church engaged in pre-marital sex. Educated parents chaperoned their daughters very carefully. Some perpetuated the Yoruba custom of sending female relatives with the bride on her wedding night to determine whether she was a virgin. Pamphlet literature and newspaper articles testify that in the early twentieth century educated Africans began to worry about pre-marital sex, and specifically about the chastity of women. At this time, some educated males began cohabiting with women they planned subsequently to marry in church. Kenneth Little and Anne Price, 'Some Trends in Modern Marriage among West Africans' in Colin Turnbull (ed.), *Africa and Change* (New York, Knopf, 1973), pp. 187–8; Barbara E. Harrell-Bond, *Modern Marriage in Sierra Leone: A Study of the Professional Group* (The Hague, Mouton, 1975), pp. 155–95; and Christine Oppong, *Marriage among a Matrilineal Elite: A Family Study of Ghanaian Senior Civil Servants* (Cambridge, Cambridge University Press, 1974), p. 65. For evidence on nineteenth-century Lagos see *LWR*, 28 March 1903, p. 4, c. 3; 17 and 26 February 1910, p. 3, c. 1; and 18 February 1911, p. 3, c. 2; and *LS*, 21 July 1915, p. 7, c. 1; and 25 August 1915, p. 4, c. 1.
114 Henry Carr, *Diocesan Synod of Western Equatorial Africa, Report of Speeches Delivered in Synod, May 1912* . . . (Newcastle-upon-Tyne, Mawson, Swan, and Morgan, 1912), p. 11.
115 Moloney to Knutsford, 30 August 1890, C.O. 147/76. Interviews in Lagos with Mrs C. O. Blaize, Mrs E. M. E. Agbebi and Archdeacon J. O. Lucas, January, March and April 1974.
116 Interviews in Lagos with Mrs Adewakun, Mrs R. A. Wright, Mrs Tinuola Dedeke and Mrs Syrian Taylor, March–May 1974. Mann, 'Women's Rights in Law and Practice', pp. 170–1.
117 *Cole v. Cole*, 1 N.L.R., p. 22.
118 'Ordinance No. 14, Lagos, 1884', pp. 453–4. G. B. A. Coker, *Family Property among the Yorubas*, pp. 246–63, S. N. Chinwuba Obi, *Modern Family Law in Southern Nigeria* (London, Sweet and Maxwell, 1966), pp. 282–3, and Alfred B. Kasunmu and Jeswald Salacuse, *Nigerian Family Law* (London, Butterworth, 1966), pp. 261–74, include fuller discussions of the effect of the Marriage Ordinance on inheritance.
119 William Geldart, *Elements of English Law* (London, Oxford University Press, 1975), p. 121; P. M. Bromley, *Family Law* (London, Butterworth, 1962), pp. 401–2 and 467; and F. R. Crane, 'Family Settlements and Succession' in R. H. Graveson and Crane (eds.), *A Century of Family Law* (London, Sweet and Maxwell, 1957), pp. 245–6.
120 'Ordinance No. 14, Lagos, 1884', pp. 443–57.

121 *LS*, 28 August 1895, p. 3, c. 3.
122 *LS*, 20 February 1895, p. 3, c. 2.
123 *LWR*, 13 March 1909, p. 4, c. 2. See also Jacob Kehinde Coker, 'Is Native Marriage Advisable or Not Advisable?'; and *LWR*, 6 August 1898, p. 4, c. 3; 15 June 1901; 22 April 1905, p. 5, c. 2; and 19 July 1913, p. 3, c. 1.
124 Obi, *Modern Family Law*, pp. 198–284; and Kasunmu and Salacuse, *Nigerian Family Law*, pp. 48–70, 183–96 and 261–90.
125 *The Book of Common Prayer and Administration of the Sacraments . . .* (London, Oxford University Press, 1861), p. 335. See also 'Christian Marriage' in Taiwo (ed.), *Henry Carr*, p. 26.
126 *LWR*, 27 February 1904, p. 4, c. 2.
127 *LS*, 10 January 1900, p. 2, c. 1.
128 *LS*, 9 June 1897, p. 5, c. 3.
129 'Petition from the Protestant Ministers on the Subject of Divorce', Denton to Knutsford, 15 August 1889, C.O. 147/71. Kasunmu and Salacuse, *Nigerian Family Law*, pp. 126–44; and Obi, *Modern Family Law*, pp. 234–5 and 363–70.
130 Johnson, *History of the Yorubas*, p. 117; Ajisafe, *Laws and Customs of the Yoruba*, p. 54.
131 Hopkins, 'Report on the Yoruba', p. 79.
132 Fadipe, *Sociology of the Yoruba*, p. 92. See also Jacob Kehinde Coker, *Polygamy Defended*, p. 13.

3 ELITE MEN AND THE MARRIAGE DILEMMA

1 Determining whether persons had made Christian marriages posed few problems. They had either wed in church or they had not. If they had, documentary evidence usually survived in marriage registers, newspapers or wills. Documenting Yoruba and outside unions proved more difficult. The colonial state did not require registration of Yoruba marriages, and few references occur in written records to specific customary or outside unions. Interviews with descendants provided the only means of obtaining information about these relationships. However, children of Christian wives sometimes tried to hide the fact that their fathers had had relations with other women. To minimize this difficulty, I began each interview by compiling a family genealogy. In this context informants usually named all the subject's offspring. Only then did I inquire about the mothers of these children and about women who did not produce children.

Ascertaining the status of non-Christian unions proved even more problematic. Faced with a similar task, anthropologist Caroline H. Bledsoe, *Women and Marriage in Kpelle Society* (Stanford, Stanford University Press, 1980), pp. 7–8, admitted the impossibility of determining marital status precisely. The difficulties are particularly great in an historical study where the parties to unions have long since died and few contemporaries survive. Not surprisingly, children usually asserted that their parents had either married in church or performed the full Yoruba marriage rites. Asked about the status of the mothers of his father's children, a typical informant retorted, 'My father did not take women off the street. He married them in the usual way.' However, when pressed the man could not say whether his father had paid bridewealth for all of these women (interview in Lagos with T. A. Doherty, April 1974). When elite males did not marry in church, women who bore them children usually acquired the status of customary wives. This was not always true if the men had married in church. The educated elite and their descendants coped with the ambiguity and fluidity of relationships between men who married in church and women other than their Christian wives by referring to these unions as 'outside' marriages. I have followed their lead in adopting this terminology.

2 Henry Carr, *Diocesan Synod of Western Equatorial Africa, Report of Speeches Delivered in Synod, May 1907 . . .* (Exeter, Townsend and Sons, 1907), p. 11.

3 *LS*, 17 March 1915, p. 4, c. 2. See also the Rev. James Johnson's statement against polygyny, *LWR*, 17 March 1894, p. 2, c. 3; and *LS*, 29 March 1899, p. 3, c. 3.
4 J. F. Ade Ajayi, *Christian Missions in Nigeria, 1841–1891: The Making of a New Elite* (Harlow, Longman, 1965), pp. 14–19; E. A. Ayandele, *The Missionary Impact on Modern Nigeria, 1842–1914: A Political and Social Analysis* (Harlow, Longman, 1966), pp. 241–6; Robert W. July, *The Origins of Modern African Thought* (New York, Praeger, 1967), pp. 130, 142–4, 180–3 and 189–93; Fred I. A. Omu, *Press and Politics in Nigeria, 1880–1937* (Atlantic Highlands, Humanities Press, 1978), pp. 103 and 114–15; Michael J. C. Echeruo, *Victorian Lagos: Aspects of Nineteenth Century Lagos Life* (New York, Macmillan, 1977), pp. 35–49 and 80–94. Leo Spitzer, *The Creoles of Sierra Leone: Responses to Colonialism, 1870–1945* (Madison, University of Wisconsin Press, 1974), pp. 9–45, discusses this phenomenon in colonial Sierra Leone.
5 *LWR*, 14 December 1895, p. 5, c. 3.
6 *LWR*, 14 April 1894, p. 2, c. 1.
7 *LS*, 29 March 1899, p. 3, c. 3.
8 *LS*, 15 March 1911, p. 5, c. 3.
9 Abner Cohen, *The Politics of Elite Culture: Explorations in the Dramaturgy of Power in a Modern African Society* (Berkeley, University of California Press, 1981), pp. 17–38 and 60–75.
10 Interviews in Lagos with Archdeacon J. O. Lucas, April 1974; Mrs Comfort Maja, August 1974; and N. E. S. Adewale, July 1974. See also *LWR*, 16 May 1903, p. 6, c. 1.
11 J. P. L. Davies's Diary, 13 December 1885, Coker 3/7.
12 *LWR*, 27 April 1895, p. 3, c. 1.
13 Ibid.
14 *LS*, 18 January 1911, p. 4, c. 1. See also *LS*, 2 September 1908, p. 4, c. 2; and 10 November 1909, p. 4, c. 2.
15 Adebesin Folarin, *England and the English: Personal Impressions during a Three Years' Sojourn* (London, John Taylor, n.d.), pp. 39–42; and Mojola Agbebi, *Inaugural Sermon Delivered at the Celebration of the First Anniversary of the 'African Church', 21 December 1902* (New York, Edgar F. Howorth, 1903), pp. 18–20. Folarin called educated Africans 'the greatest race of imitators . . . that ever existed on the globe'.
16 *LS*, 7 February 1900; 22 July 1908, p. 6, c. 1.
   An article reprinted in *LWR*, 17 February 1912, referred to the 'high status' accorded Christian marriage in the Gold Coast. Barbara E. Harrell-Bond, *Modern Marriage in Sierra Leone: A Study of the Professional Group* (The Hague, Mouton, 1975), pp. 3, 54 and 287, notes that educated Africans in colonial Freetown also regarded Christian marriage as more prestigious than African marriage. She argues that this belief has carried over among contemporary Sierra Leonean professionals.
17 See pp. 77–87 above.
18 For evidence on Dr Ṣapara's engagement to Ore Green see *In re Ṣapara*, in Peter Awoonor Renner, *Reports, Notes of Cases and Proceedings and Judgments in Appeal . . . Relating to the Cape Coast Colony and the Colony of Nigeria from 1861 to 1914*, 2 vols. (London, Sweet and Maxwell, 1915), vol. 1, pp. 611–12. *LS*, 20 September 1911 through 13 March 1912, provides additional information.
19 Interviews in Lagos with Archdeacon J. O. Lucas, April 1974; and Mrs C. O. Blaize, January 1974. See also 'Education of Women' in C. O. Taiwo (ed.), *Henry Carr: Lectures and Speeches* (Ibadan, Oxford University Press, 1969), p. 34.
   The emphasis in women's education on deportment and domestic economy made good sense given these concerns.
20 Spencer H. Brown, 'A History of the People of Lagos, 1852–1886', unpublished Ph.D. thesis, Northwestern University, 1964, p. 135.
21 MacGregor to Chamberlain, 14 August 1901, C.O. 147/156.

22 Wills often made bequests to children 'for their sole use and benefit'. Sometimes bequests to daughters specified 'sole use and benefit . . . independently of . . . husbands'. See for example the wills of J. P. L. Davies, Wills, vol. 2, pp. 409–15; and Charles Joseph George, vol. 2, pp. 424–34, Lagos Probate Registry.
23 Interview in Lagos with Archdeacon J. O. Lucas, April 1974. See also *LS*, 20 August 1913, p. 4, c. 2.
24 Blyden to Chancellor B, n.d., Macaulay 22/8. See also Coker to ?, 16 July 1913, Coker 2/1/10; and *LWR*, 18 July 1908, p. 4, c. 3; and 23 November 1912, p. 4, c. 2. Peter C. Lloyd, 'The Status of the Yoruba Wife', *Sudan Studies*, 2 (1963), p. 40, notes that in more recent times Yoruba men still objected to ordinance marriage on these grounds.
25 *LWR*, 10 April 1897, p. 4, c. 1. See also *LWR*, 16 September 1899, p. 3, c. 3; and 19 October 1907, p. 4, c. 2; Jacob Kehinde Coker, 'Is Native Marriage Advisable or Not Advisable?', p. 10, Coker 4/2/53, and *Polygamy Defended* (Lagos, 1915), p. 14.
26 Samuel Johnson, *The History of the Yorubas* (London, Church Missionary Society, 1921), p. 115; Ajayi Kolawole Ajisafe, *The Laws and Customs of the Yoruba People* (Lagos, Church Missionary Society Bookshop, 1924), pp. 75–6; and N. A. Fadipe, *The Sociology of the Yoruba* (Ibadan, Ibadan University Press, 1970), pp. 67 and 141.
27 *LWR*, 11 July 1908, p. 3, c. 1.
28 Coker, *Polygamy Defended*, p. 14.
29 *LWR*, 22 June 1901, p. 3, c. 2; see also Coker, 'Is Native Marriage Advisable or Not Advisable?', p. 9; and Blyden to Chancellor B, n.d., Macaulay 22/8.
30 *LS*, 20 August 1913, p. 4, c. 2.
31 Interview with Mrs E. M. E. Agbebi, Lagos, March 1974.
32 See pp. 12, 16–17, 19–21 and 39–40 above.
33 Interviews in Lagos with Kunle Akinṣemoyin, January 1974; Mrs Kwao Sagoe, February 1974; and A. K. Lamilisa, January 1974. See also Anthony G. Hopkins, 'Richard Beale Blaize, 1845–1904: Merchant Prince of West Africa', *Tarikh*, 1 (1966), pp. 70–8, and 'An Economic History of Lagos, 1880–1914', unpublished Ph.D. thesis, University of London, 1964, pp. 75–8; and Jean Herskovits Kopytoff, *A Preface to Modern Nigeria: The 'Sierra Leonians' in Yoruba, 1830–1890* (Madison, University of Wisconsin Press, 1965), pp. 283–301.
34 Interviews in Lagos with T. A. Doherty, April 1974; Mrs E. I. Oni, August 1974; and H. O. Davies, April 1974.
35 Coker, *Polygamy Defended*, p. 14.
36 I owe this insight to Jane I. Guyer.
37 *LS*, 27 February 1901, p. 5, c. 1. Also interviews with T. A. Doherty, Lagos, April 1974; Akin Adeshigbin, Ikeja, April 1974 and July 1980; and Dr da Rocha-Afodu, Lagos, April 1974.
38 *LS*, 29 March 1899, p. 3, c. 2. Also Mrs Abigail C. Oluwoli[e], *Christian Marriage* (Coventry, Curtis and Beamish, n.d.), p. 13.
39 *LS*, 31 January 1900, p. ?, c. 1. See also *LS*, 22 April 1903, p. 2, c. 3; 17 November 1915, p. 4, c. 2; and 4 March 1914, p. 4, c. 3.
40 Interviews in Lagos with Dr da Rocha-Afodu, April 1974; Mrs E. I. Oni, August 1974; and T. A. Doherty, April 1974.
41 'The Debate on the European Marriage Custom, 2 November 1888' in Mojola Agbebi, *Africa and the Gospel: Sermons, Debates, and Lectures* . . . (Lagos, T. A. King, n.d.), p. 20. Samuel A. Coker, *The Rights of Africans to Organize and Establish Indigenous Churches, Unattached to and Uncontrolled by Foreign Church Organizations* (Lagos, Tika Tore Press, 1917), pp. 26–7.
42 *LWR*, 17 April 1897, p. 4, c. 1.
43 *LWR*, 22 April 1905, p. 5, c. 2. See also *LWR*, 6 August 1898, p. 4, c. 3; *LS*, 10 August 1898, p. 5, c. 2; and *Report of the Proceedings of the First and Second Sessions of the First*

Synod of the Diocese of Western Equatorial Africa (Exeter, Townsend and Sons, 1907), pp. 127–31.
44 See for example the wills of E. A. Caulcrick, Wills, vol. 3, pp. 327–9; and Andrew W. Thomas, vol. 6, pp. 202–8, Lagos Probate Registry.
45 'Resolution Adopted at the Conference of Bishops', Lagos, March 1906, C.M.S.-Y.M. G3A2-012.
46 See pp. 41–3 above.
47 Interviews in Lagos with Archdeacon J. O. Lucas, April 1974; T. A. Doherty, April 1974; Mrs E. I. Oni, August 1974; and Lady Ayo Alakija, March 1974.
48 Interviews with Mrs G. C. Agbe, Lagos, February 1974; and Jack Randle, Ikeja, August 1974. Jacob Kehinde Coker, 'Is Native Marriage Advisable or Not Advisable?', p. 3, Samuel A. Coker, *The Rights of Africans to Organize Indigenous Churches*, pp. 24–9, and 'The Debate on the European Marriage Custom', p. 22, emphasize the unhappiness of Christian marriages. See also *LS*, 2 September 1908, p. 4, c. 2.
49 I would like to thank Mrs Comfort Maja for showing me this photograph. Interviews in Lagos with Archdeacon J. O. Lucas, April 1974; and Mrs Ayo Manuwa, May 1974.
50 Interviews with Dr Mobolaji Alakija, Lagos, January 1974; and Mrs Afolabi Johnson, Lagos, July 1974.
51 Interviews with C. E. Nylander, Lagos, August 1974; and Ajani Olujare, Lagos, January 1974.
52 Interview in Lagos with Archdeacon J. O. Lucas, April 1974.
   Fadipe, *Sociology of the Yoruba*, p. 97, said of this situation, 'Married life with many a young Christian begins with legal monogamy and ends with customary polygyny.'
53 Interview with Archdeacon J. O. Lucas, Lagos, April 1974.
54 Henry Carr, *Diocesan Synod of Western Equatorial Africa, Report of Speeches Delivered in Synod, May 1912* . . . (Newcastle-upon-Tyne, Mawson, Swan, and Morgan, 1912), p. 12; and *LWR*, 16 May 1903, p. 6, c. 1.
55 Initially, I hypothesized that more first-generation repatriates than second- and third-generation repatriates would have made Yoruba marriages as a way of building an economic and political base in Lagos. This was not the case.
56 Studies of contemporary educated elites report a similar finding. Peter C. Lloyd, 'Introduction' in Lloyd (ed.), *The New Elites of Tropical Africa* (London, Oxford University Press, 1966), pp. 28–31; Kenneth Little and Anne Price, 'Some Trends in Modern Marriage among West Africans' in Colin Turnbull (ed.), *Africa and Change* (New York, Knopf, 1973), p. 197; and Christine Oppong, *Marriage among a Matrilineal Elite: A Family Study of Ghanaian Senior Civil Servants* (Cambridge, Cambridge University Press, 1974), pp. 2 and 153.
57 Lloyd, 'The Status of the Yoruba Wife', pp. 39–40, drew a similar conclusion in the 1960s.
58 Christopher Fyfe, *A History of Sierra Leone* (London, Oxford University Press, 1962), pp. 127–498 passim; Kopytoff, *Preface to Modern Nigeria*, pp. 31–6; and July, *Origins of Modern African Thought*, pp. 142–4, 182 and 191.
59 July, *Origins of Modern African Thought*, p. 130.
60 Interview with Mrs C. O. Blaize, Lagos, January 1974; and *In re Ṣapara*, in Renner, *Reports, Notes of Cases and Proceedings*, vol. 1, pp. 605–14.
61 Brown, 'A History of the People of Lagos', pp. 33–44.
62 James Bertin Webster, *African Churches among the Yoruba, 1888–1922* (Oxford, Clarendon Press, 1964), pp. 7–41.
   Governor Gilbert Carter refused to permit Dr John Randle to withdraw a resignation that he had earlier tendered. Carter commented in defense of his decision, 'I can see no excuse for the tone of his original communication, and I am strongly of the opinion that such a person is not fit for Her Majesty's service. It is, moreover, well known that he has behaved in a scandalous manner to his wife.' Carter to Knutsford, 7 July 1892, C.O. 147/

85. See also Moloney to Knutsford, 13 March 1889, C.O. 147/70; and McCallum to Chamberlain, 23 June 1897, C.O. 147/114.
63 Justice Osborne stated in the case *In re Ṣapara*, 'This has been a very painful case, and a very repulsive case . . . Dr Ṣapara is a member of an honourable and learned profession who . . . might have been in a position to confer lasting benefits on his race . . . [T]o the obloquy of all self-respecting persons in the community, of whatever creed or colour . . . he stands [condemned].' See Renner, *Reports, Notes of Cases and Proceedings*, vol. 1, p. 613.
64 Kristin Mann, 'Women's Rights in Law and Practice: Marriage and Dispute Settlement in Colonial Lagos' in Margaret Jean Hay and Marcia Wright (eds.), *African Women and the Law: Historical Perspectives*, Boston University Papers on Africa, vol. 7 (1982), pp. 151–71.
65 Interviews in Lagos with J. A. Akitoye, November 1973; Victor Abiodun Dawodu, March 1974; and J. O. Haastrup, January 1974.
66 Interviews with Akin Adeshigbin, Ikeja, April 1974 and July 1980; J. A. Akitoye, Lagos, November 1973; and Victor Abiodun Dawodu, Lagos, March 1974.
67 Interviews with T. A. Doherty, Lagos, April 1974; Akin Adeshigbin, Ikeja, April 1974 and July 1980; and Mrs H. F. Pereira, Lagos, February 1974 and July 1980.
68 See for example George Peter Murdock, *Social Structure* (New York, Macmillan, 1949), pp. 184 and 250–9; Sidney M. Greenfield, 'Industrialization and the Family in Sociological Theory', *American Journal of Sociology*, 67 (1961), pp. 312–22; William J. Goode, *World Revolution and Family Patterns* (New York, Free Press, 1963), pp. 1–26, 164–202 and 366–80; and Morris Zeldich, 'Cross-Cultural Analysis of Family Structure' in H. T. Christensen (ed.), *Handbook of Marriage and the Family* (Chicago, Rand McNally, 1964), p. 469.
69 Few elite males married before age twenty-five or after age fifty. The oldest members of the 1851 to 1890 cohort began marrying in the late 1870s. Only a handful of the youngest members of the 1810 to 1850 cohort continued to make marital decisions after the 1890s.

Changes in the composition of elite males do not account for changes in the group's marital behavior. The percentage of locals and second- and third-generation repatriates, men prone to Yoruba marriage, increased among the 1851 to 1890 cohort. However, this increase was more than offset by a rise in the percentage of professionals, colonial servants and second- and third-generation educated Christians, men prone to Christian marriage.
70 See pp. 21–2 above.
71 Interviews in Lagos with E. M. E. Willoughby, January 1974; and Mrs R. A. Wright, April 1974.
72 See for example *LS*, 29 March 1899, p. 3, c. 2; 31 January 1900, p. ?, c. 1; and 27 February 1901, p. 5, c. 1.
73 Interviews in Lagos with T. A. Doherty, April 1974; Mrs E. I. Oni, August 1974; and Iya Onigari, March 1974; and in Ikeja with Akin Adeshigbin, April 1974 and July 1980.

Hopkins, 'An Economic History of Lagos', pp. 58, 291 and 422, lists leading African merchants between 1880 and 1889, 1890 and 1905, and 1906 and 1914. Fifty-five percent of the first group, 66 percent of the second group, and 80 percent of the third group made Yoruba or outside marriages. Among educated Christians who were new recruits to his lists for 1890 to 1905 and 1906 to 1914, 73 percent and 75 percent respectively formed Yoruba or outside unions.
74 Ayandele, *The Missionary Impact on Modern Nigeria*, pp. 246–8 and 252–60; Omu, *Press and Politics in Nigeria*, pp. 107–15; July, *Origins of Modern African Thought*, pp. 349–58; and Patrick Cole, *Modern and Traditional Elites in the Politics of Lagos* (Cambridge, Cambridge University Press, 1975), pp. 75–89. See also *LWR*, 19 May 1906, p. 6, c. 3.
75 *LWR*, 21 January 1911, p. 4, c. 1.
76 Jacob Kehinde Coker, 'Is Native Marriage Advisable or Not Advisable?', pp. 3–4. This point of view emerged gradually in editorials by John Payne Jackson in the *Lagos Weekly*

Notes to pp. 72–3

Record, and can also be found in correspondence in his paper. *LWR*, 10 April 1897, p. 4, c. 1; 16 September 1899, p. 3, c. 1; 15 June 1901, p. 4, c. 1; 27 February 1904, p. 4, c. 2; 1 September 1906, p. 6, c. 1; and 11 September 1915, p. ?, c. 1. See also *LS*, 27 September 1899, p. 3, c. 3; 26 April 1905, p. 5, c. 2; 12 August 1908, p. 6, c. ?; 13 August 1913, p. 4, c. 3; and 1 September 1915, p. 4, c. 2.

77 Quoted in Omu, *Press and Politics in Nigeria*, p. 112.
78 *LS*, 17 March 1915, p. 4, c. 2. See also *LS*, 2 September 1908, p. 4, c. 2.
79 *LWR*, 18 May 1907, p. 3, c. 2. Educated Africans apparently reached this position of cultural relativism quite independently. In the United States, Franz Boas grappled with problems of race, culture and evolution at roughly the same time. I find no evidence that the Lagos elite knew about his work. Possibly Boas's ideas influenced the elite indirectly, through lectures, newspapers and periodicals. On the development of Boas's thought see George W. Stocking, *Race, Culture and Evolution: Essays in the History of Anthropology* (New York, Free Press, 1968), pp. 115–235 passim.
80 See for example *LWR*, 21 January 1905, p. 4, c. 1; 25 April 1908, p. 4, c. 2; 13 March 1909, p. 4, c. 2; 19 July 1913, p. 3, c. 1; and *LS*, 27 September 1899, p. 3, c. 3; 9 September 1908, p. 6, c. 1; and 9 November 1910, p. 5, c. 2.
81 Ayandele, *The Missionary Impact*, pp. 248–50. See an editorial on this subject in *LWR*, 13 April 1907, p. 4, c. 1; and Bishop James Johnson's response, *LWR*, 27 April 1907, p. 5, c. 2. See also Keyinde Okoro, *Views of Some Native Christians of West Africa on the Subject of Polygamy* (Lagos, General Printing Press, 1887), p. 24.
82 *LWR*, 27 April 1907, p. 5, c. 2. See also *LWR*, 1 February 1902, p. 4, c. 2; 28 August 1909, p. 4, c. 1; and 11 September 1915, p. ?, c. 1; and *LS*, 2 September 1908, p. 4, c. 2.
83 *LS*, 27 November 1895, p. 3, c. 3; and 25 March 1896, p. 2, c. 2. *LWR*, 27 February 1904, p. 5, c. 2; 27 April 1907, p. 5, c. 2; 28 August 1909, p. 4, c. 1; and 21 January 1911, p. 4, c. 1.
84 *LWR*, 10 April 1897, p. 4, c. 1; and 16 September 1899, p. 3, c. 3. *LS*, 13 July 1910, p. 6, c. 1. Also Jacob Kehinde Coker, *Polygamy Defended*, p. 14.
85 *LWR*, 29 January 1910, p. 4, c. 1. See also *LS*, 25 March 1896, p. 2, c. 2; 10 November 1909, p. 4, c. 2; and 1 September 1915, p. 4, c. 2; and *LWR*, 27 February 1904, p. 4, c. 2; and 7 June 1913, p. 4, c. 2.
86 *LWR*, 20 May 1905, p. 4, c. 3.
87 *LWR*, 17 April 1897, p. 4, c. 1.
88 *LS*, 22 September 1897, p. 2, c. 3.
89 Webster, *African Churches among the Yoruba*, pp. 42–91; E. A. Ayandele, *A Visionary of the African Church: Mojola Agbebi, 1860–1917* (Nairobi, East African Publishing House, 1971), pp. 12–20; Gabriel A. Oke, *A Short History of the United Native African Church*, part 1 (Lagos, Jehovah Shalom Press, 1918), pp. 1–10; and Herbert S. H. Macaulay, *The History of the Development of Missionary Works in Nigeria, with Special Reference to the United Native African Church* (Lagos, Adedimeto Printing Works, 1941), pp. 11–12.
90 Okoro, *Views of Some Native Christians*, pp. 7, 12, 17 and 27; Agbebi, *Inaugural Sermon*, pp. 18–19; Samuel A. Coker, *Three Sermons on the Christian Ministry* (London, T. Fisher Unwin, 1904), pp. 29–32; Jacob Kehinde Coker, *Polygamy Defended*, pp. 1–19; *LS*, 22 September 1897, p. 2, c. 3; 24 May 1911, p. 4, c. 3; and 8 September 1915, p. 7, c. 3; and *LWR*, 29 January 1910, p. 4, c. 1.
91 Blyden to Chancellor B, n.d., Macaulay 22/8. See also Okoro, *Views of Some Native Christians*, pp. 5, 8–9, 13 and 17; Jacob Kehinde Coker, 'Is Native Marriage Advisable or Not Advisable?', p. 3; Samuel A. Coker, *The Rights of Africans to Organize Indigenous Churches*, p. 24; and 'The Debate on the European Marriage Custom', p. 19.
92 *LWR*, 10 April 1897, p. 4, c. 1.
93 *LWR*, 26 February 1898, p. 5, c. 2.
94 *LWR*, 28 September 1907, p. 4, c. 2. See also *LWR*, 15 June 1901, p. 4, c. 1; 24 September 1904, p. 4, c. 2; 4 July 1908, p. 5, c. 1; 1 July 1908, p. 3, c. 1.

95 Interview in Lagos with Archdeacon J. O. Lucas, April 1974.
96 For an account of the Vidal–Fowler wedding see *LS*, 25 March 1896, p. 2, c. 2. For other discussions of 'Native Christian' marriage see *LS*, 7 April 1915, p. ?, c. 1; 28 July 1915, p. ?, c. 2.
97 July, *Origins of Modern African Thought*, pp. 374–91; T. N. Tamuno, *The Evolution of the Nigerian State: The Southern Phase, 1898–1914* (Harlow, Longman, 1972), pp. 111–21; Cole, *Modern and Traditional Elites*, pp. 89–101; and Omu, *Press and Politics in Nigeria*, pp. 132–70.
98 Pauline H. Baker, *Urbanization and Political Change: The Politics of Lagos, 1917–1967* (Berkeley, University of California Press, 1974), pp. 115–62; James S. Coleman, *Nigeria: Background to Nationalism* (Berkeley, University of California Press, 1958), pp. 169–86; and Richard L. Sklar, *Nigerian Political Parties* (Princeton, Princeton University Press, 1963), pp. 41–54.
99 Interview in Lagos with Archdeacon J. O. Lucas, April 1974.
100 Cole, *Modern and Traditional Elites*, pp. 73–104; and Anthony G. Hopkins, 'The Lagos Chamber of Commerce, 1888–1903', *Journal of the Historical Society of Nigeria*, 3 (1965), p. 248.
101 Interview in Lagos with Archdeacon J. O. Lucas, April 1974.
102 Interview in Lagos with Mrs Henrietta Lawson, August 1974. See also *In the Matter of the Estate of Herbert Samuel Heelas Macaulay*, 13 West African Court of Appeals, p. 304.
103 'Class, Status, Party' in H. H. Gerth and C. Wright Mills (eds.), *From Max Weber: Essays in Sociology* (New York, Oxford University Press, 1958), pp. 187–9.
104 E. A. Ayandele, *The Educated Elite in Nigerian Society* (Ibadan, Ibadan University Press, 1974), p. 29.
105 Ibid. pp. 55–93. See also Cole, *Modern and Traditional Elites*, pp. 46 and 48–9.
106 Echeruo, *Victorian Lagos*, p. 35.
107 Ibid. pp. 16 and 25–30; and Tamuno, *The Evolution of the Nigerian State*, pp. 110–21.
108 Jean Herskovits, 'The Sierra Leoneans of Yorubaland' in Philip D. Curtin (ed.), *Africa and the West* (Madison, University of Wisconsin Press, 1972), pp. 77–98.
109 Omu, *Press and Politics in Nigeria*, pp. 100–70.

4 THE DANGERS OF DEPENDENCE: ELITE WOMEN AND CHRISTIAN MARRIAGE

1 Interviews in Lagos with Mrs C. O. Blaize, Archdeacon J. O. Lucas, Mrs Tinuola Dedeke, T. A. Doherty, and Mrs R. A. Wright, January, April, May and July 1974.
2 *Savage* v. *Macfoy*, in Peter Awoonor Renner, *Reports, Notes of Cases and Proceedings and Judgments in Appeal . . . Relating to the Cape Coast Colony and Colony of Nigeria from 1861 to 1914*, 2 vols. (London, Sweet and Maxwell, 1915), vol. 1, p. 505.
3 *LS*, 31 January 1900, p. ?, c. 1.
4 *LS*, 29 January 1896, p. ?, c. 2.
5 Jacob Kehinde Coker, 'Is Native Marriage Advisable or Not Advisable?' Coker 4/2/53, p. 6.
6 Interview with Mrs T. E. Williams, Lagos, April 1974.
7 Interview with Mrs Adeniyi Williams, Ibadan, May 1974.
8 Interviews in Lagos with Archdeacon J. O. Lucas, Mrs Tinuola Dedeke, Mrs Syrian Taylor and Mrs R. A. Wright, April, May and July 1974. For a discussion of non-elite women's motives for entering customary unions, see pp. 102–8 and 124–6 above.
9 Interview with Mrs C. O. Blaize, Lagos, January 1974.
10 Barbara E. Harrell-Bond, *Modern Marriage in Sierra Leone: A Study of the Professional Group* (The Hague, Mouton, 1975), pp. 3, 54 and 287, notes that educated Africans in colonial Freetown regarded Christian marriage as more prestigious than African mar-

Notes to p. 78

riage. She argues that this belief persists among contemporary Sierra Leonean professionals.

11 Ester Boserup, *Woman's Role in Economic Development* (New York, St Martin's Press, 1970), pp. 53–65; Polly Hill, *Migrant Cocoa-Farmers of Southern Ghana* (Cambridge, Cambridge University Press, 1963), pp. 42, 65, 116–17, 165 and 168; Sara S. Berry, *Cocoa, Custom and Socio-Economic Change in Rural Western Nigeria* (Oxford, Clarendon Press, 1975), p. 165; Jane I. Guyer, 'Food, Cocoa, and the Division of Labour by Sex in Two West African Societies', *Comparative Studies in Society and History*, 22 (1980), pp. 355–73; Jan S. Hogendorn, *Nigerian Groundnut Exports: Origins and Early Development* (Ibadan, Oxford University Press, 1978), pp. 77–116; and Donal B. Cruise O'Brien, *The Mourides of Senegal: The Political and Economic Organization of an Islamic Brotherhood* (Oxford, Clarendon Press, 1971), pp. 2–3, 190–2 and 202–17. As yet we know little about the impact of the growth of palm-produce exports on the division of labor and resources by sex.

For an excellent survey of the effects on African women of colonial rule and integration into the world economy see Margaret Strobel, 'African Women', *Signs*, 8 (1982), pp. 109–31.

12 Boserup, *Woman's Role in Economic Development*, pp. 94 and 99; Catherine Coquery-Vidrovitch, 'De la traite des esclaves à l'exportation de l'huile de palme et des palmistes au Dahomey: XIXe siècle' in Claude Meillassoux (ed.), *The Development of Indigenous Trade and Markets in West Africa* (London, Oxford University Press, 1971), pp. 107–23; Rowena M. Lawson, 'The Supply Response of Retail Trading Services to Urban Population Growth in Ghana' in ibid. pp. 377–98; George E. Brooks, Jr, 'The *Signares* of Saint-Louis and Gorée: Women Entrepreneurs in Eighteenth-Century Senegal' in Nancy J. Hafkin and Edna G. Bay (eds.), *Women in Africa: Studies in Social and Economic Change* (Stanford, Stanford University Press, 1976), pp. 19–44; Kwame Arhin, *West African Traders in Ghana in the Nineteenth and Twentieth Centuries* (Harlow, Longman, 1979), pp. 104 and 127; Nina Emma Mba, *Nigerian Women Mobilized: Women's Political Activity in Southern Nigeria, 1900–1965* (Berkeley, Institute of International Studies, 1982), pp. 47–52 and 67; E. Frances White, 'Women, Work, and Ethnicity: The Sierra Leone Case' in Edna G. Bay (ed.), *Women and Work in Africa* (Boulder, Colo., Westview Press, 1982), pp. 20–1 and 25–31; Dorothy Remy, 'Underdevelopment and the Experience of Women: A Nigerian Case Study' in Rayna Reiter (ed.), *Toward an Anthropology of Women* (New York, Monthly Review Press, 1975), pp. 358–71; and Claire Robertson, 'Ga Women and Change in Marketing Conditions in the Accra Area', *Rural Africana*, 29 (1975–6), pp. 157–71. Unfortunately most of the major new studies of West African economic history say little or nothing about the effects of changes in trade on women. See for example Philip D. Curtin, *Economic Change in Precolonial Africa: Senegambia in the Era of the Slave Trade* (Madison, University of Wisconsin Press, 1975); David Northrup, *Trade Without Rulers: Pre-Colonial Economic Development in Southeastern Nigeria* (Oxford, Clarendon Press, 1978); Ray A. Kea, *Settlements, Trade, and Politics in the Seventeenth-Century Gold Coast* (Baltimore, Johns Hopkins University Press, 1982); and Patrick Manning, *Slavery, Colonialism and Economic Growth in Dahomey, 1640–1960* (Cambridge, Cambridge University Press, 1982). Stephen Baier, *An Economic History of Central Niger* (Oxford, Clarendon Press, 1980), provides an exception.

13 See the articles by Okonjo and Van Allen in Hafkin and Bay (eds.), *Women in Africa*, pp. 45–85; and Mba, *Nigerian Women Mobilized*, pp. 38–47 and 67.

14 See the articles by Wright and Mann in Margaret Jean Hay and Marcia Wright (eds.), *African Women and the Law: Historical Perspectives*, Boston University Papers on Africa, vol. 7 (1982), pp. 31–50 and 151–71. See also Claire Robertson, 'Ga Women and Socioeconomic Change in Accra, Ghana' in Hafkin and Bay (eds.), *Women in Africa*,

pp. 123–4; Mba, *Nigerian Women Mobilized*, pp. 52–8 and 67; and Manning, *Slavery, Colonialism and Economic Growth in Dahomey*, p. 191.
15 Martin Chanock, 'Making Customary Law: Men, Women, and Courts in Colonial Northern Rhodesia' in Hay and Wright (eds.), *African Women and the Law*, pp. 57–66.
16 Boserup, *Woman's Role in Economic Development*, pp. 122, 212 and 220–2; Kenneth Little, *African Women in Towns: An Aspect of Africa's Social Revolution* (Cambridge, Cambridge University Press, 1973), pp. 30–1 and 180–3; and Filomina Chioma Steady, 'Protestant Women's Associations in Freetown, Sierra Leone' in Hafkin and Bay (eds.), *Women in Africa*, 220–37.
17 See pp. 45–6 above.
18 Interviews in Lagos with Percy Savage, T. A. Doherty, Mrs Ayodele Adeshigbin and Mrs Syrian Taylor, January–July 1974. Interview with Adetokunbo Ademola, Lagos, July 1980.
19 Spencer H. Brown, 'A History of the People of Lagos, 1852–1886', unpublished Ph.D. thesis, Northwestern University, 1964, p. 135.
20 Interview with Mrs Ayo Manuwa, Lagos, May 1974.
21 Jean Herskovits Kopytoff, *A Preface to Modern Nigeria: The 'Sierra Leonians' in Yoruba, 1830–1890* (Madison, University of Wisconsin Press, 1965), pp. 206–7; and Brown, 'A History of the People of Lagos', p. 132. See also Evans to Knutsford, 17 October 1887, C.O. 147/62.
22 Stella Davies's Diary, 1898, Coker 3/7, records the daily routine of an elite woman. For newspaper accounts of women's activities see *LWR*, 12 December 1891, p. 2, c. 3; 21 May 1892, p. 3, c. 1; 24 December 1898, p. 3, c. 3; 15 February 1902, p. 3, c. 3; and 24 May 1902, p. 3, c. 1; and *LS*, 6 February 1895, p. 2, c. 1; 20 February 1895, p. 3, c. 2; 30 January 1901, p. 2, c. 2; 27 February 1901, p. 2, c. 3; 17 May 1911, p. 5, c. 3; 5 May 1915, p. 5, c. 3; and 20 October 1915, p. 5, c. 1.
23 Keith Thomas, 'The Double Standard', *Journal of the History of Ideas*, 20 (1959), p. 210.
24 N. A. Fadipe, *The Sociology of the Yoruba* (Ibadan, Ibadan University Press, 1970), p. 78. Anthony G. Hopkins, 'A Report on the Yoruba, 1910', *Journal of the Historical Society of Nigeria*, 5 (1969), p. 81, comments, 'The right to the wife's person is infringed . . . by any other man having sexual intercourse with her.'
25 Interviews with Mrs J. T. A. Williams, Mrs C. G. Agbe, Mrs R. A. Wright, Mrs Ayo Manuwa and T. A. Doherty, Lagos, January–May, 1974.
26 Crowther to Davies, 16 November 1888, Coker 6/1.
27 Interviews with Archdeacon J. O. Lucas, Mrs C. O. Blaize and Mrs Ayo Manuwa, Lagos, April, January and May 1974.
28 Kenneth Little and Anne Price, 'Some Trends in Modern Marriage among West Africans' in Colin Turnbull (ed.), *Africa and Change* (New York, Knopf, 1973), pp. 187–8; and Christine Oppong, *Marriage among a Matrilineal Elite: A Family Study of Ghanaian Senior Civil Servants* (Cambridge, Cambridge University Press, 1974), p. 65.
29 Interview with Archdeacon J. O. Lucas, Lagos, April 1974.
30 *In re Ṣapara*, Judges' Notebook in Civil Cases, 1911–12, pp. 366, 411–16, 423–4 and 443–51, Lagos High Court Archives. *LS*, 20 September 1911 through 13 March 1912, published much of the testimony in the trial. For an abbreviated version see Renner, *Reports, Notes of Cases and Proceedings*, vol. 1, pp. 605–14.
31 Interview with Archdeacon J. O. Lucas, Lagos, April 1974.
32 Interviews in Lagos with E. M. E. Willoughby, the Rev. S. A. Pearce, T. A. Doherty and Percy Savage, January, March, April and July 1974.
33 Interviews in Lagos with Mrs E. M. E. Agbebi, Mrs Adewakun, Mrs Tinuola Dedeke and Mrs Syrian Taylor, March, April, May and July 1974.
34 Abner Cohen, *The Politics of Elite Culture: Explorations in the Dramaturgy of Power in an African Society* (Berkeley, University of California Press, 1981), p. 82, notes that

Notes to pp. 81–4

economically independent Creole women in modern Sierra Leone identify their status with that of their husbands.

35 Hilda Martindale, *Women Servants of the State, 1870–1938: A History of Women in the Civil Service* (London, Allen and Unwin, 1938), p. 192; and Dorothy Evans, *Women and the Civil Service: A History of the Development of the Employment of Women in the Civil Service, and a Guide to Present-Day Opportunities* (London, Sir Isaac Pitman and Sons, 1934), p. 62.

36 On the disabilities English women faced in medicine and law see A. H. Bennett, *English Medical Women: Glimpses of their Work in Peace and War* (London, Sir Isaac Pitman and Sons, 1915), pp. 10–57; E. Moberly Bell, *Storming the Citadel: The Rise of the Woman Doctor* (London, Constable and Co., 1953); and Neal A. Ferguson, 'Women in Twentieth Century England' in Barbara Kanner (ed.), *The Women of England from Anglo-Saxon Times to the Present* (Hamden, Conn., Archon Books, 1979), p. 362.

37 Leith Mullings, 'Women and Economic Change in Africa' in Hafkin and Bay (eds.), *Women in Africa*, pp. 248–9, 251 and 255; White, 'Women, Work and Ethnicity', pp. 19–33; and Christopher Fyfe, *A History of Sierra Leone* (London, Oxford University Press, 1962), p. 143. The emergence of a money economy and private land ownership, the dependence of large-scale traders on extensive European credit and the use of privately owned land as security for loans all may have put women traders at a disadvantage.

38 'Return of . . . Schools', *Blue Books, Lagos Colony*, 1880–9.

39 Fadipe, *Sociology of the Yoruba*, p. 97.

40 *LWR*, 21 January 1899, p. 5, c. 1.

41 Coker, 'Is Native Marriage Advisable or Not Advisable?', pp. 14–15.

42 Ibid. Oppong, *Marriage among a Matrilineal Elite*, p. 65, argues that ordinance marriage gives modern Ghanaian women a measure of security.

43 Interviews in Lagos with Mrs C. O. Blaize, Archdeacon J. O. Lucas and Mrs Comfort Maja, January, April and July 1974.

44 See p. 53 above.

45 For a brief biography of Mrs Blaize see her obituary, *LWR*, 24 August 1895, p. 6, c. 1. Interview with Kunle Akinṣemoyin, Lagos, January 1974.

46 Will, Richard Beale Blaize, Wills, vol. 6, pp. 341–6, Lagos Probate Registry.

47 David Kimble, *A Political History of Ghana: The Rise of Gold Coast Nationalism, 1850–1928* (Oxford, Clarendon Press, 1963), pp. 209, 407 and 456. I am grateful to Roger Gocking for these references and for additional information about Robert Hutchinson.

48 *LWR*, 30 January 1904, p. 3, c. 1.

49 *LWR*, 10 December 1904, p. 5, c. 2.

50 Interviews in Lagos with Michael Ayo Vaughan, Mrs Comfort Maja, Mrs R. A. Wright and Jack Randle, March, April and August 1974.

51 *LS*, 22 April 1903, p. 2, c. 3. See also *LS*, 9 June 1897, p. 5, c. 3; 29 March 1899, p. 3, c. 2; 16 August 1908, p. 4, c. 2; and 17 November 1915, p. 4, c. 2.

52 Interview with Mrs Henrietta Lawson, Lagos, August 1974.

53 Kristin Mann, 'Marriage and the Consolidation of Status among the Educated African Elite in Lagos Colony, 1880–1915', p. 18, unpublished paper presented to the Southeastern Regional Seminar in African Studies, February 1981. I am currently engaged in a study of inheritance among the elite using wills and other legal documents.

54 Will, Andrew Wilkinson Thomas, Wills, vol. 6, pp. 202–8 and 375–80, Lagos Probate Registry. Interview with Mrs C. G. Agbe, Lagos, February 1974.

55 *Cole v. Cole*, 1 N.L.R., pp. 15–23. In the High Court Archives I was unable to locate the Judges' Notebook in Civil Cases, 1897–8, which should contain records of this case. *LS*, 3 August 1898, p. 3, c. 2, provided supplementary evidence, as did an interview in Lagos with Georgius Cole, January 1974.

56 Interviews with Mrs R. A. Wright, Lagos, March and April 1974.

163

Notes to pp. 84–7

57 Interviews in Lagos with Mrs H. F. Pereira, Mrs R. A. Wright, Archdeacon J. O. Lucas and Mrs Comfort Maja, February–May 1974. See also 'Petition from the Protestant Ministers on the Subject of Divorce', Denton to Knutsford, 15 August 1889, C.O. 147/71.
58 *LWR*, 18 September 1915, p. 3, c. 3.
59 *Shyngle* v. *Shyngle*, 4 N.L.R., pp. 94–7.
60 For a fuller discussion of the settlement of marital disputes see Kristin Mann, 'Women's Rights in Law and Practice: Marriage and Dispute Settlement in Colonial Lagos' in Hay and Wright (eds.), *African Women and the Law*, pp. 151–71.
61 Randle to Davies, 19 November 1895, Coker 6/2.
62 Randle to Davies, 21 October 1898, Coker 1/4/2. For an equally vituperative letter see Randle to Davies, 21 August 1902, Coker 6/3. Interview with Jack Randle, Ikeja, August 1974.
63 For an example of disciplinary action taken by a church see 'Findings of the Minor District Synod held . . . to hear the appeal . . . against a sentence of eighteen months exclusion from membership', Macaulay 23/6.
64 MacGregor to Chamberlain, 22 March 1901, C.O. 147/154.
65 Allen to Davies, 24 July 1889, Coker 6/2.
66 T. Olawale Elias, *The Nigerian Legal System* (London, Routledge and Kegan Paul, 1963), p. 69.
67 Ibid. pp. 73–5.
68 In 1983, after the completion of this study, I located a large collection of Magistrates' Court Records at the Igboṣere Road Magistrates' Court. These records are neither organized nor shelved, and I had very little time to examine them. I believe they contain documents from the Magistrates' Court that in the nineteenth century stood at Tinubu Square.
69 The Registers of Civil Cases and the Judges' Notebooks are housed in the Lagos State High Court Archives.
70 Fadipe, *Sociology of the Yoruba*, p. 7. See also 'Petition from the Protestant Ministers on the Subject of Divorce', Denton to Knutsford, 15 August 1889, C.O. 147/71; *LWR*, 18 March 1911, p. 4, c. 1; and Omoniyi Adewoye, *The Judicial System in Southern Nigeria, 1854–1954* (Atlantic Highlands, Humanities Press, 1977), pp. 52, 75–8, 124–8, 143–59, 180–200 and 230–46.
71 G. B. A. Coker, *Family Property among the Yorubas* (London, Sweet and Maxwell, 1958), pp. 253–63.
72 Note the disagreement among chiefs who testified on Yoruba marriage in the case *In re Ṣapara*, Judges' Notebook in Civil Cases, 1911–12, pp. 366, 411–16, 423–4 and 443–51, Lagos High Court Archives; and *LS*, 20 September 1911 through 13 March 1912.
73 In addition to the *Lagos Standard's* coverage in *In re Ṣapara* see *LS*, 6 February 1907, p. 6, c. 2.
74 See Justice Griffith's judgment in *Cole* v. *Cole*, 1 N.L.R., p. 22.
75 S. N. Chinwuba Obi, *Modern Family Law in Southern Nigeria* (London, Sweet and Maxwell, 1966), pp. 235 and 244.
76 Peter C. Lloyd, 'Yoruba Inheritance and Succession' in John Duncan Derrett (ed.), *Studies in the Laws of Succession in Nigeria* (London, Oxford University Press, 1965), pp. 150–2.
77 *LS*, 15 March 1911, p. 5, c. 3.
78 Randle to Davies, 21 August 1902, Coker 6/3.
79 Interviews with Archdeacon J. O. Lucas, April 1974.
80 *LWR*, 21 January 1899, p. 5, c. 1.
81 *LWR*, 22 May 1897, p. ?, c. 1. See also Samuel A. Coker, *The Rights of Africans to Organize and Establish Indigenous Churches, Unattached to and Uncontrolled by Foreign*

Notes to pp. 88–91

    Church Organizations (Lagos, Tika Tore Press, 1917), pp. 28–9; and Coker to Cousin, 16 July 1913, Coker 2/1/10.
82 See Will, Thomas George Hoare, Wills, vol. 1, pp. 35–8; and Will, Adeyemo Alakija, Wills, vol. 12, pp. 289–96, Lagos Probate Registry.
83 *In re Ṣapara*, Renner, *Reports, Notes of Cases and Proceedings*, vol. 1, p. 606. Mrs Ayodele Wright defended polygyny while travelling in England. *LWR*, 16 July 1904, p. 5, c. 1.
84 Interview with Mrs Sarah Adadevoh, Lagos, March 1974.
85 Williams to Coker, 11 March 1908, Coker 1/4/4; and Thomas to Coker, 16 September 1907, Coker 1/4/3.
86 Abigail C. Oluwoli[e], *Christian Marriage* (Coventry, Curtis and Beamish, n.d.), pp. 19–20.
87 Abigail C. Oluwoli[e], *The Training of Children* (Coventry, Curtis and Beamish, n.d.), pp. 22–3.
88 *LS*, 22 May 1901, p. 3, c. 2.
89 *LWR*, 21 January 1899, p. 5, c. 1.
90 *LS*, 7 April 1915, p. 4, c. 3. See also *LS*, 25 January 1905, p. 3, c. 1; and 19 July 1911, p. 5, c. 1.
91 *LS*, 29 March 1899, p. 3, c. 2.
92 *LS*, 25 January 1905, p. 5, c. 2. See also *LS*, 7 December 1904, p. 4, c. 1; and 18 January 1905, p. 6, c. 3.
93 *LWR*, 8 December 1906, p. 7, c. 3; and 19 January 1907, p. 3, c. 1. See also *LS*, 27 July 1910, p. 6, c. 2.
94 *LWR*, 24 February 1906, p. 2, c. 3.
95 *LS*, 27 July 1910, p. 6, c. 2; and 10 August 1910, p. 6, c. 1.
96 *LS*, 22 January 1896, p. 2, c. 2.
97 *LS*, 5 April 1911, p. 6, c. 3; 19 July 1911, p. 4, c. 1 and 2; and 28 February 1912, p. 4, c. 2.
98 *LS*, 7 April 1915, p. 4, c. 3.
99 Interview with Mrs Ayodele Smith, Ibadan, 1974. See also *LS*, 18 January 1915, p. 6, c. 3. 'List of Important Farmers', Moseley to Lyttelton, 11 June 1904, C.O. 147/170, contains information about R. A. Wright's farm.
100 Interview with Mrs Ebun Lucas, Lagos, February 1974.
101 *LWR*, 25 July 1908, p. 7, c. 1.
102 *LS*, 8 December 1909, p. 4, c. 2
103 *LS*, 1 January 1913, p. 6, c. 3; and 16 July 1915, p. 2, c. 2. I would like to thank Professor Gabriel O. Olusanya for permitting me to consult his unpublished paper 'Sisi Obasa – Philanthropist, Social Worker, Champion of Women's Rights and Cultural Nationalist'. Cheryl Jeffries Johnson, 'Nigerian Women and British Colonialism: The Yoruba Example with Selected Biographies', unpublished Ph.D. thesis, Northwestern University (1978), pp. 97–131, contains a short biography of Mrs Obasa.
104 Interviews with Dr J. T. Nelson Cole, Iju, Lagos State, August 1974 and July 1980.
105 Interview with Mrs Ayodele Adeshigbin, Lagos, April 1974.
106 Kofoworola Aina Moore, 'The Story of Kofoworola Aina Moore, of the Yoruba Tribe, Nigeria' in Margery Perham (ed.), *Ten Africans* (London, Faber and Faber, 1936), p. 331. The author contrasts her thorough education with the 'finishing course' her mother received abroad.
107 Interview with Dr Irene Thomas, Lagos, July 1974.
108 Martha Vicinus, 'Introduction' in Vicinus (ed.), *A Widening Sphere: Changing Roles of Victorian Women* (Bloomington, University of Indiana Press, 1977), pp. ix–xix.
109 See for example *LS*, 3 July 1907, p. 5, c. 1; 22 March 1913, p. 4, c. 1; and 2 July 1913, p. 4, c. 1.

5 MARRIAGE AND THE CONSOLIDATION OF STATUS

1. Abner Cohen, *The Politics of Elite Culture: Explorations in the Dramaturgy of Power in a Modern African Society* (Berkeley, University of California Press, 1981).
2. Information about elite men's and women's Christian marriage partners comes from newspapers, marriage registers and interviews with their descendants. Marriage registers give age, occupation, abode, marital status, father's name and father's occupation for both husband and wife.
3. See pp. 45, 78–9 and 89–91 above.
4. 'Notes on Zenobia Phillips', Phillips 1/1/6; and interview with Mrs E. M. E. Agbebi, Lagos, March 1974.
5. Interview with Mrs Afolabi Johnson, Lagos, March 1974.
6. Interviews in Lagos with Mrs Korowo, March 1974; and Mrs T. Banjo, April 1974.
7. Interviews in Lagos with Mrs C. O. Blaize, January 1974; and Mrs Comfort Maja, August 1974 and July 1980.
8. Interviews in Lagos with T. A. Doherty, April and May 1974.
9. Notes on Aminatu Alayo, n.d., Macaulay 21/10.
10. For a description of the Dawodu–Hoare wedding see *LO*, 21 January 1888.
11. *LS*, 16 June 1909, p. 3, c. 2.
12. Will, Thomas George Hoare, Wills, vol. 1, pp. 35–8, Lagos Probate Registry.
13. Interview with Michael Ayo Vaughan, Lagos, March 1974.
14. E. A. Ayandele, *Holy Johnson: Pioneer of African Nationalism, 1836–1917* (London, Frank Cass, 1970), pp. 15–20 and 251.
15. Pamphlet published by St Peter's Church, Ake, Abeokuta, commemorating the anniversary of the death of the Rev. William Moore.
16. C. B. Moore's Account Book, 1882–1902, in the possession of Mrs Jack McEwen, Lagos. I want to thank Mrs McEwen for permission to consult this document.
17. Information about these marriages comes from newspapers, marriage registers and interviews in Lagos with Mrs C. O. Blaize, Mrs Jack McEwen, Lady Ademola, A. K. Lamilisa, Olufemi Ibare-Akinsan, Michael Ayo Vaughan and Kunle Akinşemoyin, January–July 1974 and July 1980. I interviewed Mrs Layinka in Ibadan, May 1974.
18. Fred I. A. Omu, *Press and Politics in Nigeria, 1880–1937* (Atlantic Highlands, Humanities Press, 1978), p. 30.
19. Information about these marriages comes from newspapers, marriage registers and interviews in Lagos with Mrs Ebun Lucas, February 1974; Percy Savage, July 1974 and July 1980; Dr J. T. Nelson Cole, August 1974 and July 1980; and Mrs Kwao Sagoe, February 1974. I interviewed Mrs Ayo Smith in Ibadan, July 1974.
20. The Lagos press and John Augustus Otonba Payne, *Lagos and West African Almanack and Diary* (London, J. S. Phillips, 1877–94), report visits of Freetown, Cape Coast and Bathurst relatives and friends to Lagos and of the Lagos elite to those towns.
21. It is only a slight exaggeration to say that among the descendants of the early Lagos elite everybody is related to everybody else. Persons often know they are related but cannot explain how.
    Cohen, *The Politics of Elite Culture*, pp. 60–75, discusses the importance of kinship and affinal ties among the Creoles of contemporary Sierra Leone. He stresses the role of family ceremonies in creating and maintaining such ties.
22. Local newspapers and Payne, *Lagos and West African Almanack and Diary*, chronicle the elite's social activities.
23. *LS*, 26 April 1911, p. 6, c. 3; and 3 May 1911, p. 6, c. 2. Allister Macmillan (ed.), *The Red Book of West Africa* (London, Collingridge, 1920), pp. 97–8, contains photographs of the interior of the Pearse home.

Notes to pp. 98–100

24 Pearse to Buxton, 25 March 1916; Buxton to Pearse, 19 April 1916; and Buxton to Pearse, 7 July 1917, ASAPS S22G232.
25 Cohen, *The Politics of Elite Culture*, pp. 76–88, emphasizes the role of women in organizing elite culture among the Creoles of contemporary Sierra Leone.
26 Interviews in Lagos with Mrs Adewakun, March 1974; and Mrs Ayo Manuwa, May 1974. Interview in Ibadan with Mrs Ayo Smith, May 1974.
    Esther N. Goody, *Parenthood and Social Reproduction: Fostering and Occupational Roles in West Africa* (Cambridge, Cambridge University Press, 1982), pp. 206–9, discusses the role of fostering in the assimilation of Creole culture and upward social mobility in Sierra Leone and Liberia.
27 Coker to Coker, 15 August 1905, Coker 1/2/1.
28 Carrena to Ajasa, 4 February 1925, Carrena Letters (9).
29 For discussions of divisions within the elite see Jean Herskovits Kopytoff, *A Preface to Modern Nigeria: The 'Sierra Leonians' in Yoruba, 1830–1890* (Madison, University of Wisconsin Press, 1965), pp. 111–62 and 176–258; Robert W. July, *The Origins of Modern African Thought* (New York, Praeger, 1967), pp. 374–91 and 415–32; Patrick Cole, *Modern and Traditional Elites in the Politics of Lagos, 1884–1938* (Cambridge, Cambridge University Press, 1975), pp. 45–119; Michael J. C. Echeruo, *Victorian Lagos: Aspects of Nineteenth Century Lagos Life* (London, Macmillan, 1977), pp. 95–105; and Omu, *Press and Politics in Nigeria*, pp. 100–203.
30 In addition to the works cited in the note above see E. A. Ayandele, *The Missionary Impact on Modern Nigeria, 1842–1914: A Political and Social Analysis* (Harlow, Longman, 1966), pp. 175–238; T. N. Tamuno, *The Evolution of the Nigerian State: The Southern Phase, 1898–1914* (Harlow, Longman, 1972), pp. 110–21, 127–47 and 309–16; James S. Coleman, *Nigeria: Background to Nationalism* (Berkeley, University of California Press, 1958), pp. 169–230; Richard L. Sklar, *Nigerian Political Parties* (Princeton, Princeton University Press, 1963), pp. 41–54; and Pauline H. Baker, *Urbanization and Political Change: The Politics of Lagos, 1917–1967* (Berkeley, University of California Press, 1974).
31 Cohen, *The Politics of Elite Culture*, pp. 5–9 and 89–215 passim.
32 Form of marriage affected intestate succession. Customary law applied to the division of the estates of persons who made Yoruba marriages. Customary inheritance itself probably changed in the late nineteenth century, but generally self-acquired property passed to male and female children. Rights to use property acquired through family membership passed to siblings. English laws of inheritance applied to persons who married under the ordinance and to their children. These laws held that if a man died intestate, his widow had rights to use one-third of his estate for life and his issue shared the remaining two-thirds. If a woman died intestate, her estate passed to her children, subject to her husband's right to use it for life.
    J. S. Eades, *The Yoruba Today* (Cambridge, Cambridge University Press, 1980), pp. 55–6; G. B. A. Coker, *Family Property among the Yorubas* (London, Sweet and Maxwell, 1958), pp. 227–83; S. N. Chinwuba Obi, *Modern Family Law in Southern Nigeria* (London, Sweet and Maxwell, 1966), pp. 280–3 and 330–5; and Alfred B. Kasunmu and Jeswald W. Salacuse, *Nigerian Family Law* (London, Butterworth, 1966), pp. 263–71.
33 This information comes from an analysis of the wills of the elite and of wealthy uneducated merchants, Wills, vols. 1–13, Lagos Probate Registry.
34 Obi, *Modern Family Law*, pp. 244–84; and Kasunmu and Salacuse, *Nigerian Family Law*, pp. 106–54, 183–96 and 261–80.
35 N. A. Fadipe, *The Sociology of the Yoruba* (Ibadan, Ibadan University Press, 1970), pp. 96–7. Interviews in Lagos with Archdeacon J. O. Lucas, April 1974; T. A. Doherty, April 1974; and Mrs R. A. Wright, March 1974.

36 Will, Hope Adelabu Nelson Cole, Wills, vol. 9, pp. 16–20, Lagos Probate Registry. Also interviews with Dr J. T. Nelson Cole, Iju, Lagos State, August 1974 and July 1980.
37 Will, Hannah Matilda Benjamin, Wills, vol. 4, pp. 200–2, Lagos Probate Registry. Also interviews in Lagos with Mrs Ebun Lucas, February 1974; and in Ibadan with Mrs Ayo Smith, May 1974.
38 Anthony G. Hopkins, 'An Economic History of Lagos, 1880–1914', unpublished Ph.D. thesis, University of London, 1964, pp. 443–4, argues that investment in children's education diverted capital from commerce and inhibited the development of large African trading companies capable of competing with expatriate firms. By the end of the nineteenth century profits from trade had fallen. African merchants experienced difficulty competing with large European firms because of changes in the organization of international trade. They probably would not have done much better had they invested in trade what they spent on their children's education. From the perspective of the elite, real estate and education provided the safest investments. Real estate yielded dividends in the form of rents, and it appreciated steadily in value. Land and houses gave families a lasting economic base in the local community. Education opened to sons lucrative, high-status careers. It enabled daughters to make good marriages.
39 Studies of marriage and family life in contemporary West African towns report chronic tension over resources between educated couples and their agnatic kin. Alison Izzett, 'Family Life among the Yoruba, in Lagos, Nigeria' in Aidan Southall (ed.), *Social Change in Modern Africa* (London, Oxford University Press, 1961), pp. 311–12; Peter C. Lloyd, 'The Elite' in Lloyd, Akin Mabogunje and Bolanle Awe (eds.), *The City of Ibadan* (Cambridge, Cambridge University Press, 1967), pp. 142–4; Kenneth Little and Anne Price, 'Some Trends in Modern Marriage among West Africans' in Colin Turnbull (ed.), *Africa and Change* (New York, Knopf, 1973), pp. 195–201; and Barbara E. Harrell-Bond, *Modern Marriage in Sierra Leone: A Study of the Professional Group* (The Hague, Mouton, 1975), pp. 208–22. Matrilineal descent exacerbates problems between couples and kin. Christine Oppong, *Marriage among a Matrilineal Elite: A Family Study of Ghanaian Senior Civil Servants* (Cambridge, Cambridge University Press, 1974), pp. 7–11, 110–13 and 149–59.
40 Jane I. Guyer, 'Household and Community in African Studies', paper commissioned by the Social Science Research Council, June 1981, pp. 6–18.
41 Sara S. Berry, 'Aspects of the Political Economy of Inequality in Africa', pp. 16–17, unpublished paper.
42 Stella to Cousin Henry, 13 August 1906, Coker 2/1.
43 Will, J. H. Doherty, Wills, vol. 7, pp. 188–96, Lagos Probate Registry.
44 Will, R. B. Blaize, Wills, vol. 2, pp. 341–6, Lagos Probate Registry.
45 Interviews in Lagos with Mrs C. O. Blaize, January 1974; and Kunle Akinṣemoyin, January 1974.
46 Will, J. H. Doherty, Wills, vol. 7, p. 195, Lagos Probate Registry.
47 Christian wives bore an average of five children for elite husbands, while customary and outside wives rarely bore more than two or three. The instability and hence short life of outside unions helps explain this difference. Polygynists more often than monogamists observed taboos against sex during lactation, and this too limited the number of children born to customary and outside wives.
48 Henry Carr, *Diocesan Synod of Western Equatorial Africa, Report of Speeches Delivered in Synod, May 1912* . . . (Newcastle-upon-Tyne, Mawson, Swan, and Morgan, 1912), p.12.
49 Information about customary and outside wives comes almost exclusively from interviews with their descendants.
50 Interviews with Mrs Afolabi Johnson, Lagos, March 1974 and July 1980.

Notes to pp. 103–7

51 See pp. 801 above. See also Will, J. E. Johnson, Wills, vol. 4, pp. 295–7, Lagos Probate Registry.
52 Coker to Cousin, 16 July 1913, Coker 2/1/10.
53 Notes on Aminatu Alayo, n.d., Macaulay, 21/10. Also interview with Victor Abiodun Dawodu, Lagos, March 1974.
54 *LS*, 16 June 1909, p. 3, c. 2.
55 *E & LC*, 31 January 1885.
56 *LO*, 21 January 1888.
57 *LS*, 12 July 1905, p. 3, c. 2; and 20 September 1905, p. 3, c. 1.
58 See pp. 58–61 above.
59 Interviews in Lagos with Mrs C. G. Agbe, February 1974; Mrs R. A. Wright, March 1974; and T. A. Doherty, April 1974. Interview in Ikeja with Akin Adeshigbin, April 1974 and July 1980. Sara S. Berry, *Fathers Work for their Sons* (Berkeley, University of California Press, forthcoming), examines the link between class and community in Yoruba social and economic change. This work shows that kinship plays an important part in enabling persons to take advantage of new economic opportunities. However, it also demonstrates that the demands of kin, and of maintaining kinship ties, dissipate resources and constrain upward mobility.
60 Interviews in Lagos with Mrs R. A. Wright, March 1974; Mrs Sarah Adadevoh, March 1974; Mrs Leila Abiodun, March 1974 and July 1980; and Mrs Comfort Maja, August 1974 and July 1980.
61 Coker, *Family Property among the Yorubas*, pp. 227–45; Obi, *Modern Family Law*, pp. 280–1; and R. Olufemi Ekundare, *Marriage and Divorce under Yoruba Customary Law* (Ife, University of Ife Press, 1969), pp. 26–7. See also Eades, *The Yoruba Today*, pp. 55–6.
62 Interviews in Lagos with Mrs R. A. Wright, March 1974.
63 The information in this chapter on testate succession comes from an analysis of wills in the Lagos Probate Registry, vols. 1–13.
64 Interviews in Lagos with Mrs R. A. Wright, March 1974; Mrs Leila Abiodun, March 1974 and July 1980; Mrs Tinuola Dedeke, April 1974; and Mrs Comfort Maja, August 1974 and July 1980.
65 Eades, *The Yoruba Today*, p. 55.
66 Interviews in Lagos with Mrs C. G. Agbe, February 1974; Mrs R. A. Wright, March 1974; Mrs Tinuola Dedeke, April 1974; T. A. Doherty, April 1974; and Archdeacon J. O. Lucas, April 1974.
67 See p. 81 above.
68 Interviews in Lagos with Archdeacon J. O. Lucas, April 1974.
69 Peter C. Lloyd, 'Yoruba Inheritance and Succession' in John Duncan Derrett (ed.), *Studies in the Laws of Succession in Nigeria* (London, Oxford University Press, 1965), pp. 161–2; Coker, *Family Property among the Yorubas*, pp. 227–45; Obi, *Modern Family Law*, pp. 332–5. See also Eades, *The Yoruba Today*, pp. 55–6.
70 Interviews in Lagos with Mrs J. J. Marinho, January 1974; Lady Bank-Anthony, March 1974; Mrs R. A. Wright, March 1974; and Mrs Leila Abiodun, March 1974.
71 Interview in Lagos with C. E. T. Nylander, August 1974.
72 Interviews in Lagos with Mrs Adewakun, March 1974; Lady Bank-Anthony, March 1974; and Mrs Ayo Manuwa, May 1974.
73 Interview in Lagos with Mrs Ayo Adeshigbin, March 1974.
74 Will, Abigail Christiana Oluwole, Wills, vol. 9, pp. 462–6, Lagos Probate Registry.
  For a discussion of the role of fostering in West African culture see Goody, *Parenthood and Social Reproduction*.
75 Interviews in Lagos with Percy Savage, January 1974 and July 1980; and Archdeacon J. O. Lucas, April 1974.

Notes to pp. 107–10

76 Interviews in Lagos with Mrs H. F. Pereira, February 1974; and Mrs Leila Abiodun, March 1974.
77 Interview in Lagos with Archdeacon J. O. Lucas, April 1974. Michael Banton, *West African City: A Study of Tribal Life in Freetown* (London, Oxford University Press, 1958), pp. 205–8, and Goody, *Parenthood and Social Reproduction*, pp. 206–10, make similar points about fostering in Freetown, Sierra Leone, and Monrovia, Liberia.
78 Interviews in Lagos with Lady Bank-Anthony, March 1974; S. O. Foresythe, April 1974; Mrs Ayo Adeshigbin, April 1974; and Dr Irene Thomas, July 1974.
79 *Cole* v. *Cole*, 1 N.L.R., pp. 15–23, reports the facts and judgment in this important case.
80 Interview in Lagos with Mrs R. A. Wright, March 1974.
81 Edmund Leach, 'Characterization of Caste and Class Systems' in A. De Reuck and J. Knight (eds.), *Caste and Race: Comparative Approaches* (Boston, Little, Brown, 1967), p. 19.
82 Hugh H. Smythe and Mabel M. Smythe, *The New Nigerian Elite* (Stanford, Stanford University Press, 1960), pp. 95–6; and Lloyd, 'The Elite', pp. 139–44.
83 See pp. 27–9 above.
84 Pauline H. Baker, *Urbanization and Political Change*, pp. 31–45.

In 1983, I attended the funeral of an informant whose father and mother belonged to the early Lagos elite. Descendants of the old elite families packed the church. A popular Lagos clergyman delivered a eulogy praising the deceased for inheriting a good name and preserving it amid the many less respectable newcomers who have come to dominate key positions in the city.

85 Cohen, *The Politics of Elite Culture*, pp. 39–59 and 216–37.

6 ECONOMY, SOCIETY AND MARRIAGE

1 Kenneth Little, *African Women in Towns: An Aspect of Africa's Social Revolution* (Cambridge, Cambridge University Press, 1973), pp. 76–129 and 166–78; Ilsa M. Schuster, *The New Women of Lusaka* (Palo Alto, Mayfield Publishing Company, 1979), pp. 66–139; Caroline H. Bledsoe, *Women and Marriage in Kpelle Society* (Stanford, Stanford University Press, 1980), pp. 81–172; Christine Obbo, *African Women: Their Struggle for Economic Independence* (London, Zed Press, 1980), pp. 87–143; Janet Bujra, 'Women "Entrepreneurs" of Early Nairobi', *Canadian Journal of African Studies*, 9 (1975), pp. 213–34; Elizabeth Mandeville, 'The Formality of Marriage: A Kampala Case Study', *Journal of Anthropological Research*, 31 (1975), pp. 183–95, and 'Poverty, Work and the Financing of Single Women in Kampala', *Africa*, 49 (1979), pp. 42–52; John L. Comaroff and Simon Roberts, 'Marriage and Extra-Marital Sexuality: The Dialectics of Legal Change among Kgatla', *Journal of African Law*, 21 (1977), pp. 97–123; Carmel Dinan, 'Pragmatists or Feminists: The Professional Single Women of Accra', *Cahiers d'Etudes Africaines*, 19 (1977), pp. 155–76; Bonnie Keller, 'Marriage by Elopement', *African Social Research*, 27 (1979), pp. 565–85; and Christine Oppong, 'From Love to Institution: Indicators of Change in Akan Marriage', *Journal of Family History*, 5 (1980), pp. 197–209. Karen Tranberg Hansen and Margaret Strobel, 'Family History in Africa' (forthcoming), review the periodical literature on the African family. For additional evidence see the articles in Christine Oppong (ed.), *Female and Male in West Africa* (London, Allen and Unwin, 1983), by Ware, Abu, Okali, Vercruijsse, Karanja, Pittin, Etienne, Sanjek and Dinan.
2 Schuster, *The New Women of Lusaka*, pp. 75–82 and 90–139; Bledsoe, *Women and Marriage*, pp. 118–72; Obbo, *African Women*, pp. 87–142; Dinan, 'Pragmatists or Feminists', pp. 155–76; Mandeville, 'Poverty, Work and the Financing of Single Women in Kampala', pp. 42–52; Oppong, 'From Love to Institution', pp. 197–209; and articles in Oppong (ed.), *Female and Male*, by Abu, Okali, Vercruijsse, Etienne, Sanjek and Dinan.

Luise White, 'Women and the Changing African Family' in Margaret Jean Hay and Sharon Stricter (eds.), *Women in Africa* (New York, Longman, forthcoming), surveys the history of the African family from the woman's perspective.

3 I first became aware of this problem through conversations with men in Lagos. Kenneth Little, *The Sociology of Urban Women's Image in African Literature* (Totowa, N. J., Rowman and Littlefield, 1980), discusses African novels that portray women in this way. Feminists have criticized Little's *African Women in Towns* for projecting a similar image. In fairness, some of the social science literature by women paints a picture that is not radically different.

4 Little, *African Women in Towns*, pp. 15–28, 76–129 and 145–78; Schuster, *The New Women of Lusaka*, pp. 66–103; Bledsoe, *Women and Marriage*, pp. 118–72; Obbo, *African Women*, pp. 87–142; Oppong, 'From Love to Institution', pp. 197–209; and the articles by Abu, Okali, Vercruijsse, Pittin, Dinan and Sanjek in Oppong (ed.), *Female and Male*. Marcia Wright, 'Justice, Women, and the Social Order in Abercorn, Northeastern Rhodesia, 1897–1903' in Margaret Jean Hay and Marcia Wright (eds.), *African Women and the Law: Historical Perspectives*, Boston University Papers on Africa, vol. 7 (1982), pp. 33–50, examines how women used the arrival of a colonial magistrate to change their domestic situations.

5 See Marcia Wright, 'Women in Peril: A Commentary upon the Life Stories of Captives in Nineteenth-Century East-Central Africa', *African Social Research*, 20 (1975), pp. 800–19; Kennell A. Jackson, 'The Family Entity and Famine among the Nineteenth Century Akamba of Kenya: Social Responses to Environmental Stress', *Journal of Family History*, 1 (1976), pp. 193–216; Martha Mueller, 'Women and Men, Power and Powerlessness in Lesotho', *Signs*, 3 (1977), pp. 154–66; Mandeville, 'Poverty, Work and the Financing of Single Women in Kampala', pp. 42–52; Keller, 'Marriage by Elopement', pp. 565–85; Colin Murray, 'Migrant Labour and Changing Family Structure in the Rural Periphery of Southern Africa', *Journal of Southern African Studies*, 6 (1980), pp. 139–56; and the articles by Okonjo, Martin, di Domenico, Date-Bah and Etienne in Oppong (ed.), *Female and Male*.

6 Jane I. Guyer, 'Household and Community in African Studies', paper commissioned by the Social Science Research Council, June 1981, pp. 24 and 26–7.

7 Henry Carr, *Diocesan Synod of Western Equatorial Africa, Report of Speeches Delivered in Synod, May 1912* . . . (Newcastle-upon-Tyne, Mawson, Swan, and Morgan, 1912), p. 13. See also *Report of the Proceedings of the First and Second Sessions of the First Synod of the Diocese of Western Equatorial Africa* (Exeter, Townsend and Sons, 1907), pp. 6 and 135; Jacob Kehinde Coker, *Polygamy Defended* (Lagos, 1915), p. 13; 'Petition from the Protestant Ministers on the Subject of Divorce', Denton to Knutsford, 15 August 1889, C.O. 147/71; and *LWR*, 22 January 1910, p. 4, c. 2; and 8 July 1911, p. 4, c. 1.

8 Two contemporary studies emphasize the close ties between Yoruba who migrate to towns and their rural relatives: J. S. Eades, *The Yoruba Today* (Cambridge, Cambridge University Press, 1980), pp. 63–4 and 88; and Sara S. Berry, 'Work, Migration and Class in Western Nigeria: A Reinterpretation', paper presented at the African Studies Association meetings, November 1982, pp. 15–16. Berry writes, 'In their efforts to avail themselves of new economic opportunities . . . while maintaining or strengthening their ties with kinsmen and community of origin, Yorubas are continually on the move. People travel constantly.'

9 *LS*, 1 November 1911, p. 7, c. 2; and Kristin Mann, 'Women's Rights in Law and Practice: Marriage and Dispute Settlement in Colonial Lagos' in Hay and Wright (eds.), *African Women and the Law*, pp. 151–71.

Sandra T. Barnes, 'Political Entrepreneurs of Lagos, Nigeria', paper presented at the Society for Economic Anthropology meetings, April 1982, p. 22, documents that patrons perform similar functions for immigrants in modern-day Lagos.

10 'Petition from the Protestant Ministers on the Subject of Divorce', Denton to Knutsford, 15 August 1889, C.O. 147/71. For references to this phenomenon in the interior see the diaries of the Rev. Charles Phillips, Phillips 3/1; and 'Notes on the Case of David Fanoreke's Marriage to Maria Fakeye', 18 May 1900, Phillips 1/1/7.

11 Anthony G. Hopkins, 'A Report on the Yoruba, 1910', *Journal of the Historical Society of Nigeria*, 5 (1969), p. 79.

12 Ibid.

13 Yoruba husbands and wives pursued independent economic activities, but studies of farm families note cooperation between spouses. See for example Niara Sudarkasa, *Where Women Work: A Study of Yoruba Women in the Market Place and in the Home* (Ann Arbor, University of Michigan Press, 1973), pp. 119–20; Sara S. Berry, *Cocoa, Custom and Socio-Economic Change in Rural Western Nigeria* (Oxford, Clarendon Press, 1975), pp. 164–5; Jane I. Guyer, 'Food, Cocoa, and the Division of Labour by Sex in Two West African Societies', *Comparative Studies in Society and History*, 22 (1980), pp. 362–70; and Eades, *The Yoruba Today*, p. 70.

Studies by Abu, Vercruijsse, di Domenico, Date-Bah and Etienne in Oppong (ed.), *Female and Male*, show that new kinds of trade and wage labor have reduced spouses' economic interdependence in other parts of West Africa. See also Claire Robertson, 'Ga Women and Socio-Economic Change in Accra, Ghana' in Nancy J. Hafkin and Edna G. Bay (eds.), *Women in Africa: Studies in Social and Economic Change* (Stanford, Stanford University Press, 1976), pp. 117–26.

14 Many studies show that West Africans have used kinship and marriage to take advantage of new opportunities in farming and trade. See for example Polly Hill, *Migrant Cocoa Farmers of Southern Ghana* (Cambridge, Cambridge University Press, 1963), pp. 43 and 75–86; Anthony G. Hopkins, 'An Economic History of Lagos, 1880–1914', unpublished Ph.D. thesis, University of London, 1964, pp. 411–12; Berry, *Cocoa, Custom and Socio-Economic Change*, pp. 72–9, 132, 156, 164–6, 172–5, 180–3 and 207–8; Steven Baier, *An Economic History of Central Niger* (Oxford, Clarendon Press, 1980), pp. 168–206; and Bledsoe, *Women and Marriage in Kpelle Society*, pp. 118–73 and 182–90.

15 'Ordinance No. 4, Lagos, 1876', in Edward Harrison Richards, *Ordinances, Orders, and Rules in Force in the Colony of Lagos, 1893* (London, Stevens and Sons, 1894); and T. Olawale Elias, *The Nigerian Legal System* (London, Routledge and Kegan Paul, 1963), p. 69.

16 S. N. Chinwuba Obi, *Modern Family Law in Southern Nigeria* (London, Sweet and Maxwell, 1966), pp. 104–88 and 198–285; Alfred B. Kasunmu and Jeswald W. Salacuse, *Nigerian Family Law* (London, Butterworth, 1966), pp. 71–89 and 171–97.

17 Hopkins, 'Report on the Yoruba', p. 79.

18 *LWR*, 19 January 1907, p. 6, c. 1.

19 MacGregor to Chamberlain, 24 November 1899, C.O. 147/145.

20 Ibid.

21 N. A. Fadipe, *The Sociology of the Yoruba* (Ibadan, Ibadan University Press, 1970), pp. 91–2. See also *LWR*, 8 July 1911, p. 4, c. 1.

Female slaves used a similar strategy to obtain their freedom. First they formed liaisons with free men; then they took their cases to the District Commissioners, who arranged 'compromises'. The woman's lover gave her owner 'presents', which 'implie[d] that the girl cease[d] to be in any way the property of any person'. If the woman could prove her master had mistreated her, he received no compensation. Often such women chose railroad workers or other government employees as their lovers, because these men had cash with which to make 'presents'. Governor MacGregor commented, 'In this way a great many girls and women have obtained their freedom.' MacGregor instructed District Commissioners that in cases involving slavery they should err in favor of the slaves.

Notes to pp. 114–18

MacGregor to Chamberlain, 27 December 1899, C.O. 147/145. See also McCallum to Chamberlain, 4 June 1898, C.O. 147/133.
22 *LS*, 9 September 1908, p. 6, c. 1.
23 Hopkins, 'Report on the Yoruba', p. 79. See also *LWR*, 21 January 1911, p. 4, c. 1; and 11 September 1915, p. ?, c. 1.
24 Anna Hinderer, *Seventeen Years in the Yoruba Country* (London, Religious Tract Society, 1877), pp. 83 and 131; Sarah Tucker, *Abeokuta; or Sunrise within the Tropics: An Outline of the Origin and Progress of the Yoruba Mission* (London, J. Nisbet, 1853), pp. 135, 165 and 257–8; Diaries of the Rev. Charles Phillips, Phillips 3/1; and *LWR*, 28 June 1913, p. 4, c. 3.
25 See for example the discussion of contemporary marriage in Eades, *The Yoruba Today*, pp. 57–9.
26 *LS*, 13 July 1910, p. 6, c. 1.
27 Peter C. Lloyd, 'The Elite' in Peter C. Lloyd, Akin Mabogunje and Bolanle Awe (eds.), *The City of Ibadan* (Cambridge, Cambridge University Press, 1967), pp. 140–3.
28 Payne to Davies, 27 April 1888, Coker 6/1.
29 Davies to Davies, 6 December 1875, Coker 6/2.
30 Ibid.
31 Davies to Davies, 12 December 1875, Coker 6/2.
32 Interviews in Lagos with Mrs C. O. Blaize, January 1974; Mrs R. A. Wright, March 1974; Archdeacon J. O. Lucas, April 1974; and T. A. Doherty, April 1974.
33 *LS*, 27 November 1895. See also *LS*, 29 January 1896, p. ?, c. 2.
34 *LWR*, 22 June 1901, p. 3, c. 2.
35 M. T. Euler-Ajayi, 'Annual Sermon' preached at African Church, Bethel, Lagos, 22 December 1907. See also Mojola Agbebi, *Africa and the Gospel: Sermons, Debates, and Lectures . . .* (Lagos, T. A. King, n.d.), p. 22; Abigail C. Oluwoli[e], *Christian Marriage* (Coventry, Curtis and Beamish, n.d.), p. 11; Coker to Cousin, 16 July 1913, Coker 2/1/10; and Samuel A. Coker, *The Rights of Africans to Organize and Establish Indigenous Churches, Unattached to and Uncontrolled by Foreign Church Organizations* (Lagos, Tika Tore Press, 1917), pp. 26–7.
36 Interviews in Lagos with T. A. Doherty, April 1974; Archdeacon J. O. Lucas, April 1974; and Percy Savage, July 1974 and August 1980.
37 Interviews in Lagos with Mrs R. A. Wright, March 1974; Mrs Tinuola Dedeke, April 1974; and Mrs Comfort Maja, August 1974 and July 1980.
38 Mr and Mrs Josiah Crowther and Dr and Mrs John Randle stand out as exceptions. These two couples endured long and acrimonious divorce trials.
39 Allen to Davies, 24 July 1889, Coker 6/2.
40 *LWR*, 22 June 1901, p. 3, c. 2. See also *LS*, 10 November 1909, p. 4, c. 2; and 18 January 1911, p. 4, c. 1; and *LWR*, 9 September 1911, p. 4, c. 1.
41 Interviews in Lagos with Mrs Tinuola Dedeke, April 1974; Mrs R. A. Wright, April 1974; Mrs Syrian Taylor, May 1974; and Mrs Henrietta Lawson, August 1974.
42 Interviews in Lagos with Mrs J. J. Marinho, January 1974; Mrs Ebun Lucas, February 1974; Mrs C. G. Agbe, February 1974; T. A. Doherty, April 1974; H. O. Davies, April 1974; and Mrs Henrietta Lawson, August 1974.
43 For discussions of this type of marriage in Lagos and other West African towns see Mary Bird, 'Urbanization, Family and Marriage in Western Nigeria' in *Urbanization in African Social Change*, Proceedings of the Inaugural Seminar held in the Centre for African Studies, University of Edinburgh, 1963, pp. 66–72; Kenneth Little and Anne Price, 'Some Trends in Modern Marriage among West Africans' in Colin Turnbull (ed.), *Africa and Change* (New York, Knopf, 1973), pp. 183–226; Lloyd, 'The Elite', pp. 138–44; Christine Oppong, *Marriage among a Matrilineal Elite: A Family Study of Ghanaian Senior Civil Servants*

(Cambridge, Cambridge University Press, 1974); and Barbara E. Harrell-Bond, *Modern Marriage in Sierra Leone: A Study of the Professional Group* (The Hague, Mouton, 1975).

44 Peter C. Lloyd, 'Introduction' in Lloyd (ed.), *The New Elites of Tropical Africa* (London, Oxford University Press, 1966), pp. 28–31; Little and Price, 'Some Trends in Modern Marriage among West Africans', p. 197; and Oppong, *Marriage among a Matrilineal Elite*, pp. 2 and 153.

45 Oppong, *Marriage among a Matrilineal Elite*, pp. 11–14 and 156–8. Oppong cites studies which discuss the impact on matrilineal descent of migration, wage labor, education, ownership of private property, and economic inequality. See especially Kathleen Gough, 'The Modern Disintegration of Matrilineal Descent Groups' in David M. Schneider and Gough (eds.), *Matrilineal Kinship* (Berkeley, University of California Press, 1961), pp. 631–52; and Mary Douglas, 'Is Matriliny Doomed in Africa?' in Douglas and Phyllis M. Kaberry (eds.), *Man in Africa* (London, Tavistock Publications, 1969), pp. 121–36.

Schuster, *New Women of Lusaka*, pp. 13–14 and 114, makes little of matriliny in her study of the capital of Zambia, where that form of descent predominates. However, the tensions inherent in matriliny in urban settings have undoubtedly contributed to the extreme sexual conflict and marital instability that she describes.

46 Oppong, *Marriage among a Matrilineal Elite*, pp. 13–14.

47 Bird, 'Urbanization, Family and Marriage', pp. 59 and 64–72; Lloyd (ed.), *The New Elites of Tropical Africa*, pp. 28–30; Little and Price, 'Some Trends in Modern Marriage among West Africans', pp. 195–8; Lloyd, 'The Elite', pp. 138–45; Oppong, *Marriage among a Matrilineal Elite*, pp. 1–14 and 85–114; and Harrell-Bond, *Modern Marriage in Sierra Leone*, pp. 198–218, 283–4 and 289–95.

48 Oppong, *Marriage among a Matrilineal Elite*, pp. 6 and 126. See also Peter Marris, *Family and Social Change in an African City* (London, Routledge and Kegan Paul, 1961), p. 139.

49 Harrell-Bond, *Modern Marriage in Sierra Leone*, p. 254. See also Oppong, *Marriage among a Matrilineal Elite*, pp. 90–1, 145 and 154–5; and Wambui Wa Karanja, 'Women and Work: A Study of Female and Male Attitudes in the Modern Sector of an African Metropolis' in Helen Ware (ed.), *Women, Education and Modernization of the Family in West Africa* (Canberra, Department of Demography, Australian National University, 1981), pp. 42–66; Marris, *Family and Social Change*, p. 65; and Lloyd, 'The Elite', p. 141.

50 Harrell-Bond, *Modern Marriage in Sierra Leone*, pp. 218–19.

51 Little and Price, 'Some Trends in Modern Marriage among West Africans', pp. 199–200.

52 Dinan, 'Pragmatists or Feminists', pp. 155–76; Schuster, *New Women of Lusaka*, pp. 66–103 and 126–39; and Oppong, 'From Love to Institution', pp. 197–209.

53 Tanya Baker and Mary Bird, 'Urbanization and the Position of Women', *Sociological Review* (NS), 7 (1959), pp. 114–15; Alison Izzett, 'Family Life among the Yoruba, in Lagos, Nigeria' in Aidan Southall (ed.), *Social Change in Modern Africa* (London, Oxford University Press, 1961), pp. 310–11; Helen Ware, 'Polygyny: Women's View in a Transitional Society, Nigeria 1975', *Journal of Marriage and the Family*, 41 (1979), pp. 185–95; Little and Price, 'Some Trends in Modern Marriage among West Africans', pp. 198–9; Oppong, *Marriage among a Matrilineal Elite*, pp. 44 and 59; and Harrell-Bond, *Modern Marriage in Sierra Leone*, pp. 124–56.

54 *Report of the Proceedings of the . . . First Synod of the Diocese of Western Equatorial Africa*, pp. 19 and 133; Henry Carr, *Diocesan Synod of Western Equatorial Africa, Report of Speeches Delivered in Synod, May 1907 . . .* (Exeter, Townsend and Sons, 1907), pp. 5–8; Jacob Kehinde Coker, *Polygamy Defended*, pp. 14 and 20–1; and 'Is Native Marriage Advisable or Not Advisable?', Coker 4/2/53, pp. 9 and 16; and Coker to Cousin, 16 July 1913, Coker 2/1/10. See also *LWR*, 21 March 1908, p. 4, c. 2; 29 January 1910, p. 4, c. 2; and 31 May 1913, p. 4, c. 2; and *LS*, 17 March 1915, p. 4, c. 2.

55 Interviews in Lagos with Samuel Akin Oni and Bolajoko Oni, July 1974.

Notes to pp. 121–5

56 Interviews in Lagos with Mrs C. G. Agbe, February 1974; Mrs R. A. Wright, March 1974; and Mrs Tinuola Dedeke, April 1974. Interview in Ikeja with Jack Randle, August 1974.
57 Will, H. A. Caulcrick, Wills, vol. 3, pp. 97–100, Lagos Probate Registry.
58 Interviews in Lagos with Archdeacon J. O. Lucas, April 1974; and in Ikeja with Akin Adeshigbin, April 1974.
59 Interview in Lagos with Michael Ayo Vaughan, March 1974.
60 Interview in Ibadan with F. O. Sogunro, May 1974.
61 Interviews in Lagos with Mrs J. J. Marinho, January 1974; Mrs C. G. Agbe, February 1974; Lady Bank-Anthony, March 1974; and Mrs Tinuola Dedeke, April 1974.
62 Interviews in Lagos with Mrs. R. A. Wright, March 1974; and Archdeacon J. O. Lucas, April 1974.
63 Interviews in Lagos with Ajayi Coker, February 1974; Mrs R. A. Wright, March 1974; and T. A. Doherty, April 1974.
64 *LS*, 15 March 1911, p. 5, c. 3.
65 Interviews in Lagos with Mrs R. A. Wright, March 1974; Mrs Tinuola Dedeke, April 1974; and Archdeacon J. O. Lucas, April 1974.
66 Jacob Kehinde Coker, *Polygamy Defended*, pp. 14 and 20–2; *LWR*, 16 September 1899, p. 3, c. 3; 14 July 1906, p. 4, c. 3; 19 October 1907, p. 4, c. 2; 4 July 1908, p. 5, c. 1; 21 March 1908, p. 4, c. 2; 4 July 1908, p. 4, c. 1; 29 January 1910, p. 4, c. 1; and 17 February 1912, p. 4, c. 1; and *LS*, 17 March 1915, p. 4, c. 2.
67 Interviews in Lagos with Mrs Tinuola Dedeke, April 1974; Archdeacon J. O. Lucas, April 1974; and Mrs Ayo Manuwa, May 1974.
68 Interviews in Lagos with T. A. Doherty, April 1974; and Mrs R. A. Wright, April 1974.
69 Interviews in Lagos with Mrs J. J. Marinho, January 1974; Mrs R. A. Wright, March 1974; and Mrs Syrian Taylor, May 1974.
70 *LWR*, 1 May 1897, p. 4, c. 3. See also *LWR*, 11 September 1915, p. ?, c. 1.
71 See for example *LWR*, 12 February 1912, p. 4, c. 1.
72 *LS*, 22 September 1897, p. 2, c. 3.
73 *LS*, 17 March 1915, p. 4, c. 2.
74 *LWR*, 22 January 1910, p. 4, c. 2. See also *LWR*, 8 July 1911, p. 4, c. 1.
75 See for example *LWR*, 21 January 1911, p. 4, c. 1; and 8 July 1911, p. 4, c. 1.
76 *LWR*, 30 March 1912, p. 4, c. 2.
77 Jacob Kehinde Coker, 'Is Native Marriage Advisable or Not Advisable?', pp. 14–15. See also *LS*, 9 June 1897, p. 5, c. 3; 29 March 1899, p. 3, c. 2; 22 April 1903, p. 2, c. 3; 16 August 1908, p. 4, c. 2; and 17 November 1915, p. 4, c. 2.
78 Interviews in Lagos with Archdeacon J. O. Lucas, April 1974; T. A. Doherty, April 1974; and Percy Savage, July 1974 and August 1980.
79 *Report of the Proceedings of the . . . First Synod of the Diocese of Western Equatorial Africa*, p. 20; and Coker to Coker, 28 May 1911, Coker 4/1/14. See also *LWR*, 27 August 1904, p. 4, c. 1; 14 July 1906, p. 4, c. 3; 29 May 1909, p. 4, c. 2; 28 August 1909, p. 4, c. 1; and 29 January 1910, p. 4, c. 1; and *LS*, 14 July 1915; p. 6, c. 3.
80 Fadipe, *Sociology of the Yoruba*, p. 66. See also *LWR*, 18 February 1911, p. 3, c. 2; and 11 September 1915, p. ?, c. 1; and *LS*, 22 September 1915, p. 7, c. 2.
81 See for example *LWR*, 14 July 1906, p. 4, c. 3; and *LS*, 13 July 1910, p. 6, c. 1; and 17 March 1915, p. 4, c. 2.
82 Interviews in Lagos with Archdeacon J. O. Lucas, April 1974; and T. A. Doherty, April 1974.
83 Hopkins, 'Report on the Yoruba', p. 83; Samuel Johnson, *The History of the Yorubas* (London, Church Missionary Society, 1921), p. 102; and Ajayi Kolawole Ajisafe, *The Laws and Customs of the Yoruba People* (Lagos, Church Missionary Society Bookshop, 1924), pp. 33–4 and 52–3.

Notes to pp. 125–6

84 *LWR*, 28 March 1903, p. 4, c. 3; 9 May 1903, p. 6, c. 1; 14 July 1906, p. 4, c. 3; 6 October, 1906 p. 6, c. 1; 29 May 1909, p. 4, c. 2; 28 August 1909, p. 4, c. 1; 19 and 26 February 1910, p. 3, c. 1; and 8 July 1911, p. 4, c. 1; and *LS*, 22 September 1915, p. 7, c. 2.
85 *Lewis* v. *Bankole*, 2 N.L.R., pp. 81–106; and *LWR*, 3 October 1891, p. 3, c. 2.
86 Bledsoe, *Women and Marriage in Kpelle Society*, pp. 182–90, Schuster, *New Women of Lusaka*, pp. 66–139, Obbo, *African Women*, pp. 101–43, and Mandeville, 'Poverty, Work and the Financing of Single Women in Kampala', pp. 42–52, make similar arguments.
87 See for example *Aina* v. *Desu*, Judges' Notebook in Civil Cases (JNCC), vol. 3, pp. 192–3; *Fanojoria* v. *Kadiri*, JNCC, vol. 3, pp. 265–75; *Roberts* v. *Mamase*, JNCC, vol. 5, pp. 37–47; and *Awa* v. *Disu*, JNCC, vol. 6, pp. 2–5.
88 Interviews in Lagos with Mrs R. A. Wright, March 1974; Mrs Tinuola Dedeke, April 1974; and Mrs Comfort Maja, August 1974.
89 'Education of Women' in C. O. Taiwo (ed.), *Henry Carr: Lectures and Speeches* (Ibadan, Oxford University Press, 1969), p. 33.

Select bibliography

INTERVIEWS

W. O. Abina, 1 Wey Lane, Lagos, July 1974
Mr and Mrs Michael Abiodun, 207 Igboṣere Road, Lagos, May 1974 and July 1980
Mrs Sarah Adadevoh, 5 Ikorodu Road, Lagos, March 1974
Sir Adetokunbo Ademola, Victoria Island, Lagos, August 1980
Lady Kofoworola Ademola, Victoria Island, Lagos, July 1974
Akin Adeshigbin, 10 Oba Akran Avenue, Ikeja, April 1974 and August 1980
Mrs Ayodele Adeshigbin, 60A Apapa Road, Ebute Metta, Lagos, April 1974
Mrs Adewakun, 72 Abuleraro Road, Ebute Metta, Lagos, March 1974
I. A. S. Adewale, Victoria Island, Lagos, May 1974 and July 1980
N. E. S. Adewale, 22 Glover Street, Lagos, July 1974
Sufianu Braimah Affini, 21 Ṣopono Street, Lagos, July 1974
Mrs C. G. Agbe, Apapa Road, Ebute Metta, Lagos, February 1974
Mrs E. M. E. Agbebi, 3 Carrena Street, Lagos, March 1974
Miss Gladys Agbebiyi, 8 Bishop Crowther Street, Surulere, Lagos, July 1974 and July and August 1980
Dr Akerele, Ikeja, January 1974
Dr J. O. Akerele, Apapa Road, Lagos, June 1974
Kunle Akinṣemoyin, Plot 968, Idejo Street, Victoria Island, Lagos, January 1974 and August 1980
J. A. Akitoye, Isale Eko, Lagos, November 1973
Dr Afolabi Alakija, 5 Alakija/Jibowu Street, Yaba, Lagos, February 1974 and July 1980
Lady Ayo Alakija, 10 Macarthy Street, Lagos, March 1974
Dr Mobolaji Alakija, 20 Abeokuta Street, Ebute Metta, Lagos, January 1974
A. W. Animashaun, 45 Martin Street/26 Shitta Street, Lagos, February 1974
Iṣmaila Lawal Apatira, Apatira Street, Lagos, December 1973
Mrs Georgiana Aromure, Bank Olemoh Street, Surulere, Lagos, February 1974
Abimbola Ali Balogun, 117 Ojo Road, Apapa, Lagos, February 1974. This interview was conducted at a family meeting and other members of the family also gave information
Atanda Balogun, Oluwole Street, near Martin Street, Lagos, July 1974
Mrs T. Banjo, 37 Alara Street, Yaba, Lagos, April 1974
Lady Bank-Anthony, Ikoyi, Lagos, March 1974
Mr and Mrs J. Benka-Laleye, 112 Freeman Street, Ebute Metta, Lagos, July 1974
Mrs Basilia Byass, Igboṣere Road, Lagos, July 1974
Miss Towobola Byass, 5 Onikepo Street, Lagos, January 1974
Mr Campbell, 76 Queen Street, Yaba, Lagos, April 1974
Eligious Esedeo Iyodeji Carrena, 69 Bamgboṣe Street, Lagos, December 1973 and July 1980
Nestor Esegra Carrena, 10 Salawu Street, Surulere, Lagos, December 1973
Abner Coker, Aderupoko Compound, Itesi, Abeokuta, June 1974
Ajayi Coker, 33 MacNeil Street, Yaba, Lagos, February 1974 and August 1980

Select bibliography

Alphonso Pike Coker, 16 Cemetery Street, Apapa, Lagos, July 1974
Mrs B. C. Coker, P.O. Box 72, Jos, Nigeria, August 1974 (information supplied by letter)
James A. Coker, Ikoyi, Lagos, August 1974
Mrs Shola Ṣapara Coker, Campbell Street, Lagos, August 1974
W. Coker, Director of Federal Surveys, Tafewa Balewa Square, Lagos, February 1974
Georgius Cole, 39 Bankole Street, Lagos, January 1974
Dr J. T. Nelson Cole, Mofolorunsho Villa, off Iju Water Works Road, Iju, Lagos State, August 1974 and July 1980
H. O. Davies, 17 Agard Street, Yaba, Lagos, April 1974
S. O. Dawodu, College of Education, University of Lagos, November 1973
Victor Abiodun Dawodu, 2 Asa Williams Street, Lagos, February and March 1974
Mrs Tinuola Dedeke, 45 Falolu Street, Surulere, Lagos, April 1974
Mrs Sally Dixon, 5 Onikepo Street, Lagos, January 1974
Samuel William Doherty, 72 Bamgboṣe Street, Lagos, July 1974
T. A. Doherty, 23 Odunlami Street, Lagos, April and May 1974
Mrs Titi Euba, University of Lagos, Lagos, July 1980
Idowu Ola Fafunwa, 16 Atin Street, Lagos, July 1974
Gbadamoṣi A. Fanimokun, 15 Bankole Street, Lagos, May 1974
The Hon. Justice Atanda Fatayi-Williams, Nigerian Supreme Court, Lagos, April 1974
S. O. Foresythe, 4 Wakeman Street, Yaba, Lagos, April 1974
Sulamon Alabi B. I. Forrest, Faji Market, Lagos, January 1974
Mrs Franklin, Jerico Hospital, Ibadan, May 1974
J. O. Haastrup, Akerele Street, Surulere, Lagos, January 1974
Alexander Sanyolu Harding, 2 Ladipo Street, Ebute Metta, Lagos, August 1974
Mrs Edith Yetunde Harrison, 8 Aje Street, Yaba, Lagos, July 1980
Olufemi Ibare-Akinsan, 43 Onitana Road, Surulere, Lagos, July 1974
Mrs T. E. Ibikitola, 16 Joseph Odunlambo Street, Lagos, July 1980
Dr J. O. Jackson, Department of Engineering, University of Lagos, January 1974
Miss A. I. Johnson, 30 Bamgboṣe Street, Lagos, December 1973
Mrs Afolabi Johnson, 57 Queen Street, Yaba, Lagos, March and July 1974 and July 1980
Mrs Jones, Ajele Street, Lagos, March 1974
Bamidele Jones, 23 Guy Street, Freetown, Sierra Leone, August 1974 (information supplied by letter)
Mrs Korowo, Librarian, Ministry of Justice, Lagos, March 1974
Mrs Lahonmi, 72 Oyerokan Road, Surulere, Lagos, July 1974
Adesola Kolajo Lamilisa, 23 Ibadan Street, Ebute Metta, Lagos, January 1974
Harry Lardner, Herbert Macaulay Street, Ebute Metta, Lagos, July 1974
Mrs Henrietta Lawson, Olatunde Crescent, Surulere, Lagos, August 1974
Mrs Layinka, Good Samaritan School for Handicapped Children, Ibadan, May 1974
Mrs Annie Efuṣeke Lowe, Faji Market, Lagos, July 1974
Mrs Ebun Lucas, 11 MacNeil Street, Yaba, Lagos, February 1974
Archdeacon J. O. Lucas, 8 Turton Street, Lagos, April, May and August 1974
Mr and Mrs Jack McEwen, Surulere, Lagos, July 1974 and August 1980
Mr and Mrs John MacGregor, Yaba, Lagos, January 1974
Oluyomi MacGregor, 36 Strachan Street, Lagos, February 1974
Dr Akinola Maja, Aje Street, Ebute Metta, Lagos, May 1974
Mrs Comfort Maja, Garber Square, Lagos, August 1974 and July 1980
Mrs T. Ayodele Manuwa, Antie Ayo School, Ikoyi, Lagos, May 1974
Mrs J. J. Marinho, Military Street, Lagos, January 1974
M. A. Mustapha, 15 Balogun Street, West, Lagos, March 1974
C. N. Norman-Williams, Public Service Commission, 57 Marina, Lagos, April 1974
C. E. T. Nylander, 14 Majaro Street, Yaba, Lagos, August 1974

Select bibliography

Daniel Akinola Ogunbiyi, 71 Igbehinadun Street, Oshodi, May 1974
Bankole Oki, Office of the Attorney General, Lagos State, July 1974
R. O. Olaniyan, 6 Isale Agbede Street, Lagos, July 1974
Olofin of Isheri, Isheri, March 1974
M. A. O. Ologundudu, 128 Griffith Street, Ebute Metta, Lagos, January 1974
Ajani Olujare, 40 Doherty Street, Lagos, January 1974
Nathaniel Akinola Olukolu, 1 Ricca Street, Lagos, July 1974
T. A. Olukolu, 12 Maloney Bridge Street, Lagos, July 1974
Bolajoko Oni, 40 Ajişomo Street, Lagos, July 1974
Mrs Elfrida Ibironke Oni, 12 Airport Road, Ikeja, August 1974
Samuel Akin Oni, 40 Ajişomo Street, Lagos, July 1974
Iya Onigari, 90 Okepopo Street, Lagos, March 1974
Mrs Oluremi Onosanyo, 37 Karimu Street, Surulere, Lagos, July 1980
Durojaiye Olajuwon Oshodi, Oshodi Palace, Oshodi Street, Lagos, January 1974
Harry Payne, Surulere, Lagos, March 1974
Solomon Adewale Pearce, Bishop Street, Lagos, March 1974
Dr Abiodun Pearse, 2 Abiona Close, off Falolu Street, Surulere, Lagos, March 1974
Mr and Mrs H. F. Pereira, 52 Olonde Street, Yaba, Lagos, February 1974 and July 1980
Jack Randle, Hausa Village, Ikeja, August 1974
Mrs Clara Rhodes, 30 Bamgboşe Street, Lagos, December 1973
Anthony Robbin, British High Commission, Lagos, April 1974
Dr da Rocha-Afodu, Medical Research Institute, Yaba, Lagos, April 1974
Mrs Kwao Sagoe, 66 Old Yaba Road, Lagos, February 1974
Miss Ibironke Şapara, 112 Bamgboşe Street, Lagos, March and April 1974
Mrs Ayodele Şapara-Peragrino, 16 Oyerokun Street, Surulere, Lagos, January 1974
Dr A. O. Şaşegbon, Nigerian Airways, Ikeja, August 1974
Mrs Evelyn Savage, Surulere, Lagos, June 1974
Percy Savage, 5 Desalu Street, Surulere, Lagos, January and July 1974 and August 1980
Vincent Akinfemiwa Savage, 23 Aşimawu Bakare Street, Surulere, Lagos, January 1974
W. R. Shitta, Bamgboşe Street, March 1974
Mrs Shoande, 20 Oyediran, Surulere, Lagos, April 1974
Charles Egerton Shyngle, Eric Manuel Crescent, Surulere, Lagos, March 1974
Mrs D. A. Silva, 6 Old Yaba Road, Lagos, July 1974
Sallustanio Elias da Silva, Ibiere Crescent, Apapa, Lagos, July 1974
Mrs Ayodele Smith, Manuwa Street, Ibadan, May 1974
O. A. Şobande, 13A Coates Street, Ebute Metta, Lagos, 1974 and July 1980
Y. P. O. Şodiende, 63 Wakeman Street, Yaba, Lagos, April and July 1974
Alhaji Sogunro, Obun Eko, Lagos, March 1974
F. O. Sogunro, Bodeja Estate, Ibadan, May 1974
Mrs Idowu Şokenu, 10 Adeniran Ogunsanya Street, Surulere, Lagos, January 1974
Mrs Syrian Adesola Taylor, 36A Offin Road, Lagos, May and July 1974
Dr Irene Thomas, 5 Taslim Elias Street, Victoria Island, Lagos, July 1974
Mrs Tubi, Herbert Macaulay Street, Ebute Metta, Lagos, June 1974
Mrs Oyejola Turner, 14B Olonode Street, Yaba, Lagos, March 1974 and July 1980
Mrs D. P. Turner-Shaw, 6 Moleye Street, Yaba, February 1974
Dr O. J. Vanderpuye, Health Department, University of Lagos, May 1974
Michael Ayo Vaughan, 99 Tokunboh Street, Lagos, March 1974
Mrs F. T. Wey, 117 Tokunboh Street, Lagos, March 1974
W. T. Wey, 3 Chapel Street, Ebute Metta, Lagos, March 1974
Mr and Mrs Adeniyi Williams, 2 Rotimi Williams Street, Ibadan, May 1974
C. B. Williams, Ebute Metta, Lagos, August 1974
Mrs J. Aganga Williams, near Yaba Baptist Church, Yaba, Lagos, August 1974

Select bibliography

Mrs J. T. A. Williams, Coates Street, Yaba, Lagos, January 1974
Samuel J. A. Williams, 35 Onitana Street, Surulere, Lagos, March 1974
Mrs T. E. Williams, Palm Grove, Ikorodu Road, Lagos, April 1974
Mrs Emily Willoughby, 6 Willoughby Street, Lagos, March 1974
Emmanuel Molade Willoughby, 6 Willoughby Street, Lagos, January 1974
Mrs R. A. Wright, 73 Oyerokun Road, Surulere, Lagos, March and April 1974

MANUSCRIPT SOURCES

GOVERNMENT ARCHIVES

The Public Record Office, London
Lagos
  C.O. 147, Original Correspondence
  C.O. 148, Acts
  C.O. 149, Sessional Papers (Legislative Council Debates)
  C.O. 150, Government Gazettes
Southern Nigeria
  C.O. 520, Original Correspondence
  C.O. 588, Acts
  C.O. 592, Sessional Papers (Legislative Council Debates)
  C.O. 591, Government Gazettes
Other
  C.O. 806, Africa, Confidential Prints
  F.O. 2, Africa (Consular Correspondence)
  F.O. 84, Slave Trade, General Correspondence
  F.O. 403, Africa, Confidential Prints

The Colonial Office Library, London
West African Lands Committee, *Committee on the Tenure of Land in West African Colonies and Protectorates, Draft Report and Minutes of Evidence*, April 1917

The Nigerian National Archives, Ibadan
C.S.O. 1–28, Records of the Colonial Secretary's Office, 1861–1958, containing dispatches, registers, reports, minute books, letter books, filed papers and miscellaneous bound volumes
Com Col I, Records of the Commissioner of the Colony, 1918–50, containing administrative files and intelligence reports
Badadiv 1–8, Records of the Badagry Divisional Office, 1865–1913, containing civil court records, criminal court records, minute books, letter books, intelligence books, diaries and correspondence registers
Epediv 4–7, Records of the Epe Divisional Office, 1889–1909, containing civil court records, criminal court records, letter books, minute books, and miscellaneous bound volumes
Church Missionary Society, Yoruba Mission Papers, containing the local records of the Church Missionary Society, including correspondence, minutes and school records
Methodist Missionary Society Papers, containing the local records of the Methodist Missionary Society
Coker Papers, containing correspondence, business records, and diaries of Jacob Kehinde Coker, J. P. L. Davies and Stella (Davies) Coker
Phillips Papers, containing correspondence, diaries and notes of the Rev. (later Bishop) Charles Phillips
Oke Papers, containing pamphlets, manuscripts and notes on the history of the African churches written or collected by the Rev. Gabriel A. Oke

Select bibliography

The Nigerian National Library, Lagos
Typescript of biographies of Lagosians prominent in the late nineteenth and early twentieth centuries. Written by Mr Dedeke

The High Court, Lagos State, Lagos
Wills, 1885–1955. In bound volumes at the Probate Registry
Registers, Civil Cases, the Supreme Court, 1876–1920
Judges' Notebooks, Civil Cases, the Supreme Court, 1876–1920

Land Registry, Lagos
Records of Crown Grants, 1863–1915
Deeds, Mortgages and Conveyances, 1863–1915

Marriage Registry, Lagos
Marriage Registers, Lagos Colony, 1884–1945

Registry of Births and Deaths, Lagos State Department of Health, Lagos
Registers of Births, 1892–1945
Registers of Deaths, 1867–1960

OTHER ARCHIVES

Rhodes House, Oxford
Papers of the Anti-Slavery Society and the Aborigines Protection Society, which merged to become the Anti-Slavery and Aborigines Protection Society
  MSS Brit. Emp. G18, Nigeria, 1860–1910
  MSS Brit. Emp. G211–13, 215–19, 221–34, 236–9, 242–3; Nigeria, 1911–25
  MSS Brit. Emp. G247–50, West Africa, 1909–19
  MSS Brit. Emp. G252–60, West Africa, 1912–36
Colonial Records Project, Nigeria, containing letters, diaries and notes of colonial officials serving in Lagos Colony and the Protectorate of Southern Nigeria, 1890–1960

The Royal Commonwealth Society, London
Papers of John Hawley Glover, 1861–75, containing official and private correspondence and notes on Lagos Colony

The Church Missionary Society, London
CA2/L, Yoruba Mission to 1880, Outgoing
CA2/0, Yoruba Mission to 1880, Incoming
G3 A2/L, Yoruba Mission post 1880, Outgoing
G3 A2/0, Yoruba Mission post 1880, Incoming

The Methodist Missionary Society, London
Correspondence, Outgoing, Secretary's Letter Books
Correspondence, Incoming, Yoruba District Files

Africana Collection, University of Ibadan Library, Ibadan
Minutes of the Central Native Council
Henry Carr Papers, containing manuscript notebooks, diaries and newspaper clippings
Herbert Macaulay Papers, containing correspondence, family papers and notes on Lagos history and politics

Select bibliography

Oged Macaulay Papers, containing correspondence, notes on Herbert Macaulay and typescripts on the history of Lagos.
Mojola Agbebi Papers, microfilm of materials in the Howard University Library, Washington, D.C.
Edward Wilmot Blyden Papers, correspondence relating to the appointment of Blyden as Agent for Native Affairs, 1895–7
Baptist Mission in Nigeria, microfilm of correspondence

Christ Church Cathedral, Lagos
Baptismal Registers transferred from St Andrew's, Badagry, to Christ Church, Lagos, 1845–1920
Marriage Register, 1864–84

Holy Trinity Church, Lagos
Baptismal Registers, 1877–1920

St Paul's Church, Lagos
Baptismal Registers, 1879–1920
Marriage Register, 1869–84

Olowogbowo Methodist Church, Lagos
Baptismal Registers, 1906–20

Trinity Methodist Church, Lagos
Baptismal Registers, 1911–20

Holy Cross Cathedral, Lagos
Baptismal Registers
Marriage Registers

First Baptist Church, Lagos
Diaries of a church deacon, 1906–9
Letters of Mojola Agbebi, 1914 and 1915
E. A. Alawode's unpublished manuscript on the history of the First Baptist Church

Private collections
A. E. Carrena Papers, containing correspondence, account books and minutes of family meetings. Located at the Carrena family home, 69 Bamgboṣe Road, Lagos. Nestor Carrena, 10 Salawu Street, Lagos, has two additional files
C. B. Moore's Account Book, 1882–1910, in the possession of Mrs J. McEwen, Surulere, Lagos
J. T. Nelson Cole Papers, containing legal documents in Cole's safe at the time of his death. In the possession of Dr J. T. Nelson Cole, Iju, Lagos State

PUBLISHED PRIMARY SOURCES

GOVERNMENT

Annual Reports, Lagos Colony, 1880–1905
Annual Reports, Southern Nigeria, 1906–15
Blue Books, Lagos Colony, 1861–1905
Blue Books, Southern Nigeria, 1906–15
Census, Lagos Colony, 1881, Colonial Office Library

Select bibliography

Census, Lagos Colony, 1891, Colonial Office Library
Census, Lagos Colony, 1901, Colonial Office Library
Census, Southern Nigeria, 1911, Colonial Office Library
Colonial Office pamphlets
    Alexander, C. W., *Memorandum on the Subject of Native Land Tenure in the Colony and Protectorate of Southern Nigeria (1910)*, Colonial Legal Pamphlet, vol. 1, no. 26
    Cameron, Donald Charles, *Notes on the Report of the Commission of Inquiry Regarding the House of Docemo*, West Africa Pamphlet, No. 213, 1933
    Cameron, Donald Charles, *Notes Regarding the Head of the House of Docemo 1933*, West Africa Pamphlet, No. 214, 1933
    Geary, William Nevill Montgomerie, *The Development of Lagos in Fifty Years*, Nigerian Pamphlet, No. 13, 1924
    Lagos Native Advisory Board Rules, 1899, West Africa Pamphlet, No. 21, 1899
    Memorial of the Inhabitants of Lagos, 1889, Nigerian Pamphlet, No. 2, 1889
    Rossiter, H. V., *The Henry Carr Library*, 1946
Nigerian Law Reports
West African Court of Appeal Reports
Parliamentary Papers
    1852 LIV (221), *Papers Relating to the Reduction of Lagos by H.M.'s Forces*
    1854 LXV (296), *Quantities of Palm-Oil Imported into the United Kingdom, 1844–53*
    1861 LXIV (1), *Slave Trade Correspondence, Africa (Consular)*
    1862 LXI (1), *Slave Trade Correspondence, Africa (Consular)*
    1862 LXI (339, 365), *Papers Relating to the Occupation of Lagos*
    1863 XXXVIII (117), *Papers Relating to the Destruction of Epe*
    1863 XXXVIII (512), *Letters from the Rev. Henry Venn on the Conduct of Missionaries at Abeokuta*
    1865 V (1, 412), *Report of Select Committee on the State of British Settlements*
    1865 XXXVII (170), *West Coast of Africa: Colonel Ord's Report*
    1865 XXXVII (533), *Papers on War between Native Tribes in the Neighbourhood of Lagos*
    1874 LXX (C. 1038), *Statistical Tables Relating to the Colonial and Other Possessions of the United Kingdom*
    1876 LII (C. 1343), *Papers Relating to H.M.'s Possessions in West Africa*
    1884 LVI (C. 4052), *Gold Coast: Further Correspondence*
    1887 LX (1, 167), *Correspondence between Native Tribes in the Interior and Negotiations for Peace Conducted by the Government of Lagos*
    1893–4 LXII (C. 7227), *Report on Governor Carter's Expedition into the Interior*
    1905 LVI (Cd. 2325), *Papers Relating to the Construction of Railways in Sierra Leone, Lagos and the Gold Coast*
    1906 LXXVIII (Cd. 2787), *Correspondence Relating to the Railway Construction in Nigeria*
    1908 LXX (Cd. 3999), *Report on the Forest Administration of Southern Nigeria for 1906*
    1909 LX (Cd. 4906, Cd. 4907), *Report and Evidence of the Committee of Enquiry into the Liquor Trade in Southern Nigeria*, Part 1 and Part 2
    1909 LXI (Cd. 4718), *Report by Prof. W. J. Simpson on Sanitary Matters in Various West African Colonies*
    1909 LXI (Cd. 4720), *Report of the Departmental Committee on the West African Medical Staff*
    1912–13 LIX (Cd. 6561), *Correspondence Respecting the Grant (to Messrs Lever Bros) of Exclusive Rights for the Extraction of Oil from Palm Fruits*
    1913 XLVIII (Cd. 6462, Cd. 6427), *Report and Evidence of the Departmental Committee Appointed to Inquire into Matters Affecting the Currency of the British West African Colonies and Protectorates*
    1916 IV (Cd. 8247, Cd. 8248), *Report and Evidence of the Committee on Edible and Oil Producing Nuts and Seeds*

Select bibliography

OTHER

Missionary periodicals
Church Missionary Intelligencer, 1870–1906 (continued as *Church Missionary Review*, 1907–13)
Methodist Magazine, 1880–1913

Local newspapers
Iwe Irohin, 1859–67
Anglo-African, 1863–5
Lagos Times and Gold Coast Colony Advertiser, 1880–93
The Observer, 1882–8
Eagle and Lagos Critic, 1883–7
The Mirror, 1887–8
Lagos Weekly Times, 1890
Lagos Echo, 1891
Lagos Weekly Record, 1891–1930
Lagos Standard, 1893–1920
Nigerian Chronicle, 1908–13
The Nigerian Times, 1910–13

Index

Abayomi, Lady Oyinkan (Ajasa), 90
Abeokuta, 17, 26, 106, 152n92
Ademola, Lady Kofoworola (Moore), 90
Adeshigbin, Ayodele (Taylor), 90
adultery, 53, 72, 80, 85–6, 114, 124–6; *see also* extra-marital sexual relations
affines, 37, 39–40, 42, 50, 60, 68, 104–5, 112–13, 126
  affinal relationships, 7, 42, 53, 58, 71, 98–9
  affinal responsibilities, 122–3
African churches, 27, 66, 68, 73–4, 116–17
  impact on elite marriages, 73–4
Africans, educated, 2, 11, 19, 24, 43, 67
  dependence of Europeans on, 20–1
  effect of racism on, 23–4
  exclusion from jobs, 24
  importance of marriage, 133n2
  influence with Europeans, 19, 57
  low standard of sexual morality, 121
  misuse of position, 21
Agbebi, Rev. Mojola (David Brown Vincent), 30, 61, 73
Ajasa, Sir Kitoyi, 24, 96, 98–9, 146n149
Ajasa, Lady Lucretia, *see* Moore, Lucretia
Ajisafe, Ajayi Kolawole, 48
Akinṣemoyin, Mobolaji Adeyemi, 31, 97
Akitoye, Daniel, 31
Akitoye, Ọba of Lagos, 12, 14
Alakija, Sir Adeyemo, 21, 24, 32, 87
Alakija, Olayimika, 21
alarede (erẹ), 50
alarena, 47
Alayo, Aminatu, 103
ale (concubines), 42
alliance and relationship networks
  Christian, 53, 67, 78, 95–100, 112
  Yoruba, 37, 40, 60, 71, 74, 103–4
  see also kinship: relationships among elite
Amaro (Brazilian liberated slaves), 17–18, 27–8, 63, 93, 102; *see also* repatriated slaves
Anglicans, 18, 20, 27, 61, 66, 69, 88
ano, 39, 42
artisans, 18, 103, 114

Awoliyi, Dr E. (Akerele), 90
aya (wife), 42
Ayandele, E. A., 71, 76

Badagry, 17
Balogun, Ali, 139n34
baptism, 44
baptismal registers, 6
Baptists, 18, 20, 27
Barber, Fanny, 26, 97
Bathurst, 93, 95, 98
Benin
  Bight of, 14
  Kingdom of, 12
Benjamin, Clara, 97
Benjamin, Fanny, 97
Benjamin, Felicia Ayodele, *see* Wright, Felicia Ayodele (Benjamin)
Benjamin, Hannah Matilda, *see* Cole, Hannah Matilda (Benjamin)
Benjamin, Hannah Matilda (Williams), 31, 90, 97, 100–1
Benjamin, Henrietta Arabella, 97
Benjamin, John Stanley, 97
Benjamin, Josuah Begandeji, 97
Benjamin, Josuah Blackall, 97, 100
Benjamin, Rowland Abiodun, 97
Berry, Sara S., 16–17
betrothal, 114
  Christian, 48–9
  Yoruba (iṣihun), 38, 49, 79
Biafra, Bight of, 14
Blaize, C. O., 96–8
Blaize, Mrs C. O., 78, 96, 98
Blaize, Emily (Cole), 83, 89
Blaize, Richard Beale, 20, 60, 83, 89, 94–6, 98, 101–2, 139n34
Blyden, Edward W., 59, 73, 115
Bott, Elizabeth, 9
Brazilians, *see* Amaro
bridewealth, 36–43, 49–50, 105, 113, 148n26, 148n30, 149n35, 154n1; *see also* betrothal; courtship; prestations
Bucknor, Joseph Samuel, 93, 103

185

Index

Campbell, Rev. James George, 42, 73, 87, 122
Cape Coast, 93, 95, 98
Carr, Henrietta (Robbin), 96
Carr, Henry, 24, 43, 51, 55, 59, 67, 96, 102, 112, 121, 126
Carrena, Albert E., 48, 99
Carter, Sir Gilbert, 20, 23, 157n62
catechists, 6, 29, 44, 103
Catholics, 18, 27, 66; see also Christianity; Société des Missions Africaines; Western education
Caulcrick, Hezekiah Africanus, 73, 107, 121
chiefs, 12, 15–16, 19, 29, 31, 41–2, 56, 103, 148n33
children, 9, 11, 41, 50, 59, 62, 95, 99–100, 102, 104–5, 107, 110, 113, 126, 146n148, 168n47
  as economic asset, 40, 58, 60
  as investment, 119–20
  and kin, 29, 36
  legitimacy of, 36, 61, 106
  outside, 83–4, 87, 107–8
  relations between Christian and outside, 106, 108, 121
  rights to, 38, 112
  treatment by elite men, 104, 106–7
Christ Church, Lagos, 27, 81
Christianity, 4, 17, 27, 43, 54, 67, 73–4, 76, 78, 115
  characteristic of elite, 28
  introduction and spread, 8, 10–11, 18, 33, 111, 115
  legitimizes social and economic change, 20
  opposition to, 5
Christian marriage, 1, 35, 42–53, 58, 60–2, 67, 71–7, 80–2, 87, 94, 100–2, 105, 116–18, 122–5, 154n1, 155n16, 157n48, 160n10
  advantages to elite, 56–7, 75, 108, 122–3
  adverse effect, 116–17
  age at, 67–8, 152n99, 158n69
  changes in, 117–18, 126
  conflict between husbands and wives, see domestic disputes
  and elite culture, 56, 75, 78, 108
  and elite status, 51, 56, 75, 82, 86–7, 91, 108
  impact of Europeans, 43–6, 54
  introduction, 8, 44
  love and companionship, 8, 44–6, 57, 60, 72, 115–16, 118, 127
  numbers of elite, 43, 54–5, 63–4, 70, 75
  pre-nuptial exchange, 49–50
  response of elite men, 10, 54–6, 62, 68, 76–7, 116
  response of elite women, 2, 10, 54, 57, 61, 68, 77–8, 91, 116
  rites, 43, 46–7, 50, 53, 82, 104
  role in elite formation and maintenance, 54, 112
  role of kin, 46–50, 77
  sign of conversion, 43
  symbol of assimilation, 57
  union of individuals, 44, 48, 115
  union of two families, 46, 48–9
  see also Christian and outside marriage; ordinance marriage
Christian and outside marriage, 61–2, 75, 80–1, 83, 86, 104–5, 120, 122
  numbers of elite, 55, 63–4, 69
Christians, 8, 18–19, 27, 58, 60, 66–9, 73, 77, 158n65, 158n73
churches, 18, 20, 24, 51, 68, 73, 85, 89, 92
Church Missionary Society, 18, 20, 24, 27, 44, 58, 95
  Female Institution, 45
  Grammar School, 18, 24, 58, 79
clergy, 5, 20, 29–31, 52, 55, 74, 85, 95
clerks, 6, 18, 20, 24, 29–31, 45, 62, 103, 114, 126
clients, 11–12, 16, 18, 36, 39
cognates, 36, 38–9, 46, 48, 101, 120, 149n35
Cohen, Abner, 7, 56, 92, 99
Coker, Adel, 43, 80–1, 103, 106
Coker, Adeyinka, 97
Coker, Dr J. O., 85, 97
Coker, Jacob Kehinde, 37, 59–60, 73, 77, 82, 97, 103, 121
Coker, Rev. R. A., 80–1, 97
Coker, Samuel A., 73
Coker, Stella (Davies), 30, 46, 85, 88, 97, 99, 101
Cole, Eleanor, 95, 98
Cole, Emily, see Blaize, Emily (Cole)
Cole, Hannah Matilda (Benjamin), 97
Cole, Mrs J. W., 84–5
Cole, James William, 84
Cole, T. F., 98
Cole, Dr William Alexander, 21, 90, 97
Cole v. *Cole*, 108
colonial administration, 20, 23–4, 30, 109
  expansion, 23
colonial government, 4–5, 11, 15–16, 19, 23–4, 26, 39, 44, 74, 76, 78, 102, 111, 113
colonialism, 8, 15, 20, 23, 76, 113
Colonial Medical Service, 31
Colonial Office, 15, 20–3
colonial servants, 5, 15, 24–5, 29, 33, 57–8, 62, 64–5, 67–8, 94, 111, 158n69
  African, 4, 6, 20–1, 79, 135n13
  salaries of elite males, 31
colonial service, 4, 24, 30, 34, 58, 70, 77, 96, 101, 107, 109
  educated Africans, 11, 20, 25
  women in, 81, 90

colonial society, 21, 57, 111
   position of educated elite, 4, 11, 24, 33, 71, 92
colonial state, 4, 15
   rise of, 5, 8, 10, 19, 33, 91, 111, 115
Comaroff, John, 42
commerce, 21, 70, 101, 109, 139n33, 168n38
   investment in, 101
   legitimate, 14, 16–17, 19, 31, 111, 113; effect of rise in, 33, 60
   women in, 58, 78, 82, 125
   see also trade
concubinage, 42, 75, 123–5
concubines, 36, 42, 51, 75
conjugal estates, 46, 100, 118
conjugal expectations, 62, 87, 121
   women, 83, 90, 91
conjugal ideals, 10, 54, 67–9, 91, 116
   Victorian, 8, 45, 79, 122
   Yoruba, 115
conjugal relationships and roles, 9, 74, 91, 110, 117, 119, 124
   Western, 44–5, 111
   Yoruba, 41–2, 60–1, 112, 116, 118, 120
conjugal responsibilities, 41–2, 82, 84–5, 106, 116, 122–4, 126
converts, 20, 43–4, 111, 116–17
court records, 6, 84–6, 126, 141n55
courts
   colonial, 15, 19, 36, 52–3, 78, 84–7, 99, 106, 113, 117
   Yoruba, 15, 106
courtship: Christian, 46, 48–9
credit, 2, 16–17, 19, 21, 32, 71, 99, 111, 113, 125, 163n37
Crowther, Bishop Samuel Ajayi, 20, 24, 59, 79, 96
cultural changes, 74, 91
cultural dilemma, 75
cultural nationalism, 34, 71–3, 89, 115–16
cultural relativism, 71–2, 159n79
culture, 18, 73
   African, 57, 67, 76; response of elite to, 7, 76
   elite, 4, 11, 75, 79, 92, 109, 134n4
   European (Western), 4, 29, 57, 67–8, 76, 81, 98; negative impact on West Africa, 72; response of educated elite, 7, 55, 76
   Yoruba, 67–8, 71–2, 74, 76, 81
customary unions, 1, 61, 71, 74–7, 80, 88, 102–4, 109
   advantages, 104–5
   ambiguity of status, 62, 122–3
   instability, 106
   social mobility, 108
   see also Yoruba marriage

Davies, James Pinson Labulo, 32, 46–7, 56, 85, 88, 115–16, 141n61, 145n123
Davies, Samuel Sogunro, 31, 145n123
Davies, Sarah Forbes Bonetta, 49, 88, 115–16
Davies, Stella, *see* Coker, Stella (Davies)
Davies, Victoria, *see* Randle, Victoria (Davies)
Dawodu, Adeline (Hoare), *see* Hoare, Adeline
Dawodu, Benjamin Charles, 94–5, 103–4
death rates, 15, 20, 23, 139n25
Denton, G. C., 24
descent, 9, 46, 101, 120
   Lagos Yoruba, 11, 35–6
   matrilineal, 174n45
   patrilineal, 11, 35, 46, 101
   relationships between couples and kin, 119–20, 168n39
   see also kinship; lineages
descent groups, 11, 35, 49
divorce, 62, 81–2, 84–7, 114, 117, 173n38
   Yoruba, 42, 53, 112
doctors, 5, 20, 25, 31, 33, 62, 67, 135n13
   women, 46, 90
Doherty, Josiah Henryson, 30–1, 61, 101–2, 139n34, 144n101, 145n134
domestic disputes, 84, 106
   with kin, 9, 112–13, 115, 119–20, 168n39
   over outside unions, 68, 123
   over polygyny, 87, 112
   over resources, 9, 100, 112, 119, 168n39
   settlement of, 84–6, 113, 117
   between spouses, 8–9, 41, 52, 54, 83–4, 100, 113, 115–17, 119, 123
domestic groups
   composition of, 11, 36, 39
   units of economic production, 39
domestic ideology, 45–6, 78–9, 91
domestic relationships and roles, 1, 8, 35, 43, 53, 56, 110, 112–13, 116, 123–4
   redefinition, 112–13, 125–6
domestic strategy, 35, 40, 62, 75, 78–9, 104, 117, 121–2, 126
double standard, 79–80, 162n24; *see also* extra-marital sexual relations
dowry, 37, 41, 50, 100; *see also* bridewealth
dual marriage, *see* Christian and outside marriage

Echeruo, M. J. C., 76
economic change, 1–2, 7, 11, 19, 25, 43, 54, 76, 78, 81, 91, 110–13, 115, 117, 124, 126–7, 134n4
economic depression: effect on educated elite, 21–2, 33, 75
educated elite
   authority of, 4, 11, 75, 92, 112

187

Index

educated elite – *contd.*
  benefits of wealth, 101
  broadening of social base, 29, 108–9
  definition of, 2, 4–5, 33, 53, 92, 98–9, 102
  economic status, 30–3
  estates, 32–3, 146nn 150–2
  formation and maintenance, 1, 5, 7, 11, 19, 25, 28, 44, 54, 109, 112
  identification of, 5–6, 25, 44, 56, 75, 78, 108
  influence of Victorian ideology, 78
  origins, 27–30, 120
education, 45, 92, 98, 101, 104, 109
  customary and outside wives, 102
  as determinant of status, 26, 28, 58, 98
  effect on marital behavior, 65–6, 69
  elite males, 26, 29, 93–4, 101–2
  as equalizer, 107
  importance for Christian marriage, 47, 94, 101
  as investment, 20, 25, 144n101, 168n38
  outside children, 107
  prestige of foreign education, 77, 102
  transmission of property through, 146n148
  women, 26, 30, 77–8, 81, 89–90, 93–4, 101, 120, 125, 155n19
  see also Western education
Edun, Annette Oyinkan (Bucknor), 30
Egerton, Sir Walter, 24
elites, 2, 4–5, 8, 134n4
  contemporary West African, 118, 120
elite theory, 2, 5
employment, 20, 24, 111
  women, 45, 77, 79, 81–2, 89–90
  see also occupations
Euba, Mrs William B., 90
Europeans, 1, 4–5, 15, 67
  attitude toward customary/outside unions, 104
  attitude toward educated Africans, 24
  dependence on educated Africans, 21
  and marriage, 1, 7–8, 43–6, 51, 54
  spread of Victorian domestic ideology, 8, 45, 78–9, 91
extra-marital sexual relations, 55, 59, 62, 69, 71, 75, 79–80, 88, 110, 113–14, 119–21, 124, 126, 162n24

Fadipe, N. A., 37, 42–3, 53, 79, 82, 86, 114, 124
Fafunwa, William Kudehinbu, 31
family
  change, 70, 113–14
  nuclear, 8, 100–1, 127
family houses, 87–8, 100
family life, 20, 29, 75
family property, 36, 100, 147n6
Fanimokun, Joseph Suberu, 24

farmers, 16, 29, 103
farming, 11–12, 31
farms, 32, 39, 90
fishing, 11–12
fornication, 125; *see also* extra-marital sexual relations
fostering, 99, 106–7
Fourah Bay College, Sierra Leone, 26
Freetown (Sierra Leone), 3, 17, 26, 93–5, 97–8, 106, 134n3, 155n16, 160n10

George, James, 61
George, Maybelle, 97
Glover, Henry, 31
Gold Coast Colony, 21
Green, Ore, 57
Griffith, Justice Brandford, 51
Guyer, Jane, 112

Harrell-Bond, Barbara E., 119
headmasters, 5, 25, 31
Herskovits, Jean, 76
Hoare, Adeline, 94, 103–4
Hoare, Margaret C., 49
Hoare, Thomas George, 94–5
Hopkins, Anthony G., 12, 15–16, 19, 23, 31–2
household composition, 36, 40, 121
households, 51
husbands
  authority within family, 31, 46
  Christian: duties and obligations, 40, 51, 104
  relations with wives, 40–1, 84–5, 116
  responsibilities, 50, 83, 116
  Yoruba: independent economic activities, 172n13
Hutchinson, Anna Sophia, *see* Şapara Williams, Anna Sophia (Hutchinson)
Hutchinson, Robert, 83

idaanọn 39, 48
Idẹjọ chiefs (heads of landowning lineages), 11–12, 138n8, 141n55
ideology, 4–5, 7–8, 20, 35, 53–4, 60, 67, 78, 111–12, 116–17, 120; *see also* domestic ideology
Ifa, 38
igbeeyawo, 39
Igbo, Braimah, 139n34
Ige, Disu, 140n49
Ijebu Expedition, 23
immigrants, 17, 35–7, 110, 112
imperialism, 33–4, 70–1
incest, 80
indirect dowry, 50
inequality, 2, 12, 19, 36, 40
infertility, 37, 47, 59, 62

Index

inheritance, 20, 102, 167n32
  by children, 30, 36, 47, 51, 61, 82, 84, 100–1, 106–8, 156n22
  effect of Christian marriage, 36, 51–2, 61, 82, 107, 167n32
  per stirpes, 36, 106
  of widows, 36, 59, 105
  by women, 36, 51, 58, 61, 82, 84, 100–1, 105, 121, 167n32
  Yoruba, 36, 51–2, 100, 105–6, 167n32
  see also family houses; family property; land; property rights; real estate
In re Şapara, 42, 158n63
intermarriage, 18, 95–100, 102, 108, 166n21
işihun, 38, 48
iyawo, 38, 42

Jackson, John Payne, 22, 55, 72–3, 82
Johnson, Alfred Latunde, 94
Johnson, G. P., 79
Johnson, Mrs. G. P., *see* Johnson, Rebecca Phillips
Johnson, Bishop James, 47, 56, 59, 85, 88, 95
Johnson, Rev. Nathaniel, 93, 96
Johnson, Rebecca Phillips, 26, 46, 79–81, 88, 97
Johnson, Sabina (Leigh), 56, 88, 95
Johnson, Zenobia (Phillips), *see* Phillips, Zenobia

kin, 29, 85, 99, 105, 126
  attitudes to marriage, 57, 67–8, 87
  conflicts with couples, 9, 113, 115, 119–20
  as economic asset, 12
  economic status of, 30, 103
  freedom from, 113, 125, 127
  role in marriage, 72, 112–13
  see also betrothal; bridewealth; courtship; inheritance
King, Dr Nathaniel Thomas, 20
kin groups, 29, 35, 46, 101, 112, 115, 120
kinship, 51, 169n59
  concentration of resources, 101–2
  relationships among elite, 7–8, 44–5, 53, 112, 166n21
  ties, 67, 171n8
kola, 38–9, 48–9, 90, 148n30
Kopytoff, Jean Herskovits, *see* Herskovits, Jean
Kosoko, *Ọba* of Lagos, 14

labor, 11–12, 39–40, 58, 60, 112, 134n4
  control over by elders, 149n35
  see also sexual division of labor; wage labor
Lagos, 11–12, 14, 16, 18–19, 22, 25, 33, 111
  annexation of, 14–15, 19, 35–6, 111
  center of international trade, 1, 17
  center of slave trade, 11–12, 17
  colonial capital, 1, 11, 15, 17, 109, 137n1
  see also trade
Lagos Chamber of Commerce, 24
Lagos School for Girls, 89
Lagos Standard, 49, 52, 55, 114, 116
Lagos Supreme Court, 20, 32, 52, 85–6, 141n55
Lagos Weekly Record, 22, 43, 52, 55–6, 59, 73, 116, 123
land, 19, 105, 107, 113, 125, 138n8
  family, 36
  investment in, 19–20, 32, 50
  transfer to wives, 50
  see also real estate
land ownership, 11, 19, 36, 141n55
  private, 36, 58, 60, 100, 111, 163n37
law, 20–1, 25, 62, 81, 90
  colonial, 2, 15, 51, 58, 61, 78, 82, 86, 106, 108, 113–14
  family, 51–2, 86, 167n32
  and marriage, 37, 82, 86, 150n45
  Yoruba, 15, 61, 78, 86, 113, 167n32
lawyers, 5, 20, 25, 31, 33, 62, 67, 86, 145n130
  women, 46, 90
Leach, Edmund, 108
legal rights and duties, 1, 35, 43, 52–3, 100, 113, 116
  impact of Christian marriage on, 51, 56, 61
  women, 78, 81–2, 85, 91, 105–6, 121, 125–6
  Yoruba, 61
Leigh, Hope Adelabu, *see* Nelson Cole, Hope Adelabu (Leigh)
Leigh, Jacob Samuel, 56, 60, 79, 88, 90, 95, 97, 100
Leigh, Sabina, *see* Johnson, Sabina (Leigh)
Leigh-Şodipe, Dr Şodiende Akisiku, 30
liberated slaves, 17; *see also* repatriated slaves
life histories, 6–7, 17, 54–5, 62, 91, 93, 135n14, 140n38
lifestyle, *see* style of life
lineages, 12, 29, 35–40, 44, 46, 101, 119, 149n35
  land- and title-owning, 11, 19, 36, 103
  see also Iḍẹjọ chiefs
literarcy: advantages of, 19–20, 141n61
Little, Kenneth, 119
Lloyd, Peter C., 115
Lumpkin, Carrie, 90

Macaulay, Abigail, 32, 79
Macaulay, Herbert Samuel Heelas, 21, 50, 74–5, 81, 88, 96
Macaulay, Dr Magnus R. L., 97–8
Macaulay, Rev. Thomas Babington, 18, 58, 79

189

Index

MacGregor, Sir William, 24, 58, 114, 172n21
Mannheim, Karl, 5
Manuwa, Ayodele (Oluwole), 90
marital attitudes, 7, 54, 108
   changes in, 54, 57, 103, 108
marital behavior, 2, 7, 42, 54, 57, 62–9, 71, 74–5, 108, 114, 158n69
marital choice, 8, 37–8, 41, 46–7, 92–5, 102
   elite males, 1, 60–9, 75, 102–3, 158n69
   elite women, 80–1, 93
marital norms, 1, 77
   changes in, 1, 119–20
   tensions between Yoruba and Christian, 116, 118
   Yoruba, 40–1, 43, 54, 68, 115, 125
Marke, Stella (Thomas), 90
marriage, 2, 7, 73, 87, 113–14, 149n35
   act of social definition, 56, 117
   age of, 49, 158n69
   conflicts between husbands and wives, *see* domestic disputes
   differences between Christian and Yoruba, 53, 59, 75
   effect of contact with Europe, 2, 42–3, 72, 111, 114–15, 124
   and elite formation, 1, 6–7, 75, 92
   increased instability, 110, 124
   responses of sexes, 8, 10, 67, 81
   role of kin, 37, 41, 46–8, 72, 112, 149n35
   and social mobility, 62, 75, 94
   taxonomy of, 42
   tensions, 119–20, 126
   tensions between Yoruba and Christian, 1, 69, 75
   views of Europeans, 1, 7, 44, 51
   see also Christian marriage; Christian and outside marriage; customary unions; 'Native Christian' marriage; outside unions; Yoruba marriage
marriage dilemma, 1, 54, 87, 91, 116
Marriage Ordinance (1884), 44, 50–2, 61–2, 74, 86, 107, 123, 153n113
   effect on Christian marriage, 61
marriage ordinances, 44
marriage registers, 6, 54, 79, 102, 152n99, 154n1, 166n2
Marriage Registries, 51–2, 74
Marx, Karl, 2, 134n4
medicine, 15, 20–1, 25, 30, 62, 107
   women, 90
Meillassoux, Claude, 149n35
men: autonomy, 113
men, elite
   advantages of elite wives, 57
   changes in composition, 158n69
   definition of, 5
   economic status, 31–3

estates, 146n151
origins, 27–8
merchants, 4–5, 16–21, 23–5, 29–30, 32–3, 57–8, 64–5, 68–9, 71, 93–5, 103–4, 108, 111, 139n34, 140n38, 158n73, 168n38
   European, 16, 19, 24
   Muslim, 5, 103
   profits of, 31–2
Methodists, 18, 20, 27, 66, 69, 73, 88
ministers, *see* clergy
missionaries, 15, 17–18, 35, 43–5, 55, 73, 77, 111
'modern West African' marriage, 8–9
monogamy, 1, 9, 60, 72, 81, 88, 101, 111, 115–16, 121, 157n52
   advantages of, 58
   and children, 59, 168n47
   and Christian marriage, 44, 51, 55
   conservation of resources, 101–2
   and elite women, 68, 78, 82, 86, 91, 101
Moore, Arabella Ibiremi (Vaughan), 30
Moore, Betsy, 96
Moore, Cornelius Bartholemew, 95–6, 98
Moore, Eliza Sabina (Williams), 95–6
Moore, Eric Olawolu, 30, 90, 96
Moore, Gwendoline, *see* Blaize, Mrs C. O.
Moore, Joseph Emanuel, 96
Moore, Louisa Matilda, 96–7
Moore, Lucretia, 96
Moore, Marian, 96
Moore, Mary Ann (Renner), 95–6
Moore, Olaṣeni, 30, 96, 98
Moore, Olympia, 96
Moore, S. J., 96
Moore, Rev. William, 95–6
Muslims, 17–18, 26, 28, 56, 60, 109; *see also* merchants

'Native Christian' marriage, 74, 77
Nelson Cole, Hope Adelabu (Leigh), 90, 97, 100–1
newspapers
   articles, 83, 113, 142n80, 143n89
   articles on marriage, 1, 37, 40, 42–3, 45–6, 50, 52, 55–6, 59–60, 71–3, 77, 117, 124, 134n3
   source of information, 6, 54, 154n1, 166n2
   see also *Lagos Standard; Lagos Weekly Record*
Nicol, Harriet Susan, 94

Ọba (king of Lagos), 12, 14–16, 19, 31, 56, 138n8, 145n127
Obasa, Charlotte O. (Blaize), 30, 46, 89–90, 94, 97
Obasa, Dr Orisadipe, 94, 97
occupations, 6, 9, 18, 20, 29, 31–2, 78

Index

elite, 5–6, 20, 25–6, 29–34, 45, 92, 94, 109, 111, *and see individual entries*
   exclusion of women, 81
   women, 6, 26, 32, 45–6, 78–9, 82, 89, 94, 103, 120, 126
Ogunbiyi, James, 140n49
Qlǫfin, 11–12
Olowo, Taiwo (Daniel Conrad Taiwo), 140n49
Olowu, Seidu, 32
Oluwole, Dr, 96
Oluwole, Mrs Abigail C., 44–5, 47, 88–9, 107
Oluwole, Bishop Isaac, 81, 83
ǫmǫiya (unit in polygynous household), 40
Omu, Fred, 71, 76
Oni, Claudius Ayodele, 121
Oppong, Christine, 9, 119
oral data, 6, 25, 93, 102, 105, 107, 140n38, 154n1, 168n49
ordinance marriage, 53, 85, 108
   advantages for elite women, 78, 82
   legal rights, 82, 100
   see also Christian marriage; Marriage Ordinance; marriage ordinances
ordinances, 15; *see also particular ordinances*
Oshodi, Alfred Ade, 31
Ouidah, 18
outside unions, 61–2, 67–9, 75–6, 83, 102–3, 109, 121–3
   advantages and disadvantages, 104–5, 108
   ambiguity of status, 55, 86, 120–3, 154n1
   defined, 154n1
   effects of, 123
   instability, 106, 123
   numbers of elite, 55, 70, 158n73
   response of elite women, 68, 77, 80, 88
   social mobility, 105, 108
   see also Christian and outside marriage
Oyejola, Dr Ayodeji, 30, 49
Oyekan, Qba of Lagos, 57, 145n127

palm produce, 14, 16–17, 21–2
   exports, 161n11
   trade, 15–16, 22–3, 148n33
Pareto, Vilfredo, 5
'parlour marriage', *see* 'Native Christian' marriage
pastors, *see* clergy
patrons, 18, 37, 41, 47, 68, 112, 171n9
Payne, John Augustus Otonba, 115–16
Payne, Martha, 116
Pearse, Samuel Herbert, 24, 98
Phillips, Bishop Charles, 44, 47–9, 93, 152n92
Phillips, Charles (catechist), 93
Phillips, Zenobia, 48, 60, 93, 152n92
political change, 1–2, 7, 11, 19, 43, 54, 57, 76, 91, 110–12, 115, 117, 124, 127, 134n4

polyandry, 81
polygamy, 55, 87, 115, 124
polygyny, 1, 35, 51–3, 58, 72, 81, 86, 112, 116, 120, 122–3, 157n52
   advantages of, 60
   attitude of African churches, 68, 73–4
   children, 9, 101–2, 168n47
   Christian attitudes toward, 43–4
   defense of, 59, 88, 165n83
   and inequality, 40
   inheritance, 36, 106
   network of relationships, 71, 104
population, 5, 18, 67, 109, 111
   domination of immigrants, 112
   elite ties to, 67–8, 74
   European, 23, 139n25
   growth, 17
   marriage practices, 1
   separation from elite, 4, 26–7, 33, 44, 53, 75, 92, 102
Porto Novo, 18
preachers, *see* clergy
pre-marital sex, 124, 153n111, 153n113; *see also* adultery; fornication; extra-marital sexual relations
press, *see* newspapers
prestations, 37–9, 49–50, 149n35, 153n109; *see also* betrothal; bridewealth
Price, Anne, 119
probate records, 32–3
professionals, 4–5, 20, 25, 29–30, 33, 45, 57–8, 64–5, 67–8, 94, 111, 158n69
professions, 4, 11, 20, 24–5, 29, 34, 81, 96, 109
   women in, 90
property, 20, 32–3, 49–52, 82, 84, 105–6, 108, 111, 146n148, 146n149
   family, 100, 147n6
   relations in marriage, 86
   transfer from husband to wife, 152n105
   see also inheritance; land; real estate
property rights, 19, 36, 40, 53, 58, 61, 100, 104, 167n32
prostitution, 59, 72, 123–6
Protestants, 17, 66

Quaker, Syrian, 96

racial discrimination, 21, 23–4, 33–4, 57, 70–1, 75, 142n69, 143n90
Randle, Dr John, 85, 157n62, 173n38
Randle, Victoria (Davies), 30, 47, 85, 87, 173n38
real estate, 19, 32, 49, 82, 100–1, 111, 118, 146n148
   as investment, 168n38
   see also land; property
rectors, *see* clergy

Index

relationship between sexes, 2, 8, 10, 36, 54, 83, 100, 106, 121–6
relationships, network of, *see* alliance and relationship networks
rent, 31–2, 58, 118, 168n38
rentier, local, 19, 100
repatriated slaves, 17–19, 78–9, 91, 111
 introduction of Christian marriage, 35, 43
 marriage choice, 63–4, 67–8, 157n35
 and origins of elite, 27–8, 120
residence, 8–9
 among elite, 51, 104, 118, 121
 Yoruba, 36, 39, 146n2
resources, 58, 82, 100, 104, 113, 119, 125, 127
 access to, 62, 105, 108, 113
 concentration within elite, 7, 9, 20, 53, 92, 98, 101–2, 112
Robbin, Christiana, 52
Robbin, Ellen, 96, 98
Rocha, Candido da, 30
Royal Navy, 12, 14
Royal Niger Company, 21, 26

St Paul's Breadfruit Church, Lagos, 27, 56
Şapara, Adel Coker, *see* Coker, Adel
Şapara, Dr Oguntola, 21, 43, 57, 61, 80–1, 89, 158n63
Şapara Williams, Anna Sophia (Hutchinson), 83
Şapara Williams, Christopher Alexander, 20, 31, 58, 81, 83
Saro (Sierra Leonean liberated slaves), 17–18, 27–9, 50, 63, 67, 144n111; *see also* repatriated slaves
Savage, Gabriel H., 97
Savage v. *Macfoy*, 77
schools, 18, 20, 27, 91, 99, 107
 attendance, 141n51; by elite, 26, 92
 curriculum, 26, 45
 enrollment, 18, 141n51
seamstresses, 26, 32, 79, 82, 94, 126
sexual behavior, change in, 124–6
sexual division of labor, 39, 115–16, 118, 161n11; *see also* domestic groups; farms; trade
sexual relationships, *see* relationships between sexes
Shyngle, Annie, 84–5
Shyngle, Joseph Egerton, 84
Shyngle v. *Shyngle*, 84
Sierra Leoneans, *see* Saro
slaves and slavery, 11–12, 14, 16–17, 36, 39, 44, 103, 140n38 172n21; *see also* repatriated slaves
slave trade, 11–12, 14–17, 31, 111, 140n38, 148n33
Smith, George, 51

Smith, Mrs George, 85
social change, 1–2, 19, 43, 54, 76, 110–12, 115, 117, 124, 127, 134n4
social mobility, 7–8, 27, 47, 56, 58, 75, 92, 94, 105, 108–9, 125, 169n59
social stratification, 2, 75, 92, 111, 134n4, 149n35; *see also* social mobility; status
Société des Missions Africaines, 18
Şogbesan, Sabina, 96
Sogunro, Edward, 121
Sogunro, Francis Olatunde, 121
Southern Baptists, *see* Baptists
status, 5, 29–30, 46–7, 51, 108, 112, 155n16
 children, 7, 30, 51, 102, 108, 112, 121–2
 determinants, 58
 elite, 2, 4–6, 10, 27, 33, 56, 58, 75, 99–100, 102, 108–9, 111, 117, 125; effect of marriage, 108, 117
 marital, 154n1
 non-elite wives, 69, 102
 transmission of, 7, 58, 92, 102, 112
 women, 36, 40, 44, 50, 58, 69, 77–9, 81–2, 86–8, 91, 93–4, 103, 105–8, 121–3, 126
status endogamy, 93–5, 98, 100, 102
status groups, 2, 4, 75–6
strangers, 11, 17, 103, 112
style of life, 4–6, 33, 102, 111
 determinant of status, 58, 75, 101
 role of marriage, 7, 53, 78, 92, 112
 see also culture
succession, 61, 100, 138n8, 167n32; *see also* inheritance
Supreme Court Ordinance (1876), 15

Taiwo, Daniel Conrad, *see* Olowo, Taiwo
Taylor, David Augustus, 32, 61
Taylor, E. J. Alexander, 90
teachers, 6, 26, 32, 62, 77, 79, 82, 93, 126
 women, 79, 82, 94, 126
Thomas, Andrew Wilkinson, 84
Thomas, Dr Irene, 90
Thomas, Keith, 79
Thomas, Peter John Claudius, 20, 32, 49, 90, 146n149
Tinubu, Madame, 12
trade, 4, 15–17, 19–20, 22–4, 34, 70
 changes in organization, 70, 11
 depression, 21, 70
 effect of new opportunities, 110
 growth of international, 5, 8, 10–11, 78, 91
 profit from, 31, 58, 168n38
 women in, 78, 81, 120
 see also commerce
traders, 6, 12, 16–18, 21, 29–31, 39, 71, 94, 103, 111, 139n33
 women, 26, 30, 32, 58, 79, 90, 95, 103–4, 126, 163n37

training schemes: women, 89–90
trousseau, 49–50; *see also* indirect dowry

universities, 20, 26, 90
urbanization: effect on marriage, 9, 110

Vaughan, Arabella Ibiremi, 96
Vaughan, Burrell Carter, 95–6, 121
Vaughan, James Churchwill, 95–6

wage labor, 110–11, 113, 125
wages, 31–2
wealth, 4, 11–12, 19, 30, 32–3, 40, 51, 58, 60, 67, 78, 82, 94–5, 100–1, 104, 111
wealth-in-people, 12, 60
Weber, Max, 2, 75
weddings (Christian), 44, 49–52, 56–7, 62
Wesleyan Girls' High School, 89
Wesleyan Methodists, *see* Methodists
West African Medical Staff, 24
Western education, 6, 26–7, 29, 106
  and educated elite, 4, 26–7
  introduction and spread, 8, 10–11, 18, 33, 76, 91, 111, 115
  necessary for elite membership, 4, 28
  opposition to, 5
  and women, 30, 78
White, Rev. James, 18
White Cap chiefs, 57
widows, 59, 77, 84, 88, 95, 121, 167n32
Williams, Eliza Sabina, *see* Moore, Eliza Sabina (Williams)
Williams, George Alfred, 52, 55, 72–3
Williams, Hannah Matilda, *see* Benjamin, Hannah Matilda (Williams)
Williams, Isaac Benjamin, 31–2, 60, 96
Williams, J. A., 103
Williams, J. S., 96
Williams, James O'Connor, 95
Williams, Remilekun, 90
Williams, Seidu, 103
Williams, Zachariah Archibald, 31–2, 95
Willoughby, Isaac Humphrey, 19–20, 31
wills, 6, 19, 32, 47, 51, 54, 61, 82, 84, 87, 95, 100, 102, 105, 107–8, 121, 146n148, 146n149, 147n6, 154n1, 156n22; *see also* inheritance
wives
  autonomy, 40–1
  background, 92–3, 102–3, 108, 121
  Christian, 45, 61, 71, 84, 87, 89, 93, 101, 116; custodian of moral values, 45–6; legal rights, 44, 51–2, 84, 86, 91; response to outside unions, 68, 83, 123
  customary: treatment by elite men, 67, 105; *see also* wives, Yoruba

  economic activities of, 60, 68, 71, 79, 104, 172n13
  as economic asset, 12, 39–40, 58, 60, 68, 78–9
  outside: treatment by elite men, 105
  relations between, 36, 83, 106, 121–2
  relations with husbands, 40–1, 44, 83–4
  shaping husbands' behavior, 62, 68–9
  social mobility, 58, 62
  status of elite men's, 58, 69, 87, 91, 93, 102–3, 105, 108
  Yoruba, 40–2, 172n13
  see also entries under marriage; women
women
  autonomy of, 10, 78, 80, 90–1, 113–14, 116–17, 120
  defense of polygyny, 88, 165n83
  relationship between, 122–3
  role in elite formation, 10
women, elite
  Christian domestic ideology, 25, 78–9, 116
  dependence on men, 10, 61, 81, 89, 91, 116–17, 125
  economic activities, 79, 81, 90
  economic status, 32–3, 81–2, 86–7, 89, 91, 120
  insistence on Christian marriage, 2, 10, 57, 75, 77, 85, 87, 91, 119–20, 126
  origins of, 27–8, 30
  reconsideration of Christian marriage, 10, 77, 88, 91
  social and cultural activities, 6, 58, 78–9, 83, 98, 104, 111
women, non-elite: unions with elite males, 125
Wright, Felicia Ayodele (Benjamin), 49, 89–91, 97, 165n83
Wright, Louisa Matilda (Moore), 96–7
Wright, Rugus Alexander, 95–7
Wright, Samuel A., 52
Wright, Rev. Thomas Benjamin, 95, 97

Yoruba interior: colonization, 23, 70
Yoruba kingdoms, 16, 138n8
Yoruba marriage, 1, 35–44, 53, 57, 61, 67–8, 72–5, 78–9, 86, 88, 104, 112, 116, 122, 124–6, 147n18, 154n1, 157n55, 167n32
  advantages to elite males, 54, 59, 61, 68, 71, 75
  ambiguity of status, 42–3, 55, 62
  changes in, 40, 113, 126
  consent of kin, 37–8, 41–2
  effect of Christianity and Western education, 114–15
  effect of colonialism, 43, 113–15
  effect on women, 105, 126

Index

Yoruba marriage – *contd.*
  as exchange, 36–8, 49
  marriage rites, 38, 47, 55, 104
  numbers, 55, 63–4, 69–70, 73, 75, 158n73
  response of elite males, 53–4, 59–62, 67–8, 70
  response of elite women, 54, 88
  role of kin in, 37–8, 41, 67, 112–13, 115
  union of lineages, 36–9, 49, 115
  see also customary unions
Yoruba rulers, 16, 23, 111
Yoruba wars/warfare, 12, 16–17, 22–3, 138n8, 142n80